About the author

Paul Scales lives in the town at the end of the line, within touching distance of Britain's most ancient woodland. He spends his days listening to other people's stories, and his nights writing his own.

You can reach him on Twitter @scales_paul

The soundtrack to this novel, *'Activity Resumed'* by Glumclub, can be found on Spotify, Apple Music, iTunes and Amazon Music.

NANCY BO & ERGONWOLD'S NEST

Paul Scales

NANCY BO & ERGONWOLD'S NEST

Vanguard Press

A CIP catalogue record for this title is
available from the British Library.

ISBN 978 1 784654 74 0

*Vanguard Press is an imprint of
Pegasus Elliot MacKenzie Publishers Ltd.*
www.pegasuspublishers.com

First Published in 2019

**Vanguard Press
Sheraton House Castle Park
Cambridge England**

Printed & Bound in Great Britain

*Inspired by the birth of my daughter,
and dedicated to all those
who do not fit where they have been put.*

1

Oakwell

There was a frenzy of activity within the corridors of Oakwell. The bell for the last day of term rang so loudly you'd have been forgiven for thinking the bell itself was relieved another school year was over. The race to evacuate was punctuated by the sound of lockers opening, doors slamming, and children's shoes squeaking on polished floors.

Nancy Bo Jones looked through the windows at her fellow students hurtling towards the school gates as if their very lives depended on it. She caught her reflection in the glass – her porcelain skin and white curls flashed back at her. She frowned and turned towards the door. It was the final day of term and she had one last detention to attend before her summer holiday could begin.

Nancy Bo cut a lone and solemn figure as she started the long trudge to Mr Tanners' Biology class. Leaving the main building, she made her way through the intertwining corridors, out into the playground, and headed towards the laboratories.

"Nancy Bo," hollered a distant voice.

The chubby outline of Jimmy James was unmistakable. He sped towards her, hair on end and his laces flapping. "Wait for me!" Then he tripped and fell, his words spilling out in a muddle: "You… detention… walking… me… with?"

Nancy stooped down and offered Jimmy her hand. "Are you all

right?"

"Er, yeah," said Jimmy, "Can I walk with you to detention?"

"Sure," replied Nancy, kindly. "You can call me Nanny Bo. That's what my friends back home used to call me."

Jimmy smiled. "Nice one. So... I'm... sort of... like... your boyfriend?"

"Just a friend, Jim Jam," said Nancy, "and a very good one." She checked her phone and changed tack. "What are your plans for the holidays?"

Jimmy rattled off a list between huffs and puffs: a fortnight at Bournemouth, camping in the New Forest, and a day-trip to Windsor Castle. "How about you?"

"My parents haven't made any plans."

A look of concern swept across Jimmy's face. "Oh, I'm sorry."

"Me, too," groaned Nancy. "We're still living out of boxes. My mother said we need time to *get straight*."

"Maybe they will surprise you?"

"No," said Nancy, with a dismissive gesture. "Six weeks of boredom, that's all I've got to look forward to. I hate it here." Her pale face wrinkled with disappointment. "There's nothing to do in the countryside."

The two walked in silence. Jimmy struggled to keep up, his legs skipping in and out of time with Nancy's long, purposeful strides. They cut through the alleyway separating the bicycle sheds from the gymnasium, and approached the Science Block where Prema Sarkander, Elijah Lincoln, and The Duke waited patiently for Mr Tanners. The Duke and Elijah grappled in a mock fight while Prema sat on a wall, shuffling a pack of elaborate picture cards.

Nancy grunted, "Hello," and joined Prema on the wall.

"You look like you're waiting for a bus," said Elijah, flexing his biceps in The Duke's face. "I need to get in and out of here as quickly as possible," he added. "I'm sick of these Friday detentions. We've had a whole term of this. I can't wait for the summer holidays."

"It's only an hour to get through," said Jimmy. "Then your wait is over."

The Duke began to giggle. "You shouldn't have raided the tuck shop, Eli."

"If it hadn't been for that interfering prefect, I would have got away with it," protested Elijah. "I don't know why you think it's so funny, Duke – you were supposed to be my lookout." Elijah pushed his friend to one side and yanked Jimmy's elasticated tie. "Come to think of it, why on earth are you in detention, Jim Jam?"

Jimmy's lips moved, but there were no words.

Elijah released the tie and sniggered as it pinged against Jimmy's neck. "Speak up, Jim Jam!"

Nancy squared up to Elijah. "Leave him alone."

"It's okay, Nanny Bo," said Jimmy. "I got locked in the tuck shop."

"And they punished you with a term of detention?" said Elijah, grinning. "That's a bit harsh."

"I panicked," whimpered Jimmy. "I thought I was going to be stuck in there forever, so I scoffed four chocolate bars, three bags of crisps, and a can of fizzy orange."

Elijah laughed out loud. "Nothing wrong with that!"

"Well, there was one problem," Jimmy added.

"What?"

"Mrs Jenkins found me, and she accused me of stealing school property."

The doors to the classroom swung open and Mr Tanners appeared. He was known affectionately as Jangles. A popular and portly teacher, he carried four sets of keys on his waistband, a half-empty tin of mints in his blazer, and a pocket full of loose change for the vending machine. Everyone could hear him jangling down the corridor half a mile away. It was the twelfth consecutive week he had used the same greeting.

Nancy mouthed it without speaking.

"Here we are, children of the light – light minds for light work. When are you going to apply yourselves and show this school your true potential?"

Jangles tapped the children's heads as they filed into his class and sat in their usual positions: The Duke and Elijah next to each other at the back of the class, Nancy and Jimmy a row ahead of them, and Prema alone at the front. Once they were settled, Jangles began to chalk their names on the revolving board.

Nancy crooked her neck as she watched Prema deal five cards onto her desk.

Jangles blew the dust from the tip of his chalk and coughed for attention. "The length of today's final detention will be determined by you and you alone."

"Let's go now, then," said Elijah. He fist-pumped The Duke, then frantically tried to silence his ringing phone.

Jangles curtailed the interruption with a swish of his cane. "Phones off. How many times do I need to remind you?"

Elijah cowered back into his chair. "Sorry, sir."

"Apology accepted. Now then, I will ask each one of you the same question, and if you answer honestly, this detention will be concluded. Then, and only then, can your summer holidays begin." He jabbed his cane at the first name: Adrian Whittle.

"Why do I have to go first, sir?" asked The Duke.

"Because you're a know-it-all," replied Elijah.

Jangles raised a finger to his mouth, then aimed it at The Duke. "Now then, can someone enlighten me as to why Adrian Whittle is known as The Duke?"

The Duke tapped his fingers rhythmically on the desk and mimicked a concert-hall pianist. "It's because I can play any song on the piano, sir."

"Oh," Jangles said, taken back at the boy's confidence. "A music man."

"My mother calls me Little Duke Ellington, after her favourite artist."

Jangles coughed into his hand. "Very impressive."

"Thank you, sir," said The Duke, graciously. "Unfortunately, Eli found out and now everyone calls me The Duke."

Laughter reverberated around the class, but it was short-lived. The sound of Jangles' cane striking the desk halted the giggles.

"Is that my question over and done with, sir?" The Duke asked.

"No," snapped Jangles. "My questions to all of you are these: what brought you here and what will you do differently in Year Eight to avoid these weekly detentions?"

The class fell silent.

"Stand up, please, Adrian. Oh, I'm sorry, stand up, please, *The Duke*."

The Duke stood. He cleared his throat and brushed his shaggy hair from his cheeks.

"Answer the questions," instructed Jangles.

"Well, I shouldn't have got caught up in the whole tuck-shop theft, sir." The Duke gave a sideways glance to Elijah. "Next year I will not get involved with silly pranks just to please my friends."

Jangles nodded enthusiastically. "Consider this a lesson not to follow others and to concentrate on what is important to you."

"Yes, sir," muttered The Duke. "I will."

Jangles turned to face Elijah Lincoln.

Elijah took a deep breath, shoved his hands into his pockets, and explained himself. "I shouldn't have attempted to rob the tuck shop, sir. I wanted to sell some sweets to the kids. It would've been extra money for the summer holidays."

Jangles stared impassively at Elijah and sighed. "Whatever next?"

"I'm going to concentrate on other money-making schemes next year," countered Elijah. "Maybe a paper round or cleaning cars, but nothing illegal, sir."

"Well done, Elijah. Responsibility is a sign of maturity."

Jimmy pushed his chair back and fiddled with his tie. He waited for Jangles' signal, then mumbled his misgivings. "I was in the wrong place at the wrong time, sir. In future, I will make sure that I think before I do anything rash."

"You are a fine pupil, Jimmy James," confessed Jangles. "I have spoken to Mrs Jenkins, who informs me she did lock the tuck shop door in haste. Maybe next term you will think before you scoff?"

"Yes, sir."

Jangles mouthed, "Good boy," as Jimmy took his seat. Then he stepped towards Prema and eyeballed the five cards. "What have we here, Prema?"

Prema placed her index finger on the first card and lowered her voice. "The first card is a wand, sir."

"I can see that for myself, dear."

"The second is a beautiful mansion, the third a slimy beast, the fourth a glass vial." Prema leaned forward and hid the final card with the palm of her hand. "What will the card reveal, sir?"

Jangles screwed his face up and stepped closer to the cards. "I have no idea, young lady. Let us see."

Nancy watched as Prema raised her hand and pushed the card into the centre of her desk. A pretty blonde girl grasping an emerald stone stared back at them, flecks of green light spilling out from the card, colouring Nancy's face.

The colour drained from Jangles' rosy cheeks, his words sticking in his throat as he steadied himself on the side of the desk. "Oh... my... goodness. The Bloodstone. She's... too... young."

"Are you unwell, sir?" Prema asked. "Is it the cards that unsettle you?"

"Oh, no. No, not at all," said Jangles. He dabbed his brow and regained his composure. "Prema, let us hear your story. Why are you in detention?"

Prema shuffled the picture cards, the fifty-two images arching from one palm to the other as she gathered her thoughts.

"Come on, Miss Sarkander," said Jangles, tapping his watch. "We haven't got all day."

Prema apologised and pushed the cards to one side. "My parents have moved back to India to care for my father's sick brother. I miss them. I have lost my appetite for school."

"I'm s-sorry to h-hear that," stuttered Jangles. "Tell us about these cards."

"My gran teaches me. She is a mystic. They are known as optical cards. They look inside us. They tell us much about the days that have yet to pass. They need my full attention, sir."

Jangles narrowed his eyes and tutted.

Prema nestled her chin into her chest and whispered, "My gran tells me they are more important than school."

"Weirdo," said Elijah, his voice echoing from the back of the class.

"Quiet!" barked Jangles; then he cupped his hand to Prema's ear. "My dear Prema, what would your parents say if they knew your grades had fallen from A to E in two terms?"

"My father would be furious."

"Next time you see them, make them proud of you."

Prema gave a gentle nod as the eyes of the class fell upon Nancy. Jangles doodled on his desk pad, his pen jittering in his fingers, his brow beaded with perspiration. There was an awkward passing of time as he twisted the ring on his little finger. It depicted a bright green iris wrapped around a dark pupil, mounted on gold, and encrusted with six miniature diamonds.

Nancy sat in silence, staring out of the window, lost in a whimsical daydream.

"Nanny Bo," whispered Jimmy, nudging her in the midriff.

"Oh… sorry," replied Nancy, her thoughts interrupted.

"It's so nice of you to grace us with your attention," said

Jangles. He peered out of the window, then back at Nancy. "Please, tell us where you were."

The Duke and Elijah shuddered in a fit of hushed giggles.

"I was thinking about home, my old home – Tooley Street, to be exact, sir."

Jangles spread his arms out wide. "Nancy Bo Jones, please enlighten us."

"Well, sir, Eli mentioned he was looking for ways to make money during the holidays and it reminded me of my weekends in Tooley Street."

"Where's Tooley Street?" The Duke asked, but Jangles hushed him and gestured for Nancy to continue.

"It's in Bermondsey, London. I used to spend every summer helping out the bellboys for loose change or handing out leaflets for the Tower of London. I got good tips and I had regulars like Mr Wuu from—"

"Mr Wuu?" interrupted The Duke.

"Will you let her speak?" pleaded Jangles.

"Mr Wuu was from Beijing. He was a businessman. He worked for the largest toy distributer in the world. I loved mixing with all the different types of people."

"Sounds interesting," said Jangles, flipping the lid off his tin of mints. "A toymaker… well, well, well."

A smile spread across Nancy's face. "It was my home. It's where I belong. You really had to have your wits about you. Now I'm here, in detention, in a place I don't know, where everyone I meet is—"

"What?" interrupted Elijah. "Not as good as you?"

"No!" said Nancy, furiously. "No one understands me. It's just different here. Different places breed different people. That's what my dad says."

"So," said Elijah, "you're *different* to us, is that it?"

Nancy pulled a face. "Everyone around here is similar. There's nothing to separate one person from another." She paused, stared up at the ceiling, and sighed heavily. "Oh, it doesn't matter."

Prema spun on her chair. "Everything matters. London is an amazing city. You must really miss it."

"I do."

Jangles left his desk and strode towards Nancy. "You need to be a special type of person to survive in our capital city, and that's what you are, Nancy Bo Jones. Special."

Nancy bit her lip and shuffled nervously on her seat.

"Now then," said Jangles, "tell us why you are here and what you will do differently next year."

"I only arrived in April, sir. I haven't bothered applying myself. I don't fit in." Nancy's voice faltered as she fought back the tears. "I really miss home. I will try harder in Year Eight."

Jangles shook his chubby cheeks. "Your self-pity is woeful. You *do* and *will* fit in at Oakwell. Do not alienate yourself. Otherwise, no one will ever understand you. If you change your outlook, Year Eight will be a whole lot easier." Jangles stomped up and down, his face twitching as he stared at Nancy. "We have been awaiting your arrival and—"

"You were expecting me?" interrupted Nancy. "How...?"

"Silence!" barked Jangles. "You need to show us what you're made of."

Elijah leaned into The Duke. "What did he mean, *we have been awaiting your arrival*?"

"How do I know?" replied The Duke from the corner of his mouth.

"Class dismissed," yelled Jangles.

The children exchanged bemused looks as they gathered their belongings and left their desks. Jangles stared out of the window, lost in thought, muttering, "It's missing," over and over.

Jimmy crept cautiously to the side of his tutor. "Are you okay, sir?"

"The Bloodstone – it must be returned. It must go back."

"I beg your pardon, sir?"

"Nothing, J-Jimmy, it's n-nothing," stuttered Jangles. "Go away. I mean, go and enjoy your summer holidays."

Nancy slid her chair beneath the desk and made her way out of the classroom.

"Wait!" bellowed Jangles.

Nancy froze. "Yes, sir."

"Make yourself known to Aunt Elma at the library. And find *The First Book of Cosmo.*"

"The what?"

But there was no time for answers. Jangles nudged Nancy out of the room and slammed the door behind her.

2
The Jagganath

Nancy woke with a start. The bright July sunshine pierced through her velvet curtains, striking the stained floorboards like shards of glass. Her bedroom was awash with hair accessories, lip balm, magazines, and strange-looking toys perched upon crooked shelves. The quartz alarm clock by the open window flashed 10.33am. It was the sound of her father mowing the lawn that prompted her to get out of bed.

All she could think of was Aunt Elma and the library. The entire detention had aroused her curiosity. For the first time since the Joneses had moved to leafy Berkshire, she had something to occupy her mind: a person to find and a book to read.

Who on earth is Aunt Elma? Nancy thought, as she wrestled with her skinny jeans. She zipped her hoodie, laced her pumps, then slid down the banister and landed feet first in the hallway. She entered the kitchen with a wide – and unfamiliar – smile. "Can I have some poached eggs?"

"Hold on a minute, babe," came the gruff reply. "I'm just finishing off this stupid survey from the council. I don't know how to attach the document to the email."

"Just click on the top right, Mum. Let me show—"

"Done it. What a ridiculous idea – a happiness survey.

Whatever will the council come up with next?"

"Don't know," replied Nancy, nonplussed.

"How on earth can you measure happiness?" asked Bessy Jones. "It's absurd. So, you fancy some poached eggs?"

"Yes, please."

Bessy stared at her little girl leaning against the fridge and smiled. "Have I got the old Nanny Bo back?"

"What are you on about? I haven't been away, I was upstairs."

"It's the first time I've seen you smiling on the inside as well as the out. Ever since we moved here you've been a fully paid-up member of the Glum Club."

There was a moment's pause before Nancy spoke. "I miss London. You dragged me here without explanation."

"It's for the best," replied Bessy, her eyes flashing with anger. "Sometimes sacrifices have to be made. In life, we have to prepare for the worst possible outcome."

Nancy considered her mother's words for a moment. "That's living in fear."

"Survivors – that's what us Joneses are – survivors," said Bessy, with a face of steel.

Nancy stepped back. She never crossed her mother – her fuse was short and her temper wild. "Can I have some sauce with my eggs?"

Bessy's anger vanished as quickly as it had arrived. "Of course you can, darlin'."

Nancy tucked into her breakfast and gulped down two mugs of tea. She wiped her mouth and thanked her mother.

Bessy acknowledged her daughter with a wink. "Make sure you say goodbye to your father before you leave."

"Okay."

Nancy skipped into the garden and yelled above the din of the mower, "I'm going out, dad!"

Teddy Jones spun around, his huge frame almost blocking out

the morning sun. The lines over his eyes, his squashed nose, and cauliflower ears were marks of his happy days boxing for Repton Boys. His curly white hair and kind eyes had been passed on to his daughter. He turned the lawnmower off and saluted his daughter. "Where you going?"

Nancy laughed. "No need to salute, dad. I'm off to the library."

Teddy returned a look of astonishment. "The library? My Nanny Bo is going to the—?"

"Yes," interjected Nancy, "I'm going to the library to find a book."

Teddy shook his head and restarted the mower.

Nancy grabbed her rucksack, walked back into the kitchen, through the hall, and slammed the front door behind her.

Her route to the library was a pretty one. The river snaked its way through three villages before it split the town centre in two. She cycled along the towpath, bobbing and weaving through a myriad of weeping willows, the tips of their spindly branches dipping into the water like gnarled fingertips.

Nancy removed her hair band and let the wind dance through her curls. She pedalled onwards, passing the grand houses that lined the riverbank, their pretty gardens meandering down to endless rows of moored barges. She cycled faster, and faster, focusing on the narrow path ahead. It wasn't long before the sweet summer air was tarnished by a foul odour. The passers-by and dog walkers appeared oblivious, but the putrid smell wafted up Nancy's nostrils and trickled down her throat. It was a vile, rotten stench that curdled her insides. She winced, squeezed her brake lever, and came to a shuddering halt. Her bicycle was now inches from a dilapidated, ramshackled vessel. Every porthole was cracked, and the smell emanating from within was enough to make the most settled of stomachs churn. She scrutinised the ruined barge. For a fleeting moment, Nancy was convinced there was someone on board. She stepped closer and stared through a grimy porthole.

Two bright red pupils glared back at her.

Then they were gone.

She peered through again. Nothing.

Then a strange reptilian hiss attacked her inner ear. *"Sssstay away, sssstay away. Don't raisssse the portal. Sssstay away."*

"Who's that?" asked Nancy, frantically looking for a body to match the voice. Her heart thumped as she placed one foot on board. The reptilian shrill returned, louder and distinct: "I have been ssssent by my master. I order you to sssstop your mission."

Nancy covered her ears. "What mission?"

"Ssssilence," hissed the voice.

Nancy wiped the porthole with her cuff and peered below deck. An oval head dripping in mucus stared back at her. She gulped, then let out a high-pitched scream.

"Ssssilence," hissed the creature. "I am one of The Jagganath. I can only stay in this realm for a limited time. So lisssssten to me, little girl, for your own sake. Sssstay away from the woods, and do not raisssse the portal."

Two hands pulled Nancy to her feet.

"Are you okay?" asked a friendly voice.

Nancy stared at the lady, finding it hard to focus on her. "I think so. There's something below deck. Something nasty."

"Nonsense," replied the woman. "This barge has been here for years. It's unattended and it's about time we informed the river police."

"But I heard a voice," proclaimed Nancy.

The lady rolled her eyes. "Did you?"

"Yes," replied Nancy, jabbing her finger at the lower deck. "There is *something* down there."

The smile disappeared from the woman's face as she descended a short flight of steps and examined the living quarters. "Nothing here," she declared from below.

"There was," shouted Nancy.

"I'm late," replied the lady, reappearing from below deck. She brushed a cobweb from her shoulder and stepped back onto dry land. "Are you sure you are okay, dear?"

"Yes," confirmed Nancy. She leaped from the vessel and landed on the riverbank. "I'm fine."

The woman shook Nancy by the hand. "Good," she said, and waddled downstream, swinging her handbag with every step.

Nancy didn't waste a second: as soon as the woman had disappeared from view, she clambered aboard. Her eyes scoured the barge for any sign of life. She stepped below. It was cold, damp and empty. She kicked a discarded lifejacket to one side and yelled, "Where are you?"

A passing boat disturbed the river, its bow cutting through the still water like a blade. Nancy wobbled on her feet as the surge of water rocked the barge from side to side. Cutlery slid from the work surface, clattering onto the floor. She left the dank room, jumped onto dry land, and considered going home.

It was then that she realised she had nothing, and no one to go home to. This wasn't London: her social circle was empty. Avoiding the river, Nancy cycled to the library. She followed signs to the shopping mall, chained her bike to a lamp-post, and sauntered into Central Square. The square was the focal point of the town centre. Shops, cafés and restaurants were sandwiched together on all sides. All Nancy could think of was the Jagganath; her mind was consumed, but she had to focus on the task at hand: finding Aunt Elma. She took a sharp left by the post office, and stared in awe at The Royal Berkshire Library.

Four banks of marbled steps led up to the grand entrance. The glass roof was gigantic – she was convinced it touched the clouds. A large double doorway was encased with elaborate brass hinges. Above the threshold, a plaque was beaded in gold: 'Here, on the Fifteenth Day of September, 1907, The Right Honourable Mayor of Berkshire, Middleton Trump, opened and funded the first library of

Berkshire. Knowledge and information free to all.'

Nancy climbed the steps. Now she could do what she did best – people watch. She studied the visitors – bow-ties, feathered hats, pinstripe suits, even military uniforms came and went. A tiny voice nestled somewhere in the thrum of the crowd. It was familiar. The squeak of a call came again. Nancy glanced over her shoulder. Prema Sarkander stood on tiptoe, waving a pencil case. "Are you okay, Nanny Bo?"

"Yes," lied Nancy. "What on earth are you doing here?"

"My gran told me to meet you."

Nancy puffed her cheeks and slumped onto the steps. "How on earth did your gran know I was here?"

Prema placed a hand on Nancy's shoulder. "The cards link hearts and minds."

"Oh, come off it, Pre. What do you take me for?"

Prema shook her head, confused. "I don't understand."

"I don't mean to shatter your dreams, but those cards are—"

"Are what?" interrupted Prema.

"They're a load of old tosh," said Nancy, trying her best not to laugh. "I've seen them in Rotherhithe. A gypsy woman sells them with her heather."

Prema waved her finger. "You are wrong." She unzipped her pencil case and pulled out a silver box. She opened it, removed the cards, and placed them in Nancy's palm. A warm residual heat crept up Nancy's arm. She arched her brow and turned the top card. A slimy creature stared back at her. The inscription on the foot of the card read: *Jagganath: Safe Keeper of Zayock.* Her stomach somersaulted. "That's it!" she cried.

"What?" asked Prema.

"The monster," whispered Nancy, unable to believe her own words.

Prema stared wide-eyed at her friend.

The blood rushed to Nancy's cheeks as she pressed her finger on the cards. "I've seen all sorts of strange things in London – magicians, sword swallowers, and the like – but never moving picture cards."

"These optical cards belonged to my great-great-grandmother from Bhopal," admitted Prema.

"Well," said Nancy, breathless, "they certainly look ancient."

"They are," confirmed Prema. "Every other pack in the world is a poor replica of these. They have been passed through our family from one generation to another." Prema reached for the card in Nancy's hand and shuffled the pack. "Only three Sarkanders have actually been able to tune into them. They act as a conduit to unravel the mysteries of the universe."

"*Tune in*? What do you mean?"

"The cards work on energy waves," replied Prema. "Only when they are held by an individual who possesses the required spiritual balance can they work their magic."

"If they're so good, what do you know of my day?"

"Please don't be angry," replied Prema. She fanned the cards and went on, "I'm still learning how to piece together the information that they present."

"*Information*?" repeated Nancy, with a bemused look.

"Yes," said Prema, quietly. "I have broken images, disjointed messages. All I know is that you were in danger and my gran told me to meet you here."

Nancy threw her hands up into the air. "I have to find Aunt Elma and a book. She's somewhere in this library. Do you want to come with me?"

"Really?" asked Prema, astounded. "You don't mind if I tag along?"

"No. Not at all."

Prema slid the optical cards back into the silver box, and the two girls walked into the library.

3
The Library

The open-plan foyer of the library resembled a busy railway station. People were milling about everywhere, trying to locate books on the endless shelves, pushing and shoving in front of the information booths, each of which displayed a sign that read 'Silence'. They were manned by an officious-looking librarian and a young assistant who fetched, carried, and sorted books.

Nancy Bo glanced up at the domed roof; she had never seen anything like it. Silver arches supported sculptures of Greek gods holding out their hands as if they were waiting to be fed. The reinforced glass ceiling allowed light to flood in. The busy book-seekers walked around the library like clockwork toys, zigzagging from one direction to the next.

Nancy dashed through the crowds, yanking Prema by the arm. "This way."

"Careful," said Prema. "We nearly bumped into—"

"Shh," interrupted Nancy. She curled a finger and walked on. "Follow me."

"I don't have a choice," complained Prema. "How are we supposed to find Aunt Elma? It's far too crowded."

Nancy pointed at Booth Nine. "Look!"

"What?"

"Haven't you noticed? It's the only one without a librarian. There's just an assistant."

"Oh," said Prema, grinning, "I see."

Nancy observed the thin, gangly book clerk in front of her, his beige uniform a size too small, the cuffs raised above his wrists as if it had been shrunk in the wash.

"Can I assist you?" asked the young man.

"I hope so," replied Nancy. "I'm looking for a lady by the name of Elma Tanners."

"The name rings a bell. Would you like me to check my staff listings?"

"Yes, please."

While the assistant thumbed through a folder, Nancy noticed the lanyard hanging around his giraffe-like neck: Oswald Goddard, Trainee, Crime Section.

"Thanks, Oswald."

Oswald Goddard returned a polite smile and continued checking the list. Nancy's eyes wandered around the library, then crept up to the magnificent glass dome. A shaft of sunlight pierced through and struck Oswald's ring.

Nancy was thunderstruck. "It's the same as Jangles'."

"What is?" asked Prema.

"The ring," replied Nancy from the corner of her mouth. "It's identical."

There was no mistaking it – an emerald iris wrapped around a pupil, mounted in gold, and encrusted with six tiny diamonds. Oswald fidgeted on the spot, twisting the ring on his little finger.

"You must know Jangles," proclaimed Nancy. She held eye contact with the lanky junior and raised her voice. "You must know Elma Tanners, too."

"Young lady, please keep your voice down."

"Do you know her?" asked Nancy, in a quiet yet demanding tone.

Oswald's lips moved, but there was no sound. His nostrils flared and his chest expanded. Then, finally, he relented. "Well, maybe, but I'm not supposed to..."

"I knew it," said Nancy. She fixed Oswald with her blue eyes and whispered, "Why did you lie to us?"

Oswald studied Nancy's face. "Are you the Jones girl from London?"

Now it was Nancy's turn to be shocked.

Prema answered for her: "Yes, she is."

Oswald stooped down and hung a 'Closed' sign over two brass hooks. He pointed to a door at the rear of the building. "You were not supposed to come here." His eyes darted left and right. "Follow me."

Nancy and Prema brushed through the crowds and followed Oswald. They scurried past the 'Science Fiction' booth and approached the fire escape. Oswald flung open the doors, and bright, radiant sunshine struck their faces. Nancy ran through and pulled a pair of sunglasses from her pocket.

They stood within a huge courtyard framed by four brick walls. Roses, clematis, and sweet peas combined to create a rainbow effect on the south-facing wall. In the far corner was a wooden door no bigger than a cat flap. Above it, a faded sign surrounded by ivy announced: Willowmead: Home For The Incurably Curious.

Oswald pointed at the doorway. "You will find Aunt Elma behind that door."

Nancy held out her hands as if surrendering to an invisible foe. "What's going on? Do you think we're stupid?"

"I'm sorry," said Oswald. "Jangles is my uncle, and Elma is his aunt. She resides at The Home For The Incurably Curious."

Nancy stepped closer to Oswald. "Jangles told me to visit Aunt Elma at *the library*."

"Jangles should've explained," said Oswald, earnestly. "It's been a long while coming. Eleven years, to be exact."

"Eleven years?" repeated Nancy, "eleven years since what?"

"Since…" Oswald paused for thought. He stared at the sign above the tiny door and realised he had said too much. "We always refer to *Willowmead* as *the library*. It was the original, you see, long before Middleton Trump built this grandiose building. Legend has it, the original Magic Circle was founded at Willowmead."

Nancy sighed, unimpressed at Oswald's ramblings. "Magic Circle; pull the other one."

Oswald tapped his watch. "I've been away from my desk too long. I'm sorry, I can't offer you more time." He twisted the ring on his finger, and slammed the door behind him.

Nancy shook her head. Nothing made sense. She stood less than twenty metres from the miniature door. She turned to Prema and huffed. "Now what?"

"I'm not sure," replied Prema, unzipping her pencil case. She removed the optical cards from the box and shuffled the pack.

Nancy stepped closer to the door. "We need to get through."

"We can't fit through there," replied Prema.

"There must be a way," insisted Nancy. "Behind that door are Aunt Elma, the book, and the Magic Circle."

Prema stared at a single card. "I've seen this before – the cards present two stars. Strange, very strange."

"Look!" screamed Nancy. "A light!" She tiptoed closer to the door. A warm, orange glow was now seeping from the fissures all around it. "Come on, Pre. What are we waiting for?"

Prema remained rooted to the spot, the optical cards hiding her face. The mesmerising light pulled Nancy closer. With each step the traction grew stronger. Just as she reached the doorway, an intoxicating mist engulfed her. Her limbs became heavy, her vision blurred, and strange, whispering voices echoed inside of her. "*There is a light that never goes out.*"

Nancy collapsed.

Prema looked up from the fan of cards. "Nanny Bo!"

Nancy stumbled to her feet. "Did you hear them?" she asked, breathless.

"What?" asked Prema.

"The voices."

"No," replied Prema.

"They were beautiful, like a choir."

"What were?"

"The voices… you must have heard them?"

"No," said Prema, "I didn't hear a thing. Are you okay, Nanny Bo?"

"Of course I am." Nancy brushed the last of the gravel from her thighs and tapped the door. "I think someone is trying to lure me inside."

Prema checked the courtyard. "But there's no one here."

"I haven't been entirely honest with you," confessed Nancy. "Something strange happened on my way to the library."

Prema punched the air. "I knew it."

Nancy stalled.

"Tell me," said Prema, excitedly.

"Okay, but no laughing."

Prema crossed her fingers and held them aloft. "I promise."

Slowly, bit by bit, Nancy pieced together the day's events, grimacing as she described the Jagganath, her face crimson. The story sounded so bizarre, she almost questioned it herself.

Prema sat in silence, deep in thought, listening, flicking through the optical cards, absorbing every word. With each passing second of silence, the agitation festered within Nancy. She stared at the doorway, the seductive orange light still glowing from within. Then she jabbed her elbow into Prema and said, "You think I'm making all of this up, don't you?"

Prema looked Nancy in the eye. "No, I don't. It all adds up to what my gran said. You are a special person, and you don't even know it."

Nancy tutted. "I don't feel special."

"The cards say you are special – you have an elevated spirit and an unusual gift for sensing what's around you."

"Too much information, Pre. Those cards freak me out – they're weird."

Prema picked a rose from the wall. "The scent reminds me of my mother. I really miss her."

Nancy watched Prema as she picked the petals from the bud. "What's she like?"

"Incredible," replied Prema. "She's the person I want to be when I grow up. And now she's gone."

"And your dad?"

"He has a goofy smile," admitted Prema; then her voice broke. "I miss them so much it hurts. You're not the only unhappy kid at Oakwell." She dropped the rose bud and lowered her voice. "I've never met anyone like you before, Nanny Bo. But I just don't understand you."

Nancy smiled. "Not many people do."

"One minute you make me feel like anything's possible, the next you act as if the world's going to end. You're so unpredictable."

Nancy shrugged. "I'm sorry, Pre. Tell me about the cards. You have my full attention."

"I'm still learning how to decipher the information that they present," explained Prema. "My gran is ninety-six. She has a lifetime of mystical knowledge to pass on. My parents forbade me to even touch the optical cards."

"Why?"

"Like you, they are sceptical. Since they left for India, my gran has seized the opportunity to teach me. Thanks to her, I now know some of the meanings and codes of the cards. I'm getting better by the day and—"

"Go on," interrupted Nancy, her appetite for knowledge rapidly increasing.

"And when I removed the cards, they presented an image."

"What image?"

"Two stars. The child of destiny and fortune."

Nancy stared at her friend. "What is that?"

"It's you."

"Me?"

"Yes, you," replied Prema. "That's what the cards say."

Nancy rubbed her thumb and forefinger together. "Am I going to be rich?"

Prema laughed. "Stop taking the mickey."

"I'm sorry; carry on."

"There is a magical force all around you," explained Prema, whispering as if she were revealing a dark secret. "And you are very close to the 'Window of Change'. You must reach for the light and it will show you the way."

Nancy was aghast. "Reach for what light? That's what the voices in my head said…"

"You asked me what I knew and, right now, that's all I can say. The cards offer me snippets of information." Prema shuffled the pack, then slid it back into its case. "Does that mean anything to you?"

Nancy's heart sank. She stared at her feet and shrugged. "I'm not sure."

"I've been dealing your cards since you arrived at Oakwell. The images are very strong. But hard to decipher."

"Why didn't you tell me?"

"Because I knew you wouldn't believe me," confessed Prema. "The creature that appeared is a Jagganath, a soldier of negative energy. To interact with such a being, you must possess a high tuning level – really high."

Nancy arched her brow. "Tuning level?"

"Yes. My gran refers to it as E.S.P." Prema placed a finger on each temple and exaggerated the three words with gusto: "Extra. Sensory. Perception."

Nancy ballooned her cheeks as Prema tried her best to explain: "My gran says it's where your head is like a radio tuned into a certain station, and you can pick up things others can't – because they're not. Tuned into it, I mean."

"Oh," said Nancy, taken aback. She narrowed her eyes as she strained to hear a secretive frequency. There was nothing; nothing but a vacuous silence.

"All I know is that you are here for a reason," said Prema, enthusiastically, "and there are forces out to encourage you, and forces to distract you. You are chosen."

"Chosen?" echoed Nancy.

"Yes. What for, I don't know; but once we know, the cards will be easier to understand. We must find Aunt Elma, and the sooner the better."

Nancy nodded. A large part of her wanted to believe Prema. The day-to-day drudgery of life at Oakwell had taken its toll. She knew the Jagganath was not a figment of her imagination and that Prema was no ordinary girl. She stood up and pulled her friend to her feet. "You don't speak like a normal kid. You sound like a fortune teller from the fairground."

"I'm the same as you – an eleven-year-old girl. Just a little bit smaller."

Nancy pushed back her locks and smiled. "Until today, all I've been dreaming about is running away. Running away from my parents' lies. You and your grandmother's cards have opened my eyes."

A broad grin stretched across Prema's face.

Nancy turned to face the minute door. "Are we going to find a way through?"

"Yes," replied Prema.

Nancy pushed her sunglasses up onto her forehead and

inspected the door. Then the mist descended again.

Her legs buckled.

The voices were now stronger than before. Her heart raced with excitement and fear in a wretched concoction of tangled emotions.

Reach for the light. You are a dual-star. We are waiting.

Over and over the voices broke upon her, like waves on a shoreline. It seemed to last a lifetime. Nancy wanted to believe the voices were real, but she couldn't. She was afraid. Afraid to trust. Afraid to disregard her mother's pessimistic mantra. She closed her eyes and blocked every negative thought. Then, as the voices unlocked her mistrust, she opened her heart and mind to the reality of the enchanted sound.

A vision formed in her mind's eye, and she pictured herself opening a door to a complete stranger. *This person is in need. I have to help.* She could hear her own voice as if through another.

Then a second voice entered her head, competing with the first. It was her mother's. "Your father told you never to let in strangers."

Nancy closed her mind to the voice of doubt. She wanted to greet the visitor. She *had* to. As the stranger crossed the threshold and lifted its head, wrinkles and creases surrounded the most beautiful green, oval eyes, while small tusks protruded from either side of a jaw, and the creature conveyed a warmth and love that lifted her spirits. The scent of warm honey wafted through the air, and her heart skipped to a joyous beat. She wanted to freeze the moment and stay in it forever, but the voices and the creature faded away and the haze lifted.

Nancy opened her eyes, unsure of where she was or what had happened.

"What's going on?" asked Prema, uneasily. "You did it again. You were sort of... all far away. I was calling you, but you didn't answer."

"It was misty," confessed Nancy, "and the voices... they returned. They were so beautiful, Pre."

The two girls were now centimetres from the diminutive door. Nancy grabbed her hair band and scrunched her ringlets back. Her sunglasses lay shattered at her feet. She unzipped her pocket, pulled out a compact mirror, and checked her face. As she did, there was a creaking noise.

Nancy's chalky face was now coloured by a warm orange light.

"The door," Prema gasped. "It's opening…"

4
Snorkel and Flippers

The hailstones pummelled the slate roof so hard that Jimmy James thought they sounded like tiny comets falling from outer space. This got him thinking. Perched on the window ledge, his hands clutching the side of his cheeks, he stared out at the bleak, rain-swept landscape.

Jimmy dreamed of saving planet Earth from the falling sky, whizzing from street to street on a motorised skateboard, taking aim with his laser gun and firing at the Earth-bound comets, disintegrating them completely. He would create a superhero appearance by wearing a cape, eye mask and leather boots equipped with jet-propelled engines to leap skywards at a moment's notice.

He would be known as 'Comet Boy'!

A familiar voice stopped the dream in its jet-packed tracks. Brenda James had waddled into the kitchen. "Snorkel and flippers. Have you packed your snorkel and flippers, Jimmy?"

"We're not leaving for another three days, mum, and my suitcase is already half-full. I'll put them in just before we leave, then they'll be at the top when I open it in Bournemouth."

"Remember last year?" frowned Brenda. "You forgot to pack them and we had to buy another set on the promenade. Then we had rain for the remainder of our holiday. Don't jinx us again."

Brenda James was a local councillor and everybody knew it. She had a headful of fluffy hair, a superstitious temperament, and a reputation for being a busybody. She was a meticulous planner, and preparations for the summer holiday had been made with military precision. Brenda had a map with pre-planned toilet breaks marked at even-numbered motorway junctions. The timings for these, and indeed for their departure and arrival, had been typed onto a spreadsheet and handed out to all. Everyone had a job, and Brenda's job was to make sure everybody fell in line.

Jimmy left the kitchen and skipped into the hallway. He stopped as a loud knock rattled the front door. Brenda shook her head and yelled, "Can you get that, dear? I'm just writing my checklist for the journey."

"Okay, mum."

Jimmy reached beneath the telephone table and pulled out a small step. He tiptoed onto the stool and released the security bolt that was high above the latch. He twisted it. As the lock was released, a slender hand wrapped itself around the edge of the door and pushed it open.

Jimmy tumbled to the floor. He looked up and saw three coloured feathers.

"Oh, dear, I didn't realise you were on the stool, Jimmy," said Cynthia Leathwaite, as she straightened her feathered hat. She raised her eyebrows and tutted. "I do hope your backside isn't bruised." Then she whispered, "Lovely boy," and marched directly into the kitchen.

Jimmy got to his feet and stared at the two women from the hallway.

"Good morning, Brenda."

"Hello, Cynthia. What's all the commotion?"

"Little Jimmy took a tumble."

"Oh," said Brenda, "I hope he doesn't forget to pack his snorkel and flippers."

"When are you leaving?"

"In three days, Cynthia – we leave in three days. Nothing is running to schedule and I still haven't completed that damn happiness survey for the council."

"That survey is preposterous," declared Cynthia.

"I know," sighed Brenda. "Hundreds of questions to gauge happiness and mood. Haven't they got anything better to do than email us that nonsense?"

Cynthia shrugged. "I just popped in to see if you wanted me to—?"

"Yes, please," interrupted Brenda. "The same as usual. Can you water the pot plants on Tuesday and Saturday and take the bins out on Monday at 8.30am prompt?"

"Of course, Brenda. Anything else before I—?"

"Please don't go, Cynthia. I feel terribly rude. I haven't even offered you a cup of tea. Just let me finish this list and I will be with you in a jiffy."

Cynthia sat at the kitchen table and removed her hat. She pressed her forefinger over her wrist and silently measured her pulse.

"Done, done, done," cried Brenda with relief, clapping her hands and letting out her trademark hyena cackle. "Now, what will it be, shortbread or digestive?"

Cynthia's answer was immediate: "Shortbread, please."

Cynthia brushed off the last of the raindrops from her shoulders and smiled. "Terrible weather, Brenda, but it's supposed to be a red-hot summer, you know? I hope it clears up for you. Bournemouth is such a beautiful place."

Brenda's checklist was now wedged between her teeth as she carried over a tray of biscuits and a pot of tea. She placed the tray down, removed the slip of paper from her mouth, and handed it to Cynthia. "It's just a little reminder of what I need you—"

"But I have been—"

"I know what you're going to say," interrupted Brenda. "You've been doing this for over ten years. You know what I'm like – I need to make sure. And I've added an emergency number if you need it."

Cynthia rolled her eyes. "Is it for the Crab Shack?" Brenda nodded, then Cynthia folded the paper in her purse, looked up, and noticed Jimmy standing in the doorway. "Have you been eavesdropping, Jimmy James?"

"No, Mrs Leathwaite."

Cynthia Leathwaite rubbed her chin and tutted. "Where on earth are you going on a day like this, Jimmy? It's pouring down."

"I'm going to see the lock-keeper. He said he had a spare crab line for my holidays."

"You can take my umbrella if you want. I've only got to step next door."

"Thanks," replied Jimmy, "I'll be fine. It's only rain."

Cynthia and Brenda smiled, then crooned in unison, "Ah."

Jimmy left the kitchen and stepped back into the hallway, ready to brave the hailstones.

Brenda yelled a final pre-holiday warning: "Make sure Mummy's Little Soldier doesn't catch a cold before his holiday."

Jimmy's face burnt crimson red. He turned and stomped back into the kitchen. "Please don't call me that in front of people."

"Oh, come on, dear. Cynthia's like the auntie you never had. It's no big deal."

"I know, but I—"

"What?"

"I don't want you to call me that if I bring friends home."

"Friends?" said Brenda, startled. "I'm still waiting to meet one of your so-called friends. You never mention anyone's name, let alone bring them home for tea." Brenda chinked her cup loudly against her saucer. "Come to think of it, you have mentioned one name."

"Who?" asked Jimmy, fiddling with the zip on his mackintosh.

"That new girl – what's her name?" Brenda scratched her head. "Nelly Jo? That's it – Nelly Jo. What a ridiculous name. Whatever were her parents thinking of?"

Jimmy stamped his boots defiantly. "It's Nancy Bo. And her friends call her Nanny Bo."

"Is she your girlfriend, Jimmy?" asked Cynthia.

"No, she is my friend."

"So, she's your *girl-friend*," said Brenda, with a suspicious nod.

"No, mum, we are friends and—"

"And she's from London, and not to be trusted," interjected Brenda. "That family and their house are bad news. Make sure you stay clear of them, otherwise you'll be grounded, okay?" Brenda James stared at her son. "What's the matter, Jimmy?"

Jimmy stalled, as if hunting for the right words. "Nothing. I'm fine. And Nanny Bo is my best friend. It doesn't matter what you say. Or do!"

"Well, explain yourself," said Brenda, affronted. "Why do you like this Nancy Bo?"

"I call her *Nanny Bo*, and she's special, a one-off."

Cynthia pulled her chair closer to the table. "And what makes this *Nanny Bo* so special?"

"She's different from all the other kids. She's brave and she sticks up for me." Jimmy wiped his nose on the cuff of his raincoat and went on: "Nanny Bo has seen so much more than I ever will. She had to find work in London because her parents couldn't afford pocket money."

Brenda rolled her eyes, then pointed at her son. "Not all children are as lucky as you, Jimmy James."

"You don't get it, do you?" retorted Jimmy. "I would love the opportunity to work for my pocket money, especially in London. Nanny Bo says it's the greatest city in the world – a place where fantasy meets reality."

"Absolute rubbish," replied Brenda. "Nanny Bo should go back to where she belongs – that run-down council estate in London."

"Just because she's different doesn't make her a bad person," said Jimmy, angrily. "You can't choose my friends for me."

The two women stared at each other, the pendulum of the grandfather clock measuring the awkward silence. Brenda looked up from her cup and saucer. "I'm sorry I have upset you. I've never seen you like this before." Her face changed from concerned to resolute. "But you are only eleven years old and it is easy to be blinded by feelings. In time you will understand my reservations towards the girl. I want you to stay away from her. Okay?"

"What do you mean, *in time I will understand*?"

Brenda coughed in an attempt to gain Cynthia's attention.

Cynthia's gaze fell to the floor. She fiddled with the buttons on her jacket, and hummed quietly.

"Cynthia," said Brenda, over Cynthia's tuneless humming.

Jimmy watched as the tension between the two women increased. "What do you mean, *in time I will understand*?"

No one answered him. He waited. And waited. "Is someone going to tell me?"

Brenda's eyes were fixed on Cynthia Leathwaite. "Cynthia, I need to tell him."

"He's too young," mumbled Cynthia, "and now is not the time."

With that, Brenda pointed towards the door that separated the kitchen from the hallway. Cynthia stood, grabbed her feathered hat, and marched towards it. Brenda followed her out into the hallway. Then the kitchen door slammed shut.

Jimmy stood alone and counted the ticks and tocks of the old clock. He stared up at the ceiling, then back at the door. He tiptoed across the kitchen floor, crouched down, and placed his ear to the keyhole.

45

"I told you never to mention this, Brenda."

"How can I possibly not mention it?"

"Let go of me," insisted Cynthia, breaking the whispers. "I have only just had this jacket cleaned."

"I'm sorry," replied Brenda. "Jimmy needs to know. It's not fair on him. I don't want that girl in my house."

Jimmy couldn't contain himself for a moment longer. He pulled open the door and shouted, "What. Do. I. Need. To. Know?"

Brenda clamped her palm over Jimmy's mouth and ushered him back to the kitchen table. "Quiet. Think of the neighbours." She removed her hand and pushed him onto a stool. "I know he's young, but we have to tell him, Cynthia."

Cynthia shook her head.

"But if my son remains friends with her, that girl could be in my home."

Cynthia drew an imaginary cross on her chest and relented. "I understand, but we must swear him to secrecy."

"I swear," said Jimmy.

Brenda leaned over the kitchen sink, grabbed a tea towel, and slapped it on the draining board. "Jimmy!"

"Yes, mum."

"I need you to promise me..."

"I promise."

"Sit down, dear – sit down," insisted Cynthia, placing her arm on Jimmy's shoulder and easing him back onto the stool. "Be patient – your mother has something to tell you."

Brenda knotted her apron strings as she walked back to the kitchen table. "Jimmy, you do know how long Cynthia and her family have lived here?"

"Years and years. Longer than us," confirmed Jimmy.

"Well, many years ago, one of Cynthia's relatives knew the person who lived in 145 Oxon Road."

Jimmy raised a finger and said, "That's Nanny Bo's house!"

"Yes, love. Nanny Bo's house," repeated Brenda in a mock-London accent. Then her eyes filled with tears and her sniffles quickly turned to sobs. "I can't do this, Cynthia."

"That's okay," replied Cynthia. "I will tell the boy all he needs to know."

Cynthia perched herself beside Jimmy and held his hand. "Now then, what I'm about to tell you must never be repeated. Agreed?" She squeezed Jimmy's hand and raised her eyebrows.

"Ouch," yelped Jimmy.

"Agreed?" repeated Cynthia Leathwaite, with a glint in her eye.

"Okay, Mrs Leathwaite," replied Jimmy. "Agreed."

"Good boy. Now then…" Cynthia paused, then expelled a jet of air through her nostrils like a yard dog. "Many years ago, my auntie lived in an old house that backed onto Roebuck Woods."

"Nanny Bo's house," confirmed Jimmy.

"Yes, although, back then, Roebuck Woods didn't actually exist."

"Oh, I thought the woods were always there."

"Jimmy James, if you want to hear this story, I will not accept rude interruptions."

"I'm sorry."

"Apology accepted. Now then, where was I? Oh, yes…" Cynthia pulled out a crumpled piece of paper from a zipped compartment in her purse, unravelled it and cleared her throat. "145 Oxon Road – that was the house my auntie spent most of her life in. Once upon a time, it overlooked a huge stately home called Bymerstone Hall. It was surrounded by acres and acres of beautiful gardens. In recent times the woods have covered the once well-manicured land."

Cynthia rubbed her chin, looked over her shoulder, then back at Jimmy. "My auntie's flimsy fence was all that kept her from the impressive gardens and stately home. On a clear day you could see the house in all its splendour, with its fine lawns surrounded by exotic shrubs, and the most beautiful greenhouse."

Jimmy's eyes widened.

"The mysterious gentleman who owned the property went by the title of Lord Vincent Bymerstone. He was an alchemist, a maker of potions – some might say a magician. He rarely left the security of his gated home. Rumour had it, he had cultivated some sort of magic tree within the grounds."

Jimmy's eyes widened. "Wow, I love magic."

"It caused much fuss at the time. People thought the berries from the tree were the Elixir of Life. Dignitaries from all over the world would visit him, yet no one actually knew him, or what he looked like. He was a recluse. One day, my auntie was pruning her roses when she heard a terrible scream."

"What was it?" asked Jimmy.

Cynthia glared disapprovingly at Jimmy. "She was convinced she had seen a monster. A slimy beast running inside the property."

Jimmy placed a hand over his mouth and inched closer to Cynthia. "What did she do?"

"She didn't know what to do, so she called for help. Luckily, her neighbour heard her. He poured her a cup of tea and told her to sit tight while he cycled to the police station for help. As time ticked by, my auntie's curiosity got the better of her. She couldn't help herself. She *had* to investigate."

"She was brave," whispered Jimmy.

"Or stupid," interjected Brenda.

"Well, my *stupid* auntie," said Cynthia, shooting Brenda a poisonous look, "grabbed the step-ladder and within a heartbeat she was over the fence and making her way through the dense rhododendron borders of Bymerstone Hall. No sooner was she within touching distance of the back door, she heard the petrified wails of Lord Bymerstone." Cynthia paused, sipped a mouthful of tea and continued: "A loud monstrous growl followed, as if something had just woken from a deep slumber. It repeated the same warning over and over: "Do not raise the portal." It didn't deter my auntie – she turned the handle and entered."

Jimmy reached for Cynthia's arm. "What happened?"

"Patience, Jimmy," groaned Cynthia. "The door was unlocked. Once inside, my aunt noticed strange hoofprints on the kitchen floor. They led into the sitting room. She said it stunk to high heaven – the smell of death. Then she heard muffled voices, but couldn't make out the words."

Jimmy glanced at his mother mopping her tears with a tissue, then turned back to face Cynthia. "Did your auntie run home?"

"No," snapped Cynthia. "She peered through a crack in the door. Lord Bymerstone was tied to an armchair. A caped monster loomed over him, dripping from head to toe in sticky mucus. She panicked, jumped into the larder, and pulled the door behind her. Her nerves were at breaking point. My auntie was terrified. She sat in darkness, shivering with fear."

"It must have been awful," said Jimmy, chewing the ends of his nails.

"After a few moments, she heard the creature growling."

"W-what did it say?"

Cynthia paused, unsure whether or not to continue. Brenda James nodded her approval, prompting Cynthia to read verbatim from the piece of paper.

"What did the monster say?" asked Jimmy, timidly.

"*Your magic has become powerful, Lord Bymerstone*," whispered Cynthia, half-heartedly. She stared at the paper, though Jimmy thought she was reading the words in her head, as if they had been etched there. "*'The Ancient Book of Cosmo' has taught you well. You should not meddle in things you do not understand. You can only come if called, and you have not been called.*"

Cynthia looked up from her notes and sighed. "My auntie said that Lord Bymerstone was a gibbering wreck. The monster warned him that his life would be in danger if he raised the portal and it would be the beginning of a terrible curse on Bymerstone Hall and 145 Oxon Road."

"Nanny Bo's house," whispered Jimmy.

"Yes," replied Cynthia. "Lord Bymerstone muttered something about finding the recipe for everlasting life. The monster vowed to return. Then there was an almighty rumble of thunder and the slimy thing was gone."

Jimmy shook his head in disbelief.

Then, from nowhere, a loud, high-pitched hiss startled them.

Brenda screamed.

Jimmy jumped from his seat.

Cynthia looked out of the window and spied two tomcats fighting on the lawn. She placed her hand on Jimmy's shoulder. "It's only the cats, dear."

Jimmy sat down and ballooned his cheeks. For the briefest moment he was convinced the monsters of Bymerstone Hall had returned. His bright mind now scrutinised Cynthia's mysterious tale. He had a pragmatic, logical, one-dimensional train of thought. Loose ends always needed tying. He scratched his temple, wrinkled his nose, and tried to articulate his thoughts.

"Spit it out, Jimmy," coaxed Cynthia. "What is it?"

"I was just thinking."

"Yes, dear."

"What happened after the monster left Bymerstone Hall? Did it come back for the recipe?"

"My auntie untied Lord Bymerstone and explained that help was on the way. Lord Bymerstone begged her not to speak a word to anyone, and somehow convinced her to remain silent."

"How?" asked Jimmy.

"Money," replied Cynthia. "Soon after this, Lord Bymerstone went missing. Year after year, his relatives sent out search parties for him, but each time they returned without him." Cynthia narrowed her eyes. "One day his gardener found a skeleton buried beneath a walnut tree in my auntie's garden. It was believed to be Lord Bymerstone wrapped in his favourite crushed-velvet dressing gown. A small funeral took place at the village church. After that, the stately home was left to fall into rack and ruin."

"And what happened to your auntie?"

"Following her encounter with Lord Bymerstone, she had a terrible run of bad luck. She used to say she was cursed by his dark magic. People would laugh at her, saying he was long dead; but one illness followed another, and her friends and relatives were all struck down in tragic circumstances."

"That's terrible."

"Yes, *terrible*," repeated Cynthia. "My auntie's sister was hit by a bolt of lightning, another relative was mysteriously poisoned by a nettle. It was all too much for my auntie. One hot, sunny day she finally lost her mind and jumped into the Thames at high tide, never to be seen again."

Cynthia held up the piece of paper. "All she left were these crumpled notes which recount the strange events and warn that 145 Oxon Road must be demolished to release the curse."

"Oh, dear," sighed Jimmy.

"Sadly, the authorities thought she was insane, and Lord Bymerstone had no traceable bloodline, so they demolished Bymerstone Hall. All that remains today are the foundations. The gardens are now smothered by woodland. My auntie's house was sold to a local family who were subsequently admitted to an asylum. Then the Clethorpes moved in. They went missing on a boat trip, never to return. And so the cycle continues…"

Jimmy held his head between his hands. "Poor Nanny Bo."

"Everybody around here knows of the curse of 145 Oxon Road," said Cynthia, "but no one dares speak of it, for fear of reprisals. The curse lives on, Jimmy, and it can be passed from one to another. So, do as your mother requests and stay clear of Nancy Bo Jones. Her house is cursed, and so is she."

The colour drained from Jimmy's face.

Cynthia folded the sheet of paper into four and placed it in her purse.

Brenda leaned over the sink, muttering words of discontent. "I don't want my little boy to be cursed. Stay away from her, Jimmy. Do not speak of this…"

"Lord Bymerstone must have raised the portal," said Jimmy, ignoring his mother's pleas.

Cynthia glared at Jimmy. "I beg your pardon."

"He must have raised the portal," repeated Jimmy, nonplussed. "That's what brought the curse on 145 Oxon Road. The creature in the cloak said there would be a curse if the portal was raised."

"I have told you enough," replied Cynthia. "You now know why your mother wants you to avoid the Jones girl. You must sever your links with her and forget this conversation ever took place." Cynthia grabbed her hat and stroked the feathers one by one.

"Maybe that book could cure Nanny Bo of the curse. I could help—"

"Book? What book?" interrupted Brenda.

"*The Cosmo Book* that Lord Bymerstone had."

Cynthia forced a nervous laugh. "Jimmy James, you are forbidden to speak of such things. *Cosmo Book*s do not exist, Lord Bymerstone is dead, and that cloaked monster is—"

"Ridiculous," pronounced Jimmy's father, as he walked into the kitchen.

"Dad," Jimmy cried.

"I think it best you leave, Mrs Leathwaite."

Cynthia returned a sharp nod, walked out of the kitchen, through the hallway, and slammed the front door behind her.

Jimmy's father wrapped his arms around his wife. "Are you okay, love?"

Brenda sunk her head into her husband's chest and bawled, "She's cursed."

"Have you packed your snorkel and flippers, son?"

"No, dad. I—"

"Best you do it then."

"But—"

"I don't want to ask you twice, Jimmy."

"Yes, dad." Jimmy removed his raincoat and trudged out of the kitchen. He was not thinking about packing his snorkel and flippers. He was daydreaming about finding *The Ancient Book of Cosmo*.

5

The Home For The Incurably Curious

The clouds parted, shimmers of light swept across the courtyard, Nancy squinted, and turned her face from the sun. The masses of tangled roses adorning the brick walls filled her nostrils with the scent of exotic perfume. She brushed the gravel from her hands and stared at the miniature door.

It was ajar.

Beside it was a weather-beaten nameplate. She placed a finger over the first letter on the sign, and whispered the name: The Home For The Incurably Curious.

Nancy pushed the door and peered through. The orange glow had all but disappeared, replaced by a tunnel of darkness. She pricked her ears and was convinced she heard the squawk of a bird. "I can hear something, Pre."

"What can you—?"

"A bird."

"A what?"

Nancy squeezed her head through the tiny opening. Her tall frame struggled in the confined space as she forced her way through.

"You can't fit through there," said Prema, tugging at Nancy's legs.

"Let go of me. My body is tingling. It's really weird, Pre."

Somehow, after much pushing and squeezing, Nancy scrambled through and landed on her knees. She attempted to stand, half-expecting to hit her head on a low ceiling. She straightened herself and waited for Prema to wriggle through.

Nancy couldn't believe what she saw. They were inside the hallway of a charming country cottage. The door they had crawled through had concealed a hidden gem: a secret, waiting to be found. Prema stooped down and pulled the tiny door. As it caught the latch, a loud, vacuous suction sealed them from the outside world.

Nancy crept forward and brushed past an unattended desk. Beyond it was a long corridor lit by a single candle. Dotted along each side were tatty leather armchairs studded with brass, resting on colourful Moroccan rugs. She continued tiptoeing along the corridor, tugging at Prema's arm.

Four doors led off in different directions, each one identified by symbols Nancy recognised from her mother's magazines as zodiac signs. Strange hieroglyphics were carved into the flagstones beneath their feet. They were difficult for Nancy to read in the flickering light. Prema raised her foot and paused momentarily to make sense of the strange lettering.

"Come on," whispered Nancy, excitedly. Further down, a door was half-open and a light shone brightly from within. Nancy spied pots and pans strewn upon the floor. She aimed her finger and whispered, "Kitchen."

At the very end of the corridor were two gigantic doors. They reminded Nancy of the entrance to the London Dungeon, heavily studded and polished to perfection. Beyond the doors she heard voices muttering over soft music and the sound of china cups chinking against their saucers.

"Penny for your thoughts," squawked a high-pitched voice, the shrill sound ripping the air like a firework.

Nancy and Prema jumped out of their skins and ran back

towards the entrance.

"Penny for your thoughts. I'm here, behind you."

A white parrot clasping a perch stared at Nancy, its beady eyes taking her in from top to bottom. Nancy glared back. *What are you staring at?* she thought. A cluck and a squawk morphed into words: "I am staring at The Chosen One, the Dual-star. I am here, *within* you. I am... Grizelda."

Nancy shook her head in defiance of the invasive voice. Her body fizzed with pins and needles, her mind being somehow controlled, her thoughts no longer private.

Prema panicked. She looked at the parrot, then at Nancy. "What's happening? Are you all right, Nanny Bo?"

"No," grimaced Nancy. "Something was controlling me."

"Like what?"

"I have no idea," confessed Nancy. She glared at Grizelda. It was her only way of showing strength – an immediate sign of recovery.

The bird stared back, unflinching.

Nancy shivered.

Grizelda ogled her. It was as if the parrot could see right through her. The bird flapped its wings and squawked, "Penny for your thoughts. Penny for your thoughts."

Prema covered her ears. "It's talking! The bird can talk!"

"Most parrots can," said Nancy, flatly. "Haven't you been to London Zoo?"

"No."

"There are loads of them there. And they all talk." Nancy bobbed her head back and forth, inspecting the bird from a distance. The name Grizelda was scratched haphazardly on the perch. Beneath it was a clay bowl containing three penny pieces and a half-eaten apple.

"Penny for your thoughts. Penny for your thoughts," repeated Grizelda, her harsh squawk disturbing the peace.

"We need to shut this parrot up," said Nancy, quickly. She pointed towards the room at the end of the corridor. "If the people in there hear us, we could be in serious trouble."

"Shut me up. Who do you think you are?" trilled Grizelda. "You sound like a street urchin. If you don't place a penny in my bowl, I will bite your nose off. Come on, dig deep, and find me a penny."

"Wow," gasped Prema. "This bird can *really* talk. It actually sounds like it's answering you."

Nancy nodded and checked her pockets.

"That includes you, little girl," crowed Grizelda.

"Me?" said Prema, aghast.

"Yes, you. I need a penny for your thoughts. Just a penny."

The girls riffled through their garments, frantically searching for a spare penny. Nancy dug deep and found some loose change, mints, and her Chinese compact mirror. She tossed the coins into the bowl. Half of them spilled onto the flag-stoned floor. A single coin rolled the length of the corridor and tapped against the studded doors.

The voices inside the room fell silent. Then the candle reached the bottom of its wick and the light left them. "Haw-haw-haw," cackled Grizelda. "Now you have woken Captain Carbunkle. You will need to explain yourselves."

Nancy stood perfectly still. There wasn't a chink of light anywhere in the room. She cupped her hands to her mouth and yelled, "Leave us alone."

"I'd like to join minds...," squawked Grizelda. "Let me help you." She ruffled her feathers and coaxed Nancy towards her. "Take one step to your left, then five steps forward."

"No."

"Just do it," snapped the parrot. "Walk towards me and place your left hand on my head-crest."

"Why?" asked Nancy, nervously.

"Two minds are stronger than one. All will be revealed."

"I can't see a thing," said Nancy.

"Come to me, or else…"

"I'm not doing anything unless you say why." All Nancy wanted was to silence the parrot, to tie its beak or, if she had to, strangle it. Grizelda's harsh voice continued to rile her, goading, calling for her to walk towards the perch. It was her only option. She had to follow the parrot's instructions. Each and every blind step took her closer to the bird. She held out her hand, feeling the space between herself and Grizelda. "Please don't bite me…"

Prema fumbled for a way out, nudging her way through the blanket of darkness, bumping into the desk and cursing herself as she searched for the tiny doorway. She called for Nancy and yelled, "Let's get out of here!"

"Just one more step," clucked Grizelda.

Nancy placed one foot in front of the other. Her left arm was now at full stretch, her fingers set rigid. Then, her index finger brushed against the parrot's crest. As it did, Grizelda's body emitted a bright, white light. Nancy's eyes closed, her tongue lolled out of the side of her mouth, and her body convulsed. A vision formed at the back of her mind. A vision of what looked like a heavenly world, a land of colour inhabited by strange creatures with exotic plumage and radiant eyes. Fountains spouting silver liquid punctuated the wooded places, ripe fruit adorned the trees, masses of petals created a multi-coloured tapestry throughout the land, and joyous music hummed above neon clouds. In the distance, a dilapidated castle watched over the enchanted land.

A connection of minds had been made – the parrot had become the conduit to Nancy's inner self. Grizelda opened her beak and spoke in a voice that seemed to be harmonised with another voice not present. "Ah… The Chosen One stands before me. Keep your hand still while I seek your mind's eye and gather your thoughts." The parrot paused, flapped her wings, and said, "We have here one of great strength and bravery and yet a wounded child with many chinks in her armour. She wants to be somebody, but only when she is happy being nobody will she actually become somebody."

Nancy's fingers caressed the parrot's yellow crest, her breathing calm and measured. Grizelda's prophetic words continued inside her hypnotic state: "You, my child, are on the verge of either moving a mountain or falling off a cliff. Which will it be?"

Just then, a door creaked open and Nancy heard the sound of footsteps. She stepped back, gulping at the air as the connection was severed.

Grizelda's harsh laugh continued to rip through the blanket of darkness. The pitter-patter of footsteps came closer still. Nancy coughed and spluttered as strange, translucent mucus spewed from her mouth.

Prema unfolded a tissue and thrusted it forward. "Here, take this."

Nancy wiped the last of the fluid from her mouth and flipped her compact mirror open. A small orb of light glowed from within the case. "Nice one, Mr Wuu," she said, pointing it towards the sound of the footsteps. There, halfway down the corridor, was a small, child-like figure. Nancy flinched as the tiny person clicked his fingers and miraculously lit six candles simultaneously. The hallway was now awash in a soft candlelit glow. Shadows danced across the walls, flickering one way, then the next. Nancy took a long, hard look at what stood before her. Never before had she seen such a creature. He was half her height, with a hooked nose and creased skin. His hands clutched an elongated ivory pipe. Ribbons of silver smoke wafted around his impish frame and strands of ginger hair poked out like rats' tails from beneath his pointed hat.

"Don't be scared," said the odd-looking man. "Grizelda means you no harm. I am Captain Carbunkle. You must be Nancy Bo Jones."

"Yes, but I prefer Nanny Bo," replied Nancy, cautiously. "That's what my friends call me; and this is —"

"Prema Sarkander, great-great-granddaughter of Sutara Sarkander," interrupted Captain Carbunkle.

"Yes," cried Prema. "How did you—?"

"I know many things, Prema, but now is not the time to explain," he said, his deep voice resonating through the hallway. He drew a breath of pungent smoke and held out his hand to Nancy. "I know of your struggle to reach us. We had our doubts, but I always had faith in you. It takes a special person to take a leap of faith." Captain Carbunkle grabbed Nancy's hand and dragged her down the corridor. "You seek Aunt Elma. You will find her here, at The Home For The Incurably Curious." The dwarf tilted his head back, flared his oversized nostrils, and sniffed. "Before I introduce you, we must step into the kitchen. I'm sure you are in need of refreshments."

Nancy marvelled at the huge kitchen – vegetables were strung up to the rafters and countless rows of onions swayed from above. The scent of vanilla wafted from a nearby oven. A trestle table stretched from one side of the room to the other. It was adorned with cakes, sweets, jars of ice cream, and jugs of cream soda. Nancy and Prema thought they had died and gone to heaven. Captain Carbunkle's green eyes sparkled with delight as he watched the girls tuck into the feast. They hardly spoke as they devoured the sumptuous offering.

"Now then," said Captain Carbunkle, his voice bursting with authority. "If we are full, I will introduce you to Aunt Elma."

Nancy licked a blob of cream from the side of her mouth and grinned. "Yes, please do."

Captain Carbunkle had the demeanour of a court jester. He rolled his arms and began to sing, his baritone vocals filling every inch of the hallway. "Follow me, follow me – a day has come for all to see – follow me..."

The hairs prickled on Nancy's skin as Captain Carbunkle left the kitchen and made his way towards the room at the end of the corridor. She followed, her heart racing, her senses alive with anticipation. Captain Carbunkle resembled a ginger ant standing in front of the huge doorway. He clicked his fingers, levitated up to the handles, and fiddled with the latch.

Nancy and Prema looked on, mesmerised.

Captain Carbunkle muttered five strange words, then glided back down to the floor. The doors creaked open and light spilled into the hallway. The hidden room finally revealed itself. A huge crystal chandelier hung from the ceiling. It was majestic – glass jewels dangled like icicles from the impressive candelabra. Nancy craned her neck and marvelled at the crystal beads reflecting prisms of light. A musky odour filtered through her nasal cavity, the scent reminded her of an old Charity Store. There were thousands of books scattered across the floor, some open, some closed, their covers dazzling to the eye. Dusty portraits hung on the cracked walls. Nicotine stained the ceiling and the carpet was so worn there were holes everywhere. The room was unkempt and dishevelled, but she sensed there was something special about it. Opposite her was a huge bookcase that stretched from floor to ceiling. Ladders on wheels were the only way of reaching the top shelf. Tucked in the far corner was a Welsh Dresser: ornate plates and ornaments were perched on the shelves, and beneath them were three drawers with glass handles.

Suddenly, the middle drawer sprung open.

Nancy watched, dumbstruck, as a small, wrinkled hand appeared.

"What's happening?" cried Prema.

"Fear not, young Prema," said Captain Carbunkle. "How did you enter The Home For The Incurably Curious?"

"Through a d-door," stuttered Prema.

Captain Carbunkle roared with laughter. "Well, here comes

Aunt Elma through a drawer."

The drawer vibrated as a frail old lady pulled herself out and introduced herself. "Good afternoon, girls. I'm so pleased you are here. I'm Aunt Elma, and we have much to discuss. You can go back to sleep now, Captain Carbunkle. All is well."

Nancy was flabbergasted. She rubbed her eyes, and stepped closer to Prema. The girls continued to stare, unable to believe what they had just witnessed. Fear, coupled with excitement, was a strange yet wonderful concoction.

Captain Carbunkle smiled at Aunt Elma, then bowed respectfully. He hopped over to the bookcase, climbed the ladder, and pulled out half a dozen books. Clouds of dust filled the room as they landed by the girls' feet. They coughed and sneezed, fanning their hands in an attempt to clear the air. Aunt Elma set a table and poured three cups of tea. Captain Carbunkle wished the girls "*Good night*," then swung from the ladder like a chimpanzee, climbing into the empty shelf and disappearing within the wall.

Nancy puffed her cheeks and waved an imaginary wand. "How do you do such magic, disappearing within walls and appearing from drawers?" She inspected the room for any sign of trickery. "I've seen illusionists at Covent Garden, but nothing like this. How do you do it?"

Aunt Elma remained tight-lipped. Nancy went on, her excitement uncontainable. "You could make thousands in London doing stuff like this."

"I believe you have spent most of today looking for me," said Aunt Elma, ignoring Nancy's revelation. She rested her cup and saucer on a small table and sat down. "Please, girls. Do join me."

"Okay," replied Nancy. She took the seat opposite Aunt Elma. On the wall hung a cracked oil painting of a chubby boy sporting a red bow-tie. It was framed in gold with a brass nameplate bearing the words *Ignatius Tanners*. Nancy clapped her hands and declared, "That's Jangles!"

"Correct," replied Aunt Elma.

All of a sudden, Nancy wanted answers. The day's events were now too much for her mind to digest. The brief interlude of sweets and disappearing tricks had distracted her from the reason why she was actually here. She gulped a mouthful of tea and spoke freely. "I'm new to this area and it's my first summer holiday here. Jangles told me to visit you, and ask for *The First Book of Cosmo*. I'm so confused, my head hurts." Nancy paused, rubbed her temples, and asked, "Why on earth am I here?"

Aunt Elma gazed up at the image of her nephew and rubbed her locket.

"You didn't tell me about *The First Book of Cosmo*," interjected Prema. Nancy offered Prema a sheepish grin and mumbled her apology, "Sorry, I forgot…"

Aunt Elma leaned forward and drew Nancy and Prema close. As their foreheads touched, her frail voice echoed in the lofty room. "For over one thousand years this little cottage has been the last outpost for the genuinely curious." She paused, observing the incredulous looks of the two girls, then continued: "People search for enlightenment here, and even for alternative life-forms."

"For real?" asked Nancy.

Aunt Elma nodded. "There are strange folk who read in our darkest corners. We have books and manuscripts on our shelves that no man can obtain from a conventional library. We only exist if you are curious enough to need us or want us. Failing that, you will never find us."

Nancy cast a sidelong glance at Prema. "So how did *we* find you?"

"You found The Home For The Incurably Curious because you *wanted* to," replied Aunt Elma. "Not everything in life is obvious, girls. There is so much we cannot always see, hear, touch, taste, or feel."

Nancy pressed her face closer to the old lady. "What do you mean?"

Aunt Elma looked over her shoulder and inspected the bookcase. "Well, it is not only our physical actions in life that have an impact on others: our thoughts, feelings, and dreams all transmit an energy that impacts and resonates with the space around us." Aunt Elma pointed directly at Nancy's heart. "They have an invisibility that only a special type of person can tune into."

"Me?" whispered Nancy. "How do you know I can—"

"You need to trust me before you believe me. And that may take a little time."

"Could you give us an example of this energy?" Prema asked, her eyes sparkling at the merest mention of the unexplainable.

"Mmm… All right," said Aunt Elma. She closed her eyes for a moment. Her left eye opened before the right, and she stared once again at the framed portrait of her nephew, before raising her crackly voice, "Love."

"Love?" queried Nancy.

"Yes, love."

Aunt Elma took hold of their hands to create a circle of one. "Think about it: you can love someone with all your heart, but what does the emotion of *love* actually look like? It doesn't look like anything to the common man. It's just a feeling that some people find harder than others to express."

"But it exists," squealed Prema with delight.

"Correct," said Aunt Elma with a stiff nod. "Here, at The Home For The Incurably Curious, we help you understand that feelings have energy, and this energy can influence the complex magnetic fields within the universe." She let go of their hands, breaking the circle. "I will give you the book. Read it well, because decisions need to be made, and time is not on our side. Think long and hard about the path you wish to follow, Nancy Bo Jones." Aunt Elma let out an exaggerated yawn. "I am tired. It has been a long day and it is my birthday tomorrow. I will take to my bed early, as I have visitors all day."

Prema smiled at the old lady. "Am I allowed to ask how old you are, Aunt Elma?"

"Of course, dear. I am ninety-nine."

"Wow, you look—"

"You haven't even told me why I am here," interrupted Nancy.

"It's all in the book," instructed Aunt Elma. "If you decide to raise the portal, you will need to come back. Then we can talk some more." Aunt Elma removed a copper key from the pocket of her apron and placed it in the recess of the table. She whispered three magical words, "*Aspertious, Spiri, Credom.*"

The table began to shake as if it was digesting something. A low, resonating hum filled the grand room. Nancy spun on her heels, her eyes searching for a swarm of bees. Then the table stopped vibrating.

The silence was brief.

A drawer slid open, squeaking on its runners.

Nancy and Prema shrieked.

Inside was a dusty, leather-bound book, its edges braided in gold. Aunt Elma took it out and kissed the cover. It was *The First Book of Cosmo*.

She placed it in Nancy's hands.

6
Fairy of the Night

Dinnertime at 145 Oxon Road was always an event, whether it was a Christmas feast, birthday celebration or just an ordinary evening meal. Teddy and Bessy Jones were a double act. Jesting, accompanied by raucous laughter, was the norm. Nancy never missed dinnertime. It was special.

"Where's my little girl?" asked Teddy Jones. He pulled a carving knife from the cutlery drawer and frowned. "She's never late for dinner."

"I'm not sure," replied Bessy. "She rode her bike to the library; maybe she got lost."

The next moment heard the tell-tale sound of the turning latch. Teddy pointed his knife at Nancy as she crossed the threshold. "There you are – we've been waiting for you. I texted you, but you didn't reply."

"Oh," said Nancy, startled. "I'm sorry. Long day. I lost track of time and my phone needs charging."

Teddy winked and gave his daughter a wry smile. "You spend way too much time on that blimmin' phone. You look nervous. Are you in trouble?"

"No, of course not," said Nancy, shielding the book from her father. "But a man holding a knife could be the first sign of trouble."

Teddy expelled a gruff laugh, placed the knife onto the work surface, and made his way to the table. "Come on, dinner's nearly ready."

Nancy patted her stomach. "Good, I'm starving."

"Look at this," said Teddy, proudly, "the best boiled bacon money can buy." Teddy carved the joint, ruminating out loud with every slice. "I met a man last week who swore blind he could tell the future by staring at the stones between the railway sleepers."

Nancy returned an empty stare.

"I know, babe – the world is full of nut jobs." Teddy clanged his knife and fork. "Let's eat!"

Nancy signalled for her father to wait. "I need to put my stuff away." She ran so fast, her feet barely touched the stairs. She skipped into her bedroom, placed the ancient book under her bed and ran back out onto the landing, before sliding down the banister and landing in the hallway. "Can I have a drink, please?"

Her mother's reply was instant: "Course you can, darlin'. What's your fancy? Gin or juice?"

Both parents erupted with laughter. Nancy shook her head and sighed. "Juice is fine. Do you have to say that *every* time I ask for a drink?"

Another peal of laughter filled the kitchen. Teddy swung back on his chair and slapped his thigh repeatedly.

Nancy sighed. "Can my friend visit tonight?"

"Who's that?" asked Bessy, as she pinched her husband's cheek.

"Prema Sarkander."

"Of course she can."

"Thanks, Mum."

Nancy swallowed her last mouthful and pushed her plate to the centre of the table. "That was lovely," she blew her father a kiss and asked, "what's for dessert?"

Teddy began to pick at his teeth with a matchstick. "Mmm, maybe a nice bowl of rice pudding."

"With a jam dollop?"

"Why not?" said Teddy. "And how did you get on at the library today?"

"Okay," replied Nancy. "I found a really old book that—

"What book?" enquired Bessy.

Nancy felt the panic rising in her throat as her mother probed her for an answer. "School's finished, love. Why would you want a book for the summer holidays?"

Nancy hesitated. All she could think of was *The First Book Of Cosmo*.

"You hate books," said Bessy, her suspicions increasing by the second. "I haven't seen you bring a book home since we moved here."

Nancy fiddled with the cutlery on her plate. Her mother's attention to detail bordered on the obsessive. If she didn't approve of her daughter's plans, they would be over before they had begun.

"Well, what book did you find?"

Nancy racked her brains for an answer. "A science book."

Bessy Jones looked down her nose and pursed her lips. "A science book?"

"Yeah, I've been struggling all term. Jangles has set a test at the start of Year Eight to make sure I'm up to speed."

"Are you sure?"

"Y-yes," said Nancy. "Prema's helping me."

Bessy Jones frowned. "Science, you say?"

"Yes, mum… Science."

Nancy stared at her mother. Waiting for her judgement was a regular and unnerving occurrence.

"Okay," said Bessy, firmly. "Best you go and start reading, then."

Nancy didn't need to be told twice. As she climbed the stairs, the sound of *Land of Hope and Glory* rang out. "When are you going to change that ringtone?"

"Never," barked Teddy; then he laughed out loud and punched his chest. "I love it."

"Can you get the door for me?" yelled Nancy from the top of the staircase.

"All right, all right, I'm on my way. Anything for my little girl."

"And put your false teeth in – you might scare Prema."

Teddy checked his teeth in the mirror and opened the door. Standing in front of him was Prema Sarkander. In one hand were the optical cards and in the other the silver carrying case. Teddy grinned, then felt the top row of his dentures drop onto his tongue. "Oops, sorry, darlin' – come in."

Nancy leaned over the banister and greeted her friend: "I'm up here, Pre."

Teddy straightened his teeth and pointed at the pack of cards. "Ooh, playing cards. I love a game of rummy. How are ya?"

"I'm fine, Mr Jones, and how are—?"

"Please don't call me Mr Jones – it makes me feel awkward. Know what I mean?"

Prema nodded.

"Call me Teddy."

"I'm sorry, Mr Jones, I mean Teddy."

Nancy summoned her friend. "Come up, Pre, don't spend too long down there with him. You won't escape."

Prema stepped to one side, gave Teddy Jones a polite smile, and tiptoed up the stairs. As soon as she reached the landing, Nancy pulled her close. "Are you mental?"

"What do you mean?" replied Prema, innocently.

"Why did you show my dad the optical cards?"

Prema tried her best to respond, but Nancy couldn't help herself. "Don't you know he tells my mother everything? She's like Sherlock blimmin' Holmes. If she finds out about this book, it's going to be game over."

Prema bowed her head. "Sorry, I didn't realise."

"That's okay. It's the first bit of fun I've had since we moved here." Nancy kicked the bedroom door and slumped onto her bed. She threw Prema a cushion, drew the curtains, and switched the bedside lamp on.

"I wish my bedroom was like this," sighed Prema. She grabbed a glossy fashion magazine and flicked through the pages. "Where did you get all this stuff?"

"London."

Prema fanned her face with the magazine and marvelled at the foreign coins scattered all around the room. She walked towards the bedroom door, where a huge London Underground map had been stapled. She squinted, then pointed at a tiny red heart inked over London Bridge. "What's that?"

"It's where I lived," replied Nancy, smiling at the slightest mention of her old life. "Our flat was in Weston Street, just behind the station."

"Cool."

"What's your bedroom like?"

"Neat, tidy, and two shelves of school books," Prema pointed at the wall behind Nancy's bed, "and none of that spray paint."

Nancy laughed. "That's graffiti."

"Oh," said Prema, shocked. "Well, my room has no *graffiti* or any of those funny toys."

Nancy stared at the weird contraptions sitting on the shelves. "Most of that is junk."

"Junk?" repeated Prema. "It doesn't look like it."

"Well, it is," said Nancy, boldly. "It belongs to Mr Wuu. He visited London every summer. I would take his daughter to the street arcades, through Borough Market, and sometimes I could get her in The Tower."

Prema waved a dollar bill. "How come you have all this foreign currency?"

"Tips."

"What for?"

"For helping at The Tower."

Prema shuffled closer to the lattice of shelves. "Lucky you."

"What's the matter, Pre?" asked Nancy, "you can't stop staring…"

"These toys look like they belong in a museum," replied Prema, "they're amazing."

Nancy pulled a face. "Mr Wuu told me never to lose them, as one day they would come in useful; maybe even save my life."

"From what?" asked Prema, her eyes fixed on the array of strange gadgets.

Nancy clutched her throat, then theatrically collapsed onto her pillow. "I have no idea."

Prema started to laugh. "You must have. Stop messing about."

"I didn't have a clue what Mr Wuu was on about," admitted Nancy. "I wanted to throw the toys away, but I made the fatal mistake of telling my mother about Mr Wuu. Ever since, she has made me keep these weird objects." She paused, then placed a finger over her mouth. "It's not wise to *tempt fate*. That's what my mum always tells me. She worries about anything and everything. It drives me crazy. Sometimes she makes me feel like the world's about to end."

"Pessimism," muttered Prema, "it's contagious." Then she grabbed a spyglass from the top shelf. "Wow, this is awesome. Why would you want to throw these toys away, Nanny Bo?"

"Because they're rubbish."

"No, they're not."

Nancy crossed her arms and watched her friend peer through the eyelet. "Trust me, none of them work."

"I can't see a thing," groaned Prema, as she twisted the lens.

"Told you!"

Prema lifted a music box from the bottom shelf, and stared in amazement at the intricate carvings of crotchets and quavers on the lid. "It's beautiful. I've never seen anything like this before."

"Turn it over," instructed Nancy. "Go on, read the message."

Prema spun the box and read the inscription: *There's a place the music plays*.

Nancy watched as her friend scrutinised the ornate box. "Open it."

Prema forced her nails beneath the lid. "I can't."

Nancy took great pleasure in proving her point. "Garbage and junk, that's what these toys are."

On the middle shelf, Prema's attention was drawn to a silver aerial attached to a small brown box with a speaker. *Aero-Strazmicator* was engraved on a brass nameplate. She pulled the aerial out to its maximum length and pressed the power button several times. "Nothing. I can't hear a single thing."

"See what I mean?" grunted Nancy. "I've never used them and I never will."

"Are you sure?"

"Of course I am," insisted Nancy. "Now sit down. I don't want my mum to hear us speaking about the *you-know-what*."

"The what?" asked Prema.

"The book, you numbskull."

"Oh, yes, of course."

Nancy reached beneath her bed and grabbed the spine. She cleared a space and placed *The First Book of Cosmo* beside them. Everything she had encountered that day darted across her memory in a nanosecond. She reached out to touch the cover, then stopped herself, her fingers centimetres from the braided edges. She stared at Prema.

Prema smiled and offered a reassuring nod. "Go on…"

Nancy reached out once more for the leather-bound book. She placed her hand on the cover. As soon as her fingers touched the book, the bedside light failed. A brief moment of darkness was banished by a bright orange light that fizzed around the outline of Nancy's hand.

The room was awash with a tangerine haze. Then came the chime of a plucked harp. "Can you hear that?" asked Nancy, waving a finger in the air.

"Yes," said Prema, softly. "It's beautiful."

From the corner of her eye, Nancy noticed something move on the shelves. "Look! The music box. It's opening."

The lid creaked on its hinges. A faint image of a miniature fairy-like figurine rose up from within, spinning effortlessly on her perch. She was beautiful. Her wand glowed as a radiant light swirled around her. "I am Shaanue, your Fairy of the Night. Open the book, Nancy Bo Jones, and I will see you on the other side. Be brave, sweetness, and listen to my song."

The mournful melody of a plucked harp oozed from the music box:

Berringer Hill is where we wait,
Not in the mountains where Zayock preys.
There is a place where the music plays.
Follow your heart and the Ergonwold ways.

"It's singing to me. The fairy is singing to me," said Nancy, hysterically.

"Open the book," insisted Prema.

Nancy removed her hand from the cover and turned it over. The moment she did, the bedside lamp flickered, and the music box closed with the click of a lock.

"Read it," said Prema, her voice fused with excitement.

Nancy blew silvery motes of dust from the first page and placed her index finger beneath the first sentence. As her nail ran along the text, sparkles of white light illuminated each letter of every word. Nancy continued, her eyes bulging, her face beaming.

CHAPTER ONE:
AN INVITATION TO ENTER ENERJIIMASS

Many minds are earth-bound, locked by one-dimensional facts. They only see what their eyes present to them, or feel what physically touches them. What lies in between is the true magic of life. Extra Sensory Perception cannot be explained or understood by those not fortunate enough to be bestowed with such a gift.

Now is the time, and you are The Chosen One, Nancy Bo Jones. There is a break in the time continuum, and you can choose to cross into the land of Enerjiimass. It is a choice, not a command. On the second day of rain and the coming of the camelback rainbow, you are invited to raise the portal and enter Enerjiimass.

Nancy paused and glared at Prema. "What's a camelback rain—?"

"Turn the page, Nanny Bo."

Nancy continued:

CHAPTER TWO
SOLDIERS OF GOOD AND BAD ENERGY

Only a specially tuned being can cross between the Earth realm and Enerjiimass. The two realms are separated by Lithonia, which is a poisonous gas that prevents the migration of creatures from one world to another. The Soldiers of Energy are not affected by Lithonia – please see list:

Elma Tanners – Housekeeper and Guardian at The Home For The Incurably Curious

Captain Carbunkle – High Priest of Enerjiimass

Inglethwip Limpweed – Potion-Maker

Mr Wuu – Maker of Instruments

Grizelda – Reader of Hearts and Minds

The Jagganath – Safe Keepers of Zayock

"Look," whispered Nancy, "Mr Wuu is on that list, and so are—"

"The Jagganath," interrupted Prema.

Nancy thumbed the page, eager for the next chapter.

CHAPTER THREE
INSTRUMENTS AND THEIR WORKINGS

Shaanue's Music Box

Aero-Strazmicator

Dual-Vision Spyglass

Ancient Optical Cards

Key-light Compact Mirror

Shape-Shifting Marbles

Multi-Language Megaphone

Decision Dice

Disappearing Dust

Shield of Pan-Coo

Mallory's Rope

To be chosen to enter the world of Enerjiimass is a daunting task. Our universe is a complex matrix of time, space, matter, and energy. To cross the threshold and survive is highly unlikely. To this end, Mr Wuu has devised some important instrumentation (see above list). Through the kind intervention of the High Priest of Enerjiimass, you should possess most of these instruments. To fully understand their workings, you will need to raise the portal.

The remainder of the book was blank. Nancy ran her fingers over the empty pages. There was nothing. She turned another page and stroked it, waiting for the words to materialise. Her smile quickly turned to a frown as she flicked through the book to the very last page. "It's a fake. A crude joke."

Prema looped her arm around Nancy's. "Calm down. There are only three completed chapters and you have read them all. *The First Book of Cosmo* must keep its secrets for beyond the portal, on the other side."

Nancy snatched *The First Book of Cosmo* and threw it under her bed. "It's a scam."

Prema pulled a single Optical card from her pocket and placed it on Nancy's duvet. An old lady and a white parrot stared back at the girls. "Look! The cards are speaking to us – maybe Aunt Elma can help."

Nancy stared at the picture card, long and hard. "You're right, Pre. I have to visit The Home For The Incurably Curious. I need help decoding the blank pages. I'm going to go tomorrow."

She drew back her curtains and gazed out onto the lush green canopy of Roebuck Woods. "*Everything* is about to change…"

7
Rubble and Dust

The morning sun blazed down on the sprawling mass of Roebuck Woods. A gentle breeze lifted the early mist, revealing sparkles of dew that glimmered like a multitude of fairy lights on the forest floor. In a small clearing, The Duke and Elijah sat silently listening to the birdsong.

Lost in thought, The Duke watched Elijah push himself to his feet, stretch his muscular frame and amble towards a tent. He unzipped the flap, dived in and tossed a sleeping bag into the air. "Where are they? I'm sure I packed them."

"What?" asked The Duke, riled at the silence being broken.

"My binoculars. I can't find them."

"Check your rucksack."

"Ah, I've found them," said Elijah, as he crawled out of the tent, "go and stand on that tree trunk."

The Duke eyeballed the mighty oak stump. "Why?"

"You can see Nanny Bo's house. It backs onto the woods."

"Really?"

"Yeah, number 145 Oxon Road – it's famous." Elijah swung his arm and threw the binoculars up into the air. The Duke cupped his hands and waited for them to fall. Elijah clapped, then wolf-whistled. "Nice catch, for a pianist."

"Thanks," said The Duke, flatly. "There's no need for applause."

Elijah grinned. "Well, what are you waiting for?"

"We shouldn't be doing this, Eli. It's wrong."

"Chicken!" cried Elijah with a haughty squawk.

"No, I'm not," protested The Duke.

"Let's see if you can spy that lanky cockney girl."

The Duke climbed up onto the tree stump and twisted the lens. "I'm not sure about this."

"What's wrong with you?"

"Nothing," snapped The Duke, "but I did promise my mum I wouldn't cycle beyond the park."

"Don't worry about it, our bikes are safe. They're chained to the fence."

"I've told her we are in your back garden, and if—"

"Are you going to use those binoculars, or what?"

The Duke raised the binoculars to the bridge of his nose and scanned the outer reaches of the forest. A small row of terraced houses came into focus. "I can see some—"

"What?" interrupted Elijah.

"Houses."

"Great. Now press the zoom button."

The Duke zoomed in, the magnification momentarily blurring his vision. He twisted the lens and regained focus. "Whooar!"

"What is it?" asked Elijah.

"It's her," said The Duke, astonished. "She's staring straight at me."

"Who?"

"Nanny Bo, you dimwit." The Duke's feet shifted one way, then the other. He took one small step backwards, lost balance, and fell off the stump.

Elijah roared with laughter. "You clumsy fool…"

The Duke threw the binoculars to the floor and stormed towards his friend. "What are you laughing at?"

"You," replied Elijah.

"But she was staring straight at me."

Elijah grabbed the binoculars. "We're too far away, there's no way she can see us."

"Well, take a look for yourself," said The Duke angrily.

Elijah scrambled up onto the fallen tree and peered into the distance. "Oh, you're right, it's definitely her. And she's smiling. Isn't that strange?"

"What's so strange about that?"

"Because that girl is always so miserable," answered Elijah. "She moans constantly that she doesn't like it here. I wish she would go back to where she came from."

"You've been fascinated with her ever since she arrived at Oakwell," replied The Duke.

Elijah snorted. "That skinny upstart of a girl. You must be joking."

"I'm not joking," replied The Duke, forcefully. "Actually, I think you're besotted by her."

Elijah denied the accusation, then he tilted the binoculars and hummed a long, tuneless note of uncertainty.

"What can you see?" enquired The Duke.

"She's just put a book in a bag, and now she's—"

"A book!" The surprise was clear in The Duke's expression. "I've never seen her in the school library."

"I know," mumbled Elijah. "It looks like she's getting ready to go out. I wonder where she's going?"

"And I'm starting to wonder what we are doing in the forest at nine o'clock in the morning," replied The Duke. "We shouldn't be spying on people. It's wrong. If Nanny Bo found out we were snooping, she would kill us."

Elijah jumped down, unzipped his rucksack, and pulled out two jam sandwiches. "You know why we are here. We've been planning this all year, and now you're chicken."

"It just doesn't feel right."

"What's wrong with you?"

"There's nothing wrong with me, Eli."

Elijah raised his arms and gestured at the enveloping foliage. "Remember our plan? Out there, somewhere in that forest, is the magician's estate. We could search for his wand, and we might find some treasure. He was a millionaire!"

"There's nothing left of Bymerstone Hall," said The Duke, his voice calm and controlled. "It's rubble and dust – that's all – just a pile of rubble and dust."

Elijah screwed his face up. "And that's where the treasure could be, you clown."

"It's cursed!"

Elijah laughed. "Who told you that?"

"Kenny Riggs. He's employed by the Forestry Commission. My dad knows him. He worked in Roebuck Woods for the council." The Duke paused, flicked the hair from his brow, and went on: "He said something wasn't right. A bad vibe…"

Elijah stared at his friend. "Nonsense."

"No, it's not. Everyone knows the history of these woods and the strange goings-on. It's best we leave."

"It's only our second day of the holidays and you're already acting like a killjoy."

The Duke ignored his friend and shifted his sights to a sign nailed to a tree: *Trespassers Will Be Prosecuted*. "Look. We are on someone else's property."

Elijah threw a stone at the sign. "The owner of this land is long dead."

"But nobody knows we are here," protested The Duke. "If something happens…"

"We've got food, drink, and a tent in case it rains. We can be home by dinnertime and no one will be any the wiser. Come on, where's your sense of adventure?"

The Duke checked his phone and stared up at the sky. "Okay, but I want to finish my breakfast first. And my mum said the forecast is for rain today."

Elijah checked the sky. "There's not a cloud in sight."

The Duke and Elijah sat by the tent and filled their stomachs with jam sandwiches and crisps. Elijah pulled a penknife from his rucksack and carved his initials onto the shaft of his torch, then he got to his feet and walked towards the trees, brushing aside the branches as if they were a doorway to another world – a world of enchanted woodland.

The Duke followed, his attention drawn to the canopy of branches interlocking above him. They reminded him of a leafy ceiling, shielding the forest from the summer sun. One step led to another. Soon, before they knew it, they were in the heart of the forest. The distant hum of the ring road had faded into silence and the murky half-light had slowed The Duke to a virtual standstill.

"Wait for me, Eli, I can't see."

Elijah marched on, ignoring The Duke's calls, swinging a stick to clear a path through the bramble. The Duke cupped his hands to his mouth and tried again. "Slow down." He stumbled on, his steps heavy and laboured as he trailed in Elijah's wake. Thorns clawed at his face like sharp fingernails, sprigs of nettles pierced his socks, and the fear of the unknown weighed down upon his weary legs. He stopped and virtually surrendered. "I can't go any further!"

"Not far now," replied Elijah. "I'm here, to your right."

The Duke finally reached his friend and fell to his haunches. "What's the rush? Why didn't you wait?"

Elijah hushed The Duke with a swipe of his stick. "Someone told me there's a rope by the entrance of Bymerstone Hall. We can use it to climb over the barbed wire."

The Duke dabbed a scratch beneath his eye and checked his fingers. "I'm not going any further. And why am I carrying your bag?"

"So I can navigate," replied Elijah. He grabbed his rucksack and strode on. "Not much further now, Duke."

The Duke reluctantly followed, his feet squelching in the mud, slipping and sliding with his arms outstretched as if he was walking the wire. The foliage grew thicker with every step, shielding the morning light from the enthralling woodland. He pressed a button on his torch, and a beam of light lit the space around him. Then the calm, eerie stillness of Roebuck Woods was interrupted by an excruciating, mechanical noise. The industrial scream penetrated the woodland, piercing the tranquillity of nature. The Duke covered his ears. There was no sign of Elijah. All he could muster was a solitary dry gulp. He jerked his head back and noticed a pair of brown eyes staring through the bracken. His tired legs sprung back to life. He ran off at breakneck speed, chasing the sound of Elijah's footsteps. The rustle of leaves beneath his feet was followed by a loud, dull, heavy thump.

The Duke opened his eyes to a blurry, incoherent world. He heard a familiar voice mumbling in the background. Then he felt someone holding him and realised the arms belonged to Elijah. "What happened?"

"You must have panicked," replied Elijah with a sheepish grin. He pointed at a low hanging branch. "You must have run into that."

The Duke sat up and rubbed his forehead. "Panicked?"

"Yes, you must have," replied Elijah.

"Well, if you hadn't left me, maybe I would've been all right, you selfish—"

"I could see the entrance to Bymerstone Hall. I was going to come back for you once I found a way in."

"Liar!"

Elijah attempted to wipe the blood from his friend's wound.

"Leave me alone," groaned The Duke, "all you ever do is bring me trouble. I must have been mad to follow you."

"Here, have some chocolate," said Elijah, "it'll boost your sugar levels."

The Duke snatched the chocolate bar and swallowed a chunk. "I was being followed, and there was this loud moaning noise – it was terrible. That's why I ran."

"I'm sorry," whispered Elijah. "That was me."

"You?" replied The Duke, astonished. "How on earth did you make such an awful noise?"

"I found the entrance to the mansion," admitted Elijah, he lowered his voice to a whisper, "it's through an archway." He pointed to the left. "It's over there."

The Duke spun his head and strained to see the entrance. "Where?"

"There," said Elijah. "I found a rope and yanked it. It released a drawbridge. It made a horrific noise, and it nearly fell on top of me. I could've been killed."

"What a shame," responded The Duke.

Elijah grinned. "There must've been a moat there years ago."

The Duke inspected the ground beneath him. "There are footprints all around us, and I—"

"Look," interrupted Elijah.

A pair of eyes peered through the coppice of trees. The Duke got to his feet and stood shoulder to shoulder with his friend, his jaw chattering. "They are the eyes that f-followed me."

The dark eyes edged closer and closer. Then, as the brambles rustled, a young Muntjac deer appeared. The animal sniffed the floor, raised its head and stared at the two frightened boys. The light from The Duke's torch flickered, then slowly faded to nothing. The Muntjac snorted, kicked out with its hind legs, and sprung off into the distance.

Elijah fumbled for his torch. "A deer," he cried. "We were scared of a Muntjac deer. Don't tell anyone at school. We will never live it down."

"Speak for yourself. I wasn't scared," lied The Duke.

The two boys shared a brief moment of laughter. Elijah took half a dozen long strides towards a stone arch that was supported by two enormous brick pillars. At the tip of the archway, 'BH' had been ornately chiselled. "It's through there."

"What is?" asked The Duke.

"Bymerstone Hall," replied Elijah in a ghoulish drawl.

The Duke laughed. "You sound ridiculous."

"Come on – just a few more steps."

"No way," replied The Duke. He crossed his arms defiantly. "I've come far enough. Let's go home."

Elijah tugged The Duke towards the arch. "Come on. Just take a look. It's incredible. There are no trees here – the sunlight gets through. Please, check it out."

The Duke relented and gazed through the leafy entrance. Thousands of red berries were scattered like a carpet of shiny marbles. Elijah stepped from beneath the arch into the grounds of the dilapidated mansion. "Come on, follow me..."

The Duke squeezed his fingers between the tangled ivy, pulled himself beneath the arch, then tiptoed onto the drawbridge. "Wow…," he said, "it's beautiful."

The drawbridge led to a perimeter of large rectangular slabs supporting two remaining walls. Beneath the crooked gable, the roof was strewn with broken tiles that clattered against the summer breeze. The remains of the stately home resembled a demolished temple. Elijah held out his arms, as if presenting his friend with a gift. "Can you believe this?"

The Duke's gaze was glued to the splendour of the ruin. "It's magical. It looks like it's glowing."

"The sun knows where to shine," said Elijah with a satisfied grin. "Roebuck Woods has kept a secret from us, and now we have found it."

"I wonder what the man who lived here was like?" mused The Duke.

Elijah walked tentatively over the drawbridge, the supporting chains on either side rattling with every step. "He was a magician, an influential man."

The Duke stood statuesque as Elijah scampered across the drawbridge into the rectangular ruins of Bymerstone Hall. "Come on, Duke, run across. I dare you."

The Duke sighed, then he grabbed a handful of berries and ran full-pelt across the drawbridge, screaming at the top of his voice, "Charge!"

Elijah ducked as the berries flew through the air. He rolled over and clattered into a row of dustbins, a metal lid landing ceremoniously on his head like an oversized crown.

The Duke erupted with laughter and scooped up more ammunition.

Elijah grabbed the dustbin lid and charged back, the berries splatting against his shield like red bullets.

The battle of the berries had begun. Golden rays of sunlight pierced through the canopy as they improvised a sword fight, rolling around like wildcats in the vast open spaces of the ruined mansion, clutching their branch-like swords in one hand and throwing their berry-bombs with the other.

"Take that," cried The Duke, as he struck out with his sword.

Elijah stepped back to cushion the blow. "My shield can take anything you throw at it."

The Duke struck again – this time, harder and faster.

"Stop!" cried Elijah.

The Duke froze, his sword aloft. "What's the matter? Have you had enough? Do you surrender to the mighty Duke and his army?"

"No, I don't," replied Elijah, angrily.

"What's wrong?"

"My foot's caught. Help me, I'm stuck."

The Duke bent down and untangled Elijah from a chain. "There you go."

Elijah rolled over and grabbed his sword. "Now, prepare to die!"

"Wait," yelled The Duke.

Elijah frowned. "What?"

The Duke pointed his branch at a pile of moss. "There. I'm certain – a door. Looks like you're sitting on an old cellar."

Elijah scraped at the moss with his sword. "Let's take a look."

The Duke stepped back. "Leave it alone, Eli."

"I want to investigate."

"It's none of our business."

Elijah began to claw at the debris, his fingers making light work of the leaf mould. "Well, let's make it our business."

The Duke watched as the layers of moss were peeled off. Two doors were revealed, they looked liked they belonged to another time, and another place. Chains looped through rusted iron handles and a black cross ran from one corner to the other. His voice faltered as he read a scribbled message: *Do not cross! Property of Zayock. Protected by the Jagganath.*

"W-what do you think that means?" he asked, half-expecting to see the lord of the manor.

Elijah tutted. "That's just a crank message from some kids who got here before us."

The Duke's bottom lip trembled as he watched Elijah pull against the handles. "Leave it, Eli. Let's get out of here."

Elijah strained as he pulled, his face flushed from the exertion. He dug his feet deep into the earth and pulled again and again. "Grab hold of me and pull."

"No way. I want to go home."

Elijah fell to the floor, out of breath, and smothered in mud. He reached for his bag and swigged from a bottle. "Maybe you're right. Come on – I've had enough. Let's get out of here."

The Duke sighed with relief and pulled Elijah to his feet, dragging him as quickly as he could back towards the drawbridge. "At least we've been inside Bymerstone Hall. Not many kids at Oakwell can say that. Why don't we ride into town when we get out of here?"

Elijah placed his arm around The Duke and smiled. "Good idea."

As they crossed the drawbridge and kicked their way through the sea of berries, a tumultuous roar shook the forest from top to bottom. Every bird fled its nest and spilled into the summer sky. The sound of beating wings filled the air like muted drums.

"What's happening?" cried The Duke, his cheeks contorting from the force of the vibrating drawbridge.

Elijah pointed at the cellar doors rattling on their hinges. "The doors – they're moving."

"Let's get out of here," screamed The Duke.

Elijah pushed The Duke to one side, turned on his heels, and sprinted back into the remains of Bymerstone Hall. "Follow me…"

The Duke refused. "Come back, Eli!"

Elijah sped towards the sound of the clanging chains. Suddenly, the bright sky morphed into patches of inky black. Forks of lightning cut the sky in two, followed by long, deep groans of thunder. Another bolt of lightning sprung down from the heavens and struck the drawbridge.

"Don't leave me," squealed The Duke.

Elijah slid to his knees and straddled the cellar doors. Only the rattling chain kept them from bursting open. He grasped the handles and pulled against them. "They're opening." Jets of pungent mucus spewed from beneath, covering him from head to foot, the sticky liquid singeing his skin.

"Sssstay away," a voice hissed.

Then it came again: a cold, icy warning that frightened the life out of the boys. Elijah ran as fast as he could, back over the smouldering drawbridge, passing The Duke, crashing through the bramble, and finally into the clear open space by the fallen trees.

The Duke lagged behind, puffing and panting, and cursing his impetuous friend. When he reached Elijah, he grabbed him by the shirt. "I don't know what happened back there, but I'm telling you, there was something behind those doors."

Elijah's mouth hardly moved. "I know."

"What was it?" asked The Duke.

"I don't know, but it smelled disgusting."

The Duke released his grip. "Let's pack up and get out of here."

Elijah pulled the tent pegs from the sodden earth and rolled the canvas into his rucksack. The final steps out of Roebuck Woods took an eternity. The distant bark of the Muntjacs kept them company as they marched towards the perimeter fence separating the woodland from the road. They squeezed through the wire like two frightened rabbits and rolled onto the grass verge that framed the busy highway. Cars zoomed past, unaware of the two boys lying flat on their backs, staring into infinity. The Duke got to his feet and stepped onto the kerbside. He blinked, rubbed his eyes, and blinked again. The curly, blonde hair was unmistakable. His heart leaped into his mouth as Nancy whizzed past on her bike. She pulled on her brakes and screeched to a standstill. "What on earth are you two doing here?"

The Duke was lost for words. He stared at her and shook his blood-stained face. He had to say something, and when he did it was feeble. "We were picking berries in the woods."

Nancy ignored him, sniffing the air repeatedly. "*Jagganath.*"

"What did you say?" asked The Duke. It was as if her whisper had awoken his senses.

"Nothing," replied Nancy, between her sniffs.

"Say it again," said The Duke, "that word."

Nancy refused. "I can't remember," she continued to inhale the summer air, "where are you two going?"

"Home, then to the park," interrupted Elijah. "What about you?"

Nancy stared at Elijah.

Elijah stared back, his expression hard. "Forgotten where you were going, Nanny Bo?"

Nancy re-mounted her bike and pedalled towards a steep hill. "I have to go. I'm late."

Elijah waited until Nancy was out of ear-shot. "We have to follow her, Duke. Something really weird is happening, and she knows what it is."

The Duke held out his hands as if he was propping up the sky. "Did you hear what she said?"

"Jagganath," answered Elijah, wiping away the last of the mucus from his torso.

"That word was written on the cellar doors."

Elijah nodded. "I know."

"How does she know about—"

"I don't know," snapped Elijah, "that's why we are going to follow her. Unlock the bikes. Let's go."

Tiny specks of rain dotted the pavement. The Duke flinched as a rumble of thunder shook the sky. He pulled up his hood; then, right on cue, the heavens opened. Rain teemed down on the two boys.

In the distance, a strange double rainbow appeared.

8
Camelback Rainbow

Nancy's legs throbbed as she felt the steep incline of the hill pull upon her tired muscles. There was no time to waste: she had to get to The Home For The Incurably Curious as soon as possible. With every push of her pedals, the incessant rain pelted her face, while the weight of her rucksack slowed her ascent like an unwanted passenger. Finally, she reached the brow of the hill, breathless and sopping wet.

Prema waited, arms folded, hood up. Her bicycle was propped against a tree. She tapped her watch and tutted.

"Sorry I'm late, Pre. I just bumped into The Duke and Eli."

Prema pointed at the sky. "Look!"

"What?" asked Nancy, shaking the rain from her coat. In her plight to climb the hill, she hadn't noticed the double rainbow glimmering on the horizon.

Prema jumped up and down, unable to contain her excitement. "Up there, Nanny Bo, there's two of them."

Nancy tilted her head towards the sky. "Wow, it looks like the letter M."

"It looks like a camel's back," added Prema; then she winked at her friend.

"Yeah, you're right – a camelback rainbow – that's exactly what it is. And today is the second day of rain."

Nancy danced in the heavy shower as if she had just solved the world's greatest mystery. "*The First Book of Cosmo* said that on the second day of rain and the coming of the camelback rainbow we could raise the portal and enter Enerjiimass."

Prema mounted her bicycle. "*You*, not *we*, Nanny Bo. The book clearly states that *you* are The Chosen One, and you alone are invited."

Nancy yanked Prema's handlebars, upturning her from the saddle. "I have no idea what is happening to me. I was dreading the summer holidays, then you turn up with your optical cards, we meet Aunt Elma, and everything changes. I know one thing – whatever's happening, it's happening to *us*... okay?"

Prema's lips curled into a smile. "Okay."

Nancy raised her fist into the air and screamed, "One for all, and all for one."

Prema raised her arm and clenched her fist. "One for all, and all for..."

But her shout was muffled by Nancy's enveloping arms. "Let's go to the library."

9
The Great Train Robbery

The Duke and Elijah pedalled frantically uphill, the storm rumbling overhead like an angry choir. Elijah was the first to reach the top. He skidded to a halt and crouched behind his bike. "We need to keep our distance, otherwise she'll see us."

The Duke sank into an exhausted squat. "Why am I carrying the tent?"

"Because I am carrying the lunch."

"That's much lighter than the tent."

"We can swap if you want," replied Elijah, trying his best not to laugh.

The Duke harrumphed. "Then you get to carry the tent downhill."

Elijah raised the binoculars to his face. "There she is, and there's someone with her."

The Duke wrestled the binoculars from Elijah. "That's Prema Sarkander."

Elijah nodded. "Do you fancy her?"

"No," snapped The Duke, as a hot flush emblazoned his face. "What's she doing hanging around with Nanny Bo?"

"How am I supposed to know? It looks like they're heading towards the town centre."

The two boys coasted downhill in pursuit of Nancy and Prema, their brakes squeaking and grinding the entire way. The route to the library made it easy for them to remain inconspicuous, twisting and turning as it did through a labyrinth of busy streets leading to the town centre and finally into Central Square.

It was market day and the smell of fresh bread and cooked meats made The Duke's mouth water. Market traders populated the square, tending their stalls and bellowing out their prices. It was organised chaos. The pavements and side streets were packed with men offering secondhand goods from overloaded suitcases. The Duke and Elijah waited for Nancy and Prema to move on. They followed, hiding behind the swell of the crowd, pushing their bikes nervously through the busy market, before reaching the grandiose library. The Duke stared up at the entrance, then scampered into a dark alleyway to the side of the building. "Quick, in here."

Elijah squeezed past a row of dustbins. The first one wobbled, then tumbled. The rest fell like dominoes. The Duke held his head in his hands. "Careful, Eli. Can't you be quiet for one minute?"

"It was an accident."

The Duke peered out from the alleyway and watched Nancy climb the marble steps, the ancient book stuffed into her rucksack, squeezing the seams to bursting point, the braided cover shimmering in the stormy half-light. "There's something sparkling in her bag."

Elijah brushed past The Duke. "Get out of my way. Let me take a look."

"Careful, Eli – she might see you."

"A golden book," whispered Elijah, his curiosity now at fever pitch. "She has a golden book. How much is that worth?"

The Duke sighed as the girls disappeared into the library. He was tired, bruised, and wet through. The day had taken its toll. All he wanted was to go home and eat. Following two girls wasn't his idea of fun. He sat on the steps and gazed up at the foreboding sky.

"Wow, look at that. A double rainbow." He waited for Elijah's response, but it didn't come. He looked around the busy courtyard for his friend. "Eli, where are you?"

Elijah was halfway up the marble staircase, striding towards the impressive entrance.

The Duke raced up the steps, cursing Elijah's impulsive nature. "Wait for me."

Once inside, they marvelled at the domed roof – an oval window to the bleak sky. The Duke's roaming eye spied a spiral of blonde hair. "She's over there."

Elijah's head twitched left to right. "Where?"

"There," said The Duke, stabbing his finger to the rear of the grand hall, "by the fire exit."

Elijah raced off. "Come on..."

"What's the rush?" asked The Duke, dodging a head-on collision with a short, plump lady carrying a handful of books.

"Keep up," replied Elijah, as he twisted through the crowded aisles. "I want to see what she's hiding in that bag."

The crowds thinned as they approached the fire exit. Oswald Goddard stood with his arms crossed, guarding the door. The Duke hid behind a bookstand and observed the librarian. "Now what do we do?"

"We need to distract him," whispered Elijah. "Then we can get through that door."

"Easier said than done."

Elijah grabbed the first thing he could lay his hands on and walked towards Oswald Goddard. "Hello."

"Oh, good afternoon," replied Oswald, unsure where the boys had appeared from. "Can I be of assistance?"

"Yes, I wondered if you had anything else on…" Elijah held out a tatty book in his right hand and checked the title. "On The Great Train Robbery?"

Oswald Goddard's face lit up. "Oh, yes, that's crime – my section of the library. I'm second-in-command, you know."

"Really?" replied Elijah, sarcastically.

"I'm sure we have at least three other books on that famous heist." Oswald walked off towards his workstation, he raised a finger and said, "Wait here, I won't be a moment."

The Duke and Elijah shuffled closer to the doorway and prepared to run.

Then Oswald stopped, scratched his head and spun around.

The Duke winced, tiny beads of sweat trickling down his brow, his heart beating a rhythm of panic. Elijah stared at the librarian open-mouthed. Oswald tapped his finger on the cover of the book. "That train never made it to Euston Station and neither did the £2.5 million on board. Mr Biggs was a Londoner, too, you know."

"Oh," said Elijah. "And a rich one."

Oswald huffed, then scurried off.

The Duke and Elijah shoulder-barged the fire door, dashed into the rain-soaked courtyard, and gawped as they caught sight of Nancy disappearing beyond the miniature doorway.

"Impossible," whispered The Duke.

"I told you they were hiding something from us," said Elijah. "They went through that door… through that *tiny* door."

The Duke's face crumpled in astonishment. "But how?"

"I don't know," said Elijah, crestfallen. "Somehow. They got through."

10

A White Feather

Nancy and Prema stood inside The Home For The Incurably Curious. The muffled sound of Captain Carbunkle's baritone vocals echoed from the room at the end of the hallway. Nancy didn't waste a second. She skipped past the sleeping parrot, along the corridor, past the kitchen, and stood at the entrance that separated her from all the answers she now craved. Her fingers tingled as she touched *The First Book of Cosmo*.

"Back again?" crowed Grizelda, awoken by the sound of footsteps. "I didn't think you had it in you, little girl."

"Don't listen to the parrot," begged Prema. "She's testing you."

Nancy refused eye contact with the bird. She stared at the double doors and whistled a three-note melody.

"Are you so scared you can't face me?" goaded Grizelda.

Nancy stomped back to where Grizelda had perched herself.

"We haven't got time for this," cried Prema.

Nancy stepped to within a hair's breadth of the parrot. "What do you mean, you didn't think I had it in me?"

"Haw-haw-haw," cackled Grizelda. "You really do have a weakness. If you manage to raise the portal, you will need to channel your frustrations and contain your temper." Grizelda shuffled sideways on her perch. "The journey of life starts with the first step. Make sure it's the right one, little girl. If not, every one thereafter will lead you astray."

Nancy wrinkled her nose and poked her tongue out.

Grizelda sprawled her wings. It was an impressive sight: white, angelic plumes wafted through the air as the parrot continued to flap. Faster and faster, her magnificent wings fluttering, until she was airborne.

Nancy reached for a falling feather and placed it in her pocket.

"Quick," hollered Prema from the end of the hallway, "we haven't got all day."

Nancy turned and ran back to the studded doors. She knocked twice and waited for an answer. The latch lifted and the door creaked open. "Welcome," said Captain Carbunkle, with arms aloft. The girls entered and stood below the radiant chandelier. Aunt Elma sat at a table, surrounded by hundreds of books, some open, some closed, but most were piled on top of one another, like leaning columns of literature. Waiting to topple at a moment's notice.

Captain Carbunkle's excitement was uncontainable. He bowed, then guided Nancy and Prema to their seats. Aunt Elma acknowledged the girls without speaking. Captain Carbunkle danced around the table, waving his arms and pirouetting. Nancy couldn't take her eyes off the strange dwarf. His tiny feet were like those of a china doll.

Aunt Elma placed her hands palm side up on the table and stretched out her fingers. "Circle of one, please, girls," she said with a dry rasp.

Nancy, Prema, and Aunt Elma linked fingers. As their hands touched, Captain Carbunkle jumped up onto the table and stood within the circle. He raised his hands towards the ceiling, tilted his head back, and began to chant rhythmically. Somehow the strange musical language seemed familiar to Nancy – like a distant dream relived.

"I send my energy to you, O' Great One," chanted Captain Carbunkle. "By the power you invest in me, I offer the girl to restore balance and harmony. She is not of age, but she is of blood."

"Blood?" repeated Nancy, incredulously.

Captain Carbunkle locked eyes with Nancy, then placed his hands ceremoniously on her head. Her body began to shake as waves of electrical energy fizzed through her veins. Her face twitched and her muscles stiffened. A brief moment of disorientation was followed by a euphoric swell in the pit of her stomach. It was as if every joyous moment in her life was condensed into that one solitary second, every doubt and worry wiped out. This was how she wanted to be, free-spirited, no feelings of isolation or self-doubt.

Captain Carbunkle removed his hands, crossed his arms, then lifted one leg off the table and balanced precariously on the other. He peeled a huge smile, his gold teeth now reflecting prisms of light from the chandelier. Slowly, he lifted his standing leg. Nancy and Prema gasped as he levitated above them. The dwarf closed his eyes and started to snore. Aunt Elma brushed wisps of grey hair from her face and pinched the locket that hung around her neck. Her soft voice drew their attention back to the circle of one. "Have you read the book?" she asked.

"Yes," replied Nancy in a hushed tone. "But some of the pages are blank and—"

"We have little time," interrupted Aunt Elma. "You have received your invitation to Enerjiimass. We need to know if you accept."

Nancy didn't answer, her empty stare holding back a thousand questions. Aunt Elma kneaded her hand. "We need an answer. The portal can only be raised when everything is aligned. The book informs us that on the second day of rain and the coming of the camelback rainbow you can raise the portal and enter Enerjiimass."

The old lady drew breath, stared into thin air, then went on: "That moment has come."

Three loud chimes rang out and the room shook. Pictures fell from the walls and dust rained down from the lattice of shelves. "Right on cue," said Aunt Elma, glancing at the clock on the wall. "Three o'clock in your Earth realm. That's nine hours before midnight."

"What happens at midnight?" asked Nancy.

"It is the end of today and the beginning of tomorrow."

"I know that, but what—?"

"Your impatience will be your undoing, Nancy Bo Jones."

"I prefer *Nanny Bo*. My grandmother called me that from birth."

Aunt Elma cocked an eyebrow. "Okay, *Nanny Bo*, your invitation to Enerjiimass is valid tonight at midnight. After that, the window of opportunity will be lost forever."

The slow tick-tock of the pendulum seemed to clunk louder as time passed. Nancy glanced at the clock, then back to the circle of one. "There is so much I don't know. I need answers to my questions before I—"

"I know, my child," interrupted Aunt Elma. "Unfortunately, I cannot give you all the answers you desire, at least not on my own. Life's answers can only be unravelled by experience and time."

"I'm lacking both," confessed Nancy. "And I'm so worried about the…" She paused and drew breath. "The future."

"People waste so much time and energy worrying about the future that they miss out on life itself," replied Aunt Elma. "I can give you as much information as you need to access Enerjiimass. It would be remiss of me not to. Your survival could depend upon it."

"Sur-vi-val?" stuttered Nancy.

"Yes. Let me explain." Aunt Elma checked the clock and continued: "If you accept the invitation, we have limited time to prepare you for your mission. Unfortunately, you are not of age.

Much of what you need to know would have been presented to you in later life."

Aunt Elma let go of Nancy's hand and broke the circle of one. Captain Carbunkle came to and fell upon the table, the china saucers clanking as he landed with an impromptu thud.

"Follow me," instructed Aunt Elma.

Captain Carbunkle got to his feet and straightened his hat. Nancy and Prema followed Aunt Elma as she carefully navigated her way through mounds of books and manuscripts. She led them to a bookshelf that leaned ominously against a supporting wall. A pile of books was used as an improvised seat. "This will suffice," croaked Aunt Elma.

The metronomic pendulum was so loud it was impossible to ignore. A time-based rhythm stimulating body and mind. Captain Carbunkle reached inside the shelf and pulled out a large book entitled *Whys and Wherefores*. Its cover was coated with tiny, square, mosaic mirrors. Reflections of light danced around them like shooting stars. Aunt Elma placed the book on her lap and gestured for Nancy to stand closer. "Now then, what do you need to know?"

Nancy's eyes widened. "Is every answer written in a book?"

"More or less," mumbled Aunt Elma. She repeated the question, this time with a sense of urgency, "What do you need to know?"

Nancy stalled, her mind a blur as she thought of all the questions that begged for an answer. She had to ask the obvious: "Why have I been invited to Enerjiimass, and where is it?"

She waited patiently, the ticking clock measuring the silence.

Aunt Elma checked the time and smiled. "Good question. I will try to be as brief as possible." She opened the book, turned a page and placed a brass monocle in her right eye. "All in your world is not as it seems. If you cannot help us, there is much imbalance and trouble ahead."

Nancy glanced sideways at Prema.

Aunt Elma thumbed the next leaf of paper. "There are many different planets beyond the reach of man. Some can be seen through telescopes, others cannot. Between these visible and invisible planets lies a parallel universe. It creates and emits energy for every planet of every solar system." Aunt Elma stroked her locket and leaned forward. "That is where we come from." She pointed at Captain Carbunkle, who lifted his hat, revealing a small clump of ginger hair. "It is a world known as Enerjiimass, where energy is refined and sent back out into the ether. Think of it as the battery of the universe, the Source." The old lady paused, her eyes narrowing between breaths. "Without harmony in the world of Enerjiimass, the life-blood of our own world is drained away and, in time, darkness will engulf planet Earth."

Nancy gulped, her eyes fixed upon the mirrored book glistening on Aunt Elma's lap.

"There are but a few who understand this, Nanny Bo. Most people are unaware that positive energy is sent from our world to Earth. Without this energy, it would cease to be."

Nancy absorbed every word, adrenaline fizzing through her veins. It was intoxicating, a feeling she craved, something that died within her the day her parents pulled her from her bed and relocated to the countryside. Then, without warning, the strange reptilian voice returned, disabling her senses: "Do not lissssten to the librarian. Sssstay away. You are cursed."

Nancy expelled a loud groan and shook her head.

Aunt Elma prodded Captain Carbunkle with her walking stick. He clicked his fingers and bellowed, "*Protect*." An orb of blue light encircled Nancy's body. Her body spasmed as the voice of the Jagganath was silenced.

"What happened?" asked Prema. "Is she all right?"

"A nasty intrusion to a moment of joy," replied Captain Carbunkle. "The dark forces of Enerjiimass are anxious." He chewed the end of his pipe and went on: "We must strive to keep a positive frame of mind. It makes us stronger as individuals, wards off the darkness, and invites the light."

Nancy stared at the ginger dwarf, his words resonating like a tonic for a vulnerable mind. She acknowledged him with a stiff nod, inhaled, then addressed Aunt Elma: "You said that my world would cease to be?"

"That I did," confirmed Aunt Elma. "Unfortunately, there is not enough positive energy created naturally in your own world."

"Can we make this energy?" asked Nancy, her nerves at breaking point.

Aunt Elma exchanged a startled look with Captain Carbunkle. "No, certainly not. It is not something that can be concocted like a potion."

"Once upon a time, someone did try," confessed Captain Carbunkle.

"That's true," said Aunt Elma. "There was once a troubled man who lived within Roebuck Woods."

"At the end of your garden…," said Prema.

Aunt Elma ignored the interruption and continued: "The man who lived there was an alchemist, a kind man who sat in solitude from the outside world. He had all the riches you could dream of. He lived in a beautiful mansion, but died lonely."

"Loneliness is a terrible thing," proclaimed Nancy, her bottom lip quivering.

"And so is greed," added Aunt Elma. "Greed drove this man to his unfortunate disappearance. Like you, he acquired *The First Book of Cosmo*."

Nancy tightened her grip on the rucksack. Aunt Elma smiled, then offered Nancy her hand. "There are no shortcuts in life, Nanny Bo. Positive energy is best generated by one good deed done to another – an act of love or a kind word to raise someone's spirits. It cannot be created through a potion mixed by an alchemist. The man in question convinced himself he was the saviour. He crossed the threshold and—"

Nancy swallowed hard. "And what?"

"He went missing, and he's never been found. Presumed dead."

A cold, tingling sensation ran the length of Nancy's spine. Aunt Elma moved closer. "Enerjiimass is a harmonious place – it shares all of its positive energy with other worlds. Only a handful of people from the Earth realm have the right attributes to cross the threshold and enter Enerjiimass."

Nancy braced herself, her gaze fixed on the old lady. "What attributes do these people have?"

Aunt Elma cleared her throat and continued: "They require an unconventional mind and possess a very special talent."

"What talent?" asked Nancy, full of curiosity.

Aunt Elma raised her finger. "A special talent. A gift. These folk are rare and, as guardian of Enerjiimass, I am tasked by the high priest to identify these special individuals."

The hairs on Nancy's neck prickled.

"I'm searching for people like you," Aunt Elma concluded.

"Me?"

"Yes, you, Nanny Bo. Ordinarily, they are of age and have been guided by myself and my army of helpers prior to crossing the threshold."

"Who are these helpers? Do they hide in the shadows?" asked Nancy, her suspicion aroused.

"It is not as sinister as you make it sound. It doesn't matter who they are. They normally identify themselves with a green-eyed ring."

"Like Oswald and Jangles."

"Yes," admitted Aunt Elma. "Like Oswald and my nephew. Not all of them have your gifts. While they are of good character, it is you, Nanny Bo, who possesses the power of Extra Sensory Perception."

"I told you!" said Prema. She punched the air victoriously and added, "E.S.P. That's your special power. That's really cool."

Nancy raised the ancient volume and presented it to Aunt Elma. "What about this book?"

"*The First Book of Cosmo* has a mysterious history. You have it at your disposal and only if you decide to enter Enerjiimass will it reveal its secrets to you. Only two people in history have managed to enter Enerjiimass and return unscathed."

"Who?"

"One of them was a holy man from the Middle East. The other shall remain nameless, for now."

The clock chimed twice on the half-hour.

Aunt Elma continued, her voice waning. "There is trouble in the world of Enerjiimass. An evil sorcerer has somehow managed to break the balance of positive energy, sending waves of negativity out into the universe. Every planet is absorbing it as we speak. He is a clever man, a thief." She shivered, as if reliving a bad dream, then slammed down her walking stick. "He has stolen the Bloodstone!" Nancy opened her mouth, but Aunt Elma gestured for silence. "The stone contains a vital ingredient for a potion that should never be made."

Nancy couldn't contain herself. "What potion?"

"The Elixir of Life," whispered Captain Carbunkle. "The search for the everlasting. It is a curse for all mankind."

Aunt Elma considered her words before they left her mouth: "Without the Bloodstone in its rightful place, Captain Carbunkle and I cannot return to Enerjiimass. Our refuge is here at The Home For The Incurably Curious. If the balance of positive energy is not restored soon, I'm afraid—"

"Our world will fall into darkness," interrupted Prema. "That *is* what you said?"

"Yes," whispered Aunt Elma. "*The First Book of Cosmo* clearly states that, without the stone in its rightful place, the Great One has limited power."

Nancy sighed, exasperated at the amount of information she was trying to digest. "*The Great One?*"

Captain Carbunkle took three steps towards Nancy. "All my power is in that stone and its rightful keeper."

"Who is the keeper?" enquired Nancy, her brow now wrinkled with confusion.

Captain Carbunkle squashed his palms together and gazed up at the smoke-stained ceiling. "It belongs to the Great One, he who gives us the reason to be. He loves us all. The true source."

Aunt Elma bent down and stroked Captain Carbunkle. "It has to be somebody from the Earth realm who crosses the threshold," she said. "We urgently need to locate the stone and restore balance. Captain Carbunkle and I would perish within seconds of setting foot within Enerjiimass right now."

"I don't understand," said Nancy, running a finger through her curls.

"Our sensitive bodies can only function in a world of harmony and positivity." Aunt Elma paused for thought, then puckered her lips and went on. "Humans are taking more from life than they are putting back. Planet Earth draws so much positive energy from Enerjiimass. To supply and maintain that constant source of energy, we need to have absolute harmony within Enerjiimass. The Bloodstone creates new energy. Without it, Enerjiimass will implode."

Captain Carbunkle tugged on Nancy's leg. "We need you to be strong. You are The Chosen One."

"That's what the book said," mumbled Nancy; "it sounds weird."

"No, it doesn't," replied Captain Carbunkle. "You *are* The Chosen One." Then he removed his hat and bowed before Nancy.

The sudden weight of responsibility hit Nancy like a sledgehammer. She reached out to the old lady. "You said my world was full of bad energy. How can you and Captain Carbunkle survive here?"

Captain Carbunkle clicked his fingers, somersaulted, and landed on a small mound of books. "The Home For The Incurably Curious is a protected refuge for us. There is a circle of love that surrounds this place. Surely someone with your sensory gifts can feel that?"

Nancy nodded. "I heard voices earlier. They sang to me like a choir. It felt amazing."

"Ah, the choral bliss of the Night Fairies," confirmed Captain Carbunkle. "Remain optimistic and they will drown out the noise of the Jagganath."

"What happens if I fail?" asked Nancy.

Aunt Elma raised an eyebrow. "You will be trapped within Enerjiimass forever. Your Earth life will be over."

Nancy reached inside her pocket and pulled out a white feather. "My dad says that if you find a white feather you should keep hold of it."

A wry grin appeared on Captain Carbunkle's face. "Why would he say such a thing?"

"Hope," replied Nancy. "A white feather always gives you hope."

"Well, best you keep hold of it," instructed the dwarf. "Inside Enerjiimass, a white feather indicates that a lost loved one is close by. Keep that feather safe, Nanny Bo."

Aunt Elma pushed down on her walking stick and stood from her makeshift seat. She placed an arm around Nancy and pressed her mouth to her ear. "The creatures of Enerjiimass are in grave danger."

"Are you okay?" asked Nancy, her slender frame now supporting the old lady.

"No," replied Aunt Elma. "I carry a burden of guilt for putting this dreadful situation upon the shoulders of a wonderful little girl like you. I know you are a lost soul, and I feel your pain."

Nancy turned her cheek and welled up.

Aunt Elma embraced Nancy. "You do not fit where you have been put. That in itself is a travesty. But there is a reason you are with us, and if you believe in yourself, all will be well."

Nancy wrapped her arms around the old lady and choked back her sadness. "There is so much I need to know. I feel so lost."

"In time, all of your questions will have answers."

"When?" asked Nancy.

"*In time,*" repeated Aunt Elma. "You have much to lose, and little time to make such a difficult decision."

Nancy pushed her forehead against Aunt Elma's. "I will do it. I will raise the portal and enter Enerjiimass."

Panic sharpened Prema's voice. "What about your family… and your life here, Nanny Bo?"

"I can do this," proclaimed Nancy. "I can find the stone and restore balance."

11
A Feathered Mentor

Captain Carbunkle checked the clock on the wall. He tapped his finger on his wrist and nodded at Aunt Elma. Nancy knew it was time to leave, so she grabbed her rucksack, looped it over her shoulder, and walked out of the inner sanctum of The Home For The Incurably Curious. She pushed against the heavy doors and stepped into the hallway. The sound of Captain Carbunkle's wooden clogs echoed as he made his way towards the empty desk. They walked in single file. There was no sign of Grizelda. Nancy ran her fingers along the edge of the desk and glanced up at the perch. Dozens of feathers were scattered below. She drew breath, puffed out a gut-full of air, and watched as they took flight, dancing and looping over and over, until they settled back onto the flagstones. She smiled, crouched down and reached for the latch.

"Wait one moment," instructed Captain Carbunkle. He climbed up onto the desk and tapped his clogs. "Time is precious, but I need a minute to offer you some help."

"I should hope so," said Prema.

The strange dwarf made the shape of a heart with his hands. "Ah, the love of a friend. You have an open heart, dear Prema." Then he curled his arms and spun 360 degrees. He rotated faster and faster, the revolutions a blur to the eye. Then he stopped abrubtly and pointed at Prema. "To assist The Chosen One on her adventure, I would like to offer her the Reader of the Cards."

"Me?" said Prema, surprised.

"Yes, you, Prema Sarkander," replied Captain Carbunkle. "If you wish to aid your friend, you have the knowledge of the optical cards. I understand that they speak of what is yet to pass."

"Y-yes," stammered Prema.

"A gift from the spirit world," said Captain Carbunkle, respectfully. "Ordinarily, it is only one person who crosses the threshold; but Nanny Bo is not of age, and the rules must be rewritten."

Nancy stepped forward and signalled her displeasure. "But—"

Captain Carbunkle cut her short, his face stern. "I'm sure the Chosen One will be *happy* to have a friend on board?"

"Maybe," replied Nancy, she paused, then frowned, "but it will be safer if I go alone, rather than risk anyone else being trapped... forever..."

"No way," protested Prema. "I'm going with you. What happened to *all for one and one for all*?"

"Okay, Pre," conceded Nancy. "Perhaps we should leave."

"Not just yet," said Captain Carbunkle. "Enerjiimass is a world that will seem strange to you. You will need all the help you can get. *The First Book of Cosmo* allows you four of the gifts that Mr Wuu bestowed upon you. Choose wisely and never, ever, give way to hatred or melancholy. Every thought or feeling you have within Enerjiimass must be a positive one. Or else..."

Nancy didn't know where to look. She knew her failings, and so did Captain Carbunkle. Her glass, like her mother's, was always half-empty. "How do I raise the portal?"

Captain Carbunkle rattled his clogs on the desk. "Look no further than the woods at the end of your garden. There is a cellar which will lead you into my world."

"Really?" said Nancy, aghast. She tried her best to visualise her back garden, squinting as she pictured the dense forest that framed her back yard.

"Yes," answered Captain Carbunkle. "You have also been awarded a guardian, young lady – someone who will share this great journey with you."

"Great," cried Prema. "A mentor. Just what we need."

There was a scratching from beneath the desk. Aunt Elma hobbled to one side and Grizelda appeared. Nancy rolled her eyes. The parrot flapped around the desktop, squawking with excitement. "Haw, haw. I am ready, Your Highness."

Nancy plugged her ears as Grizelda's harsh squawk echoed through the hallway. She shook her head and point-blank refused Captain Carbunkle's offer. "I'm not taking her."

"Hold your tongue," said Aunt Elma, sharply. "Grizelda is a Reader of Hearts and Minds. Captain Carbunkle has already told you to accept all the help that comes your way. You would be foolish to reject such a gift."

"You have to be joking," replied Nancy. "That bird drives me crazy."

Grizelda clawed the desktop, her talons tearing the leather inlay to shreds. Aunt Elma attempted to pacify the bird, stroking her head-crest, reassuring her quietly. "Settle down, Grizelda, I am sure Nanny Bo will treat you well on this journey."

"Will you take care of Grizelda?" asked Captain Carbunkle, with a pointed look.

Nancy tutted. "All right."

"That's yes, Your Highness," squawked Grizelda.

Aunt Elma hobbled over to Nancy and cupped a hand to her ear. "Captain Carbunkle is revered within Enerjiimass. He is the high priest, the teacher of magic, otherwise known as *Your Highness.*"

"Oh," said Nancy, crestfallen. She offered a half-hearted curtsey. "I'm so sorry, *Your Highness*."

Captain Carbunkle opened his arms and grinned. "Don't be sorry, you do not have to address me that way. I'm sure Grizelda was only trying to help."

"Yes, Your Highness," clucked the parrot. "Trying to help."

"Now then," said the ginger dwarf, "there is one more thing you may wish to consider for your journey."

Nancy furrowed her brow. "What's that?"

"Loyalty and trust," added Captain Carbunkle. "There is a boy who would run to the ends of the earth for you. And I am sure he would strengthen your cause."

Nancy blushed. "Jim Jam! I can't be responsible for Prema, Jim Jam, *and* the parrot."

Captain Carbunkle smiled, his gold teeth glistening like polished jewels. Aunt Elma slid the latch and a loud vacuum of air sucked Nancy, Prema, and Grizelda through the door and back out into the courtyard.

Nancy crash-landed on her back, dazed and confused. Grizelda's claws were clamped around her wrist, blistering her skin. *The First Book of Cosmo* was strewn on the floor, its decorative pages flapping against the wind.

A large shadow loomed over Nancy.

"Look who's turned up," snorted Elijah. His arms were folded and his face steely. "You visit a library and return with a parrot. What the heck is going on?" He offered Nancy his hand and grunted, "Spill the beans."

Nancy slid the book inside her rucksack, pushed Elijah's arm to one side, and got to her feet. "Leave me alone. I don't need your help."

Elijah attempted to grab the rucksack.

Grizelda retaliated, her talons puncturing the boy's skin. Elijah yelped in pain, prancing and squealing his way around the courtyard. Grizelda followed, flapping, clucking and squawking.

Nancy laughed as the parrot gave chase. "You'd better run faster than that, Eli…"

Elijah scampered past the laughing children, swatting the parrot's claws that dangled precariously over his scalp. "Stop this blasted parrot, before I punch it!"

"Only if you tell me why you are here," replied Nancy, her laughter now loud and hysterical.

The Duke answered, between fits of stifled laughter. "He was being nosey, Nanny Bo. We followed you here to see what you were up to, and now he has been attacked by a parrot." The Duke couldn't hold it in a moment longer: he erupted with a loud guffaw. "He even tried to convince me you went through that tiny door."

"We did," said Prema.

"I told you," screamed Elijah from a distance. "But you wouldn't believe me, would you?"

Nancy gave Prema a look of contempt. "I think you have said enough. We need to leave." She held out her forearm, and called the parrot.

Grizelda circled above and landed obediently.

Elijah skidded in the shingle. "There's something really weird happening. I want to know what it is."

"Your imagination is playing tricks on you," said Nancy, with an unforgiving smirk, "now, leave us alone."

Elijah persisted, trailing two steps behind Nancy. "We visited a derelict mansion in Roebuck Woods today." He paused, eager for Nancy's attention; then he said, "We found a cellar…"

Nancy brooded for a moment. "What did you say?"

Elijah stepped closer to Nancy. "We found a cellar."

"It was chained," said The Duke, "then they burst open."

"Have you heard of the Jagganath?" asked Elijah.

Nancy froze.

Elijah waited, desperate for an answer.

Nancy pursed her lips. The passing of time was now at the forefront of her mind. To navigate through woodland at midnight was one thing; finding the portal was another. She cocked her head and prodded her finger into Elijah's chest. "If you know where the cellar is, meet me in Roebuck Woods tonight."

Prema's eyes widened. "Nanny Bo!"

Nancy held a finger to her lips.

"What time?" enquired Elijah.

Nancy's eyes flitted between Grizelda and Elijah. "How long does it take to get there?"

"Not long – it's at the end of your garden. Once we are inside the perimeter fence, about twenty minutes."

Nancy was mindful of Aunt Elma's midnight warning. "Okay, meet me in my garden at eleven-thirty."

"Nice one," said Elijah, with thumbs aloft, "and then you can spill the beans."

Nancy sighed, unsure if she had done the right thing. "Maybe."

"I'll bring The Duke," added Elijah.

"Oh, no you won't," said The Duke.

Elijah bent his arms and mimicked a bird's wings. "What's the matter? You chicken?"

"No. I just don't fancy walking around the woods twice in one day."

"So you *are* chicken."

"No, I am not."

Elijah continued to goad his friend. "Why don't you come with me and Nanny Bo, then?"

"All right, I will," said The Duke. "Now give it a rest, Eli."

Nancy reached for *The First Book of Cosmo* and offered it to Prema. Grizelda rustled her feathers. There was a brief moment of telepathy. Nancy recoiled and shook her head to dispel the uninvited parrot squawks. She clicked her fingers and whispered, "*Inside.*" The parrot sprung from her arm and landed obediently in the empty rucksack.

Elijah's face morphed into a crumpled look of wonder. "So, the three of us will meet at eleven-thirty tonight?"

"No," replied Nancy, refusing eye contact as she made her way towards the library door.

Elijah shrugged. "What? I thought you said—"

"They'll be five of us – where I go, Prema goes. And there's one more."

"Who?" asked The Duke, his curiosity kindled.

Nancy pushed the fire escape and disappeared into the library.

12
Four Gifts

The hustle and bustle of market day in Central Square had slowed to a respectable rumble. The noisy market traders were now quietly counting their takings as the last of the shoppers made their way home and the innkeepers prepared themselves for the rowdy night crowd. Nancy unchained her bike and stared up at the sky. The summer sun burned crimson red – the storm had passed, and the camelback rainbow was all but a distant memory.

Her ride home was downhill. She steadied her handlebars and freewheeled. She let the wind dance through her curly mop and pondered how quickly life can change: London to West Berkshire, and now The Home For The Incurably Curious. She whizzed around a tight bend and hollered, "I think it's number one."

"What is?" asked Prema, gripping *The First Book of Cosmo* in one hand and manoeuvring with the other.

Nancy squeezed her brakes and screeched to an impromptu halt. "Jim Jam's house!"

Prema stopped in the nick of time, her front wheel nudging into Nancy's rear. The net curtains began to twitch at number three. Cynthia Leathwaite's narrow face appeared. The colour drained from her cheeks as Nancy gave a regal wave.

"Who's that?" asked Prema.

"My mum calls them *nosey parkers*."

Nancy made her way up the path to number one. She stood with her arm over the knocker and eyeballed a family portrait hanging over the fireplace. Jimmy's huge smile beamed back at her. He looked so happy and content. She thought twice about whether to knock, then threw caution to the wind and rattled the knocker.

Brenda James opened the door. "Hello."

"Hello," said Nancy, nervously. "Is Jim Jam there?"

Brenda snorted. "Jim Jam?" She thumbed a page on her notepad. "I think you mean Jimmy, young lady. Now, who might you be?"

"Tell him it's Nanny Bo."

A look of horror swept across Brenda James' face. She held her hand over her mouth, then slammed the door.

Prema pointed to the frosted window at the top of the house. "Look!"

Jimmy James opened the window and waved. "Hello."

"Hello, Jim Jam," said Nancy, grinning.

Jimmy stared at the rucksack looped over Nancy's shoulders. "Is that a parrot?"

Nancy glared at Grizelda. Grizelda disappeared back into the rucksack. "Er, yes," answered Nancy. "There's no time to explain, Jim Jam. We need to talk."

"I'm supposed to be packing," replied Jimmy in a nervous whisper. "We leave tomorrow for Bournemouth. And I'm not allowed to talk to you."

"Why? What have I done?"

Jimmy rolled his eyes. "Long story."

Nancy shrugged; then she turned to Prema. "Take the bikes, Pre, and wait on the corner for me."

"Okay."

Nancy glanced up at Jimmy and made the 'okay' signal with her left hand. Then she pulled at the metal pipe that ran from the top of the house down to the drain. She stepped back, spun around, and ran full-pelt towards the drainpipe. Her fingers clamped the pipe as her feet pushed against the pebbledashed wall. Fragments of pea shingle rained down on the path, the pitter-patter of gravel forcing Jimmy into a painful wince. He pressed his finger to his mouth as Nancy shunted her way up. She reached agonisingly for the window ledge, speaking in short, punctuated breaths, "Jim Jam. I-need-your-help. Something-has-been-stolen."

"What has?"

Nancy strained, her grip slowly waning. "You wouldn't believe me if I told you."

"I will," said Jimmy, watching Nancy's blanched fingers twitch around the pipe. "Are you okay?"

"I need to get down. If you want to help, meet me in my garden. I'll be waiting beneath the walnut tree."

"When?"

Nancy slid down the pipe and crashed to her knees. "Tonight. Eleven-thirty."

The latch to the front door clicked. Brenda James stepped out and yelled: "How dare you bother my little Jimmy." She pushed Nancy back down the path, shunting her with every word. "Cursed-child-leave-us-alone."

Nancy mounted her bike and muttered *"Cursed child"* under her breath.

"Did you tell him?" asked Prema.

"Yes," replied Nancy, "I didn't have much time to explain, though."

A few minutes later, the girls reached 145 Oxon Road. Bessy Jones greeted them with a cautious smile. "What's in ya' bag, babe?"

"Not much," lied Nancy.

"Not much?" replied Bessy. "It's moving."

Nancy felt the air thin. She gambled. She removed her rucksack and offered it to her mother with a sardonic grin. "If you don't believe me, take a look."

Bessy Jones extended her arm.

Nancy glared at Bessy, then at the bag.

Bessy Jones reached for the rucksack, then retracted her arm. "I'll take a look later. Go up to your room, there are two cans of lemonade waiting for you."

The girls climbed the stairs and fell onto the bed in a fit of hushed giggles. "Phew, that was close," said Nancy, "I thought we were done for."

"Me, too," replied Prema. "I thought she was going to look in the bag."

"So did I," admitted Nancy, "but then Grizelda did something…"

"What?"

"I heard her squawk in my head; she sent my mother a message that the bag wasn't important. And somehow, I don't know how, she changed her mind."

The girls sipped their lemonade and gazed in wonder at *The First Book of Cosmo*, its gilded cover shimmering in the late-afternoon sun. Nancy glanced across the room to Mr Wuu's peculiar contraptions and held four fingers aloft. "We can only take four toys with us. That's what Captain Carbunkle said." A loud scratching noise distracted her. She paced across the bedroom and opened the wardrobe door.

"Those *toys* that you refer to are highly prized artefacts," crowed Grizelda.

"Be quiet," said Nancy, pulling an imaginary zip over her mouth.

"Manners," squawked the bird.

"If you don't shut up, I'll take you down to the pet shop and sell you." Nancy closed the door and began to riffle through an assortment of toys and gadgets, throwing them around the room in a torrent of frustration, cursing herself and Grizelda, and anything else that came to mind.

Prema tried her best to decrypt what she could from *The First Book of Cosmo*, making notes with a pencil against each numeric passage. As she turned to page eighty-eight, her eyes sparkled. The optical cards were etched across two wrinkled pages in a variety of different watercolours. For each and every card on show, strange letters shone brightly in the margins of the ancient book, flashing intermittently, spinning around the parchment's edge like a roulette wheel. Then it all stopped, leaving only one sparkling sign: an elaborate question mark, blinking on and off. A prompt.

Prema slammed the book shut. "It's time to decide."

"Easy for you to say," groaned Nancy, scurrying around the room, inspecting Mr Wuu's gadgetry, her indecision fuelling her temper. "All this junk, and I have to choose four toys. I'll be here all night trying to decide what to take. Why can't that stupid book—"

"Calm down," interrupted Prema. She reached for her pack of cards and dealt four onto the duvet. "Turn the cards."

Nancy kicked a clockwork robot across the floor, then kneeled beside her friend. "Which one?"

Prema pointed to the card closest to the window. "Start with this one."

Nancy lifted the edge of the optical card and turned it face up. Staring back at her was the spyglass, its shaft extending and retracting like a mechanical squeeze box. "Amazing, truly amazing," whispered Nancy, surveying the room for the telescope. She flipped the second card and revealed a music box. "I'm so sorry I doubted you, Pre."

"That's okay," replied Prema. "And the next one."

Nancy lifted the card and watched in amazement as her compact mirror flicked itself open and shut. Each time it moved, a blue light flickered, its rays morphing into the shape of a key.

Finally, she revealed the last card and punched the air. The Aero-Strazmicator's aerial moved up and down, searching for an unknown frequency. "Unzip my bag, Pre. Let's pack these things before my mum calls me down for dinner."

"Okay."

Nancy whistled and hummed as she tidied her bedroom. She tossed the compact mirror into the bag and snatched a torch from her bottom drawer. "Once I find some batteries for this, we have everything we need," she unscrewed the lens and inspected the empty shaft of the torch, "well, sort of..."

"What else is there?" asked Prema.

"Jim Jam," confessed Nancy. "I'm not sure he'll show up. He's going to Bournemouth tomorrow, and I didn't have time to explain."

"We can do this ourselves," insisted Prema. "Eli will lead us to the cellar, and from there we have Mr Wuu's components, Grizelda, and the magic book to guide us."

"I know," said Nancy, "but I have this nagging feeling we are going to need Jim Jam." She stared out of her window, her sights fixed on the lush green canvas of Roebuck Woods. She crossed her fingers and sighed. *I hope we make it before midnight.*

Prema shuffled the optical cards, then placed them in her pocket. "I need to go," she said, interrupting Nancy's thoughts. "My grandmother will be expecting me."

Nancy nodded. "Can you see yourself out?"

"Sure. See you at eleven-thirty."

"Yeah, I'll see you then."

Bessy Jones' foghorn call shook the rafters. "Dinner's ready!"

13
The Prophecy

Nancy stood at the threshold of her bedroom and listened to her father bidding Prema good night. The front door slammed and Teddy Jones made his way back into the kitchen. Nancy stepped back into her room, slumped onto the bed and cradled her head in the palms of her hands. *How on earth can they expect me to do this?*

The thought of being labelled The Chosen One troubled her. Responsibility for others was a load she had never been asked to carry in the past. Settling into a new home and school was one thing, and finding a magic book was another; but having to save two worlds was something way beyond her comprehension – and maybe a monumental error of judgement by Aunt Elma and Captain Carbunkle. "They must've got the wrong person. I'm just… a normal girl."

"There's no such thing as normal."

Nancy ignored Grizelda's muffled clucks and tried to piece everything together as if it was a jigsaw. It was impossible. Her thoughts constantly returned to the night she moved – they always did in times of uncertainty. As much as she tried to block it from her thoughts, the same recurring question plagued her. *Why did we move?*

It had happened at 2.00am on the morning of her eleventh birthday. Her mother frantically packed a bag, while her father loaded a van. Every time she asked what they were doing, her mother would bark, "It's for the best."

They left Weston Street and headed west, along the South Bank, over Westminster Bridge, around Parliament Square, through Victoria and on to Hammersmith. Once they were on the motorway, Nancy slept, her head resting on her mother's shoulder. When she woke, her heart broke in two. Her father was tearing down the boards that covered the windows of 145 Oxon Road.

It looked like a haunted house.

Her mother's screams pulled her from her memories. The second call for dinner was even louder than the first. "Dinner's ready!"

Grizelda clucked and clawed incessantly within the wardrobe. Nancy pressed her face to the door. "I'm going downstairs for my dinner."

"All right for some," crowed Grizelda. "I'm hungry, too."

Nancy pulled the door. "Please be quiet! What do parrots eat?"

"I like monkey nuts."

"Okay, okay," replied Nancy, desperately begging for silence. "My dad has a stash in the larder. I'll bring some up after dinner. Now, please be quiet. Any more of your noise and my mother will be up here quicker than Jack Flash."

Grizelda gave a wry smile. "I know someone by that name."

"Don't be silly," replied Nancy, puckering her face. "That's one of my dad's sayings." She closed the wardrobe door and made her way downstairs.

Her mother and father sat at the kitchen table, looking at their dinner plates, waiting patiently for their daughter, both of them humming simultaneously, in and out of tune with the radio. Nancy hovered at the door and stared at them, time suspended, her thoughts whirring. Then, as the past finally caught up with her, the volcano erupted: "Why did you bring me here?"

Teddy and Bessy looked up from their steaming plates of food. The question provoked an uncomfortable silence. "I know you both miss London as much as I do," croaked Nancy, "it just doesn't make sense. We've been here three months now, and you haven't told me why—"

"Your dinner is getting cold, young lady," interrupted her mother. "Don't make us wait a moment longer."

Nancy stood firm. "I want to know why we moved."

Bessy stared at her husband, then at her daughter, her resilience wavering. Teddy Jones held out his arms and stepped forward. "It was for the best." He shuffled towards his daughter, but Nancy backed off, shaking her head and waving her hands.

"You have no idea what it's been like for me, or what the future holds."

Teddy stared impassively at his wife. "It's time, Bessy."

"Time for what?" asked Nancy, her eyes flitting to the clock above the stove.

Bessy shot her husband a disapproving look. "She doesn't need to know."

"She does," answered Teddy. "She *really* needs to know."

Nancy watched as her parents exchanged frowns, gestures, and muted whispers. Then, as the stand-off intensified, she yelled, "What's the big secret?"

Bessy pushed the bench from beneath her. "This is your home, Nanny Bo, your new life. Make the most of it. We made a decision and we love you lots. That's all you need to know."

"Not good enough," said Nancy, her body shaking with emotion as she confronted her parents.

Bessy tipped her chin and grunted. Two rollers came loose and fell to the floor. She picked them up and pointed at the wooden bench. Nancy sat obediently. "It's the hardest thing I've ever had to do," said her mother.

Teddy wrapped his arms around his wife. "It's okay. We were protecting our baby."

"I know," said Bessy, choking back her tears. "But we pulled her from her happy life, Teddy. Look at her. She's never been the same since."

Teddy turned to face his daughter and, for the first time, opened up. "It's a long story… but here goes… I met your mother under Tom Thumb's Arch."

"Where?" asked Nancy.

"Bow – the East End of London. It was years ago. Your mother came across the river to deliver a parcel." Teddy reached for a tissue and placed it in Bessy's hand. There was a loud sniffle, then he continued. "Well, I was minding my own business when I heard this loud scream. I ran around the corner and there she was, lying on the ground beneath the arch with the parcel next to her."

"What happened?" asked Nancy.

"I sat her up and asked if she was all right, but she couldn't remember what had happened or who the parcel was for. I took her back to my flat and gave her a brandy."

"Medicinal," interrupted Bessy. She wiped her nose and tucked the tissue up her sleeve.

"Oh, yeah. Medicinal," said Teddy. He winked at Nancy and went on, "We had no idea why ya' daft old mum was delivering that parcel. I swear someone had hypnotised her."

Nancy perched herself on the very edge of her seat. "What was inside the parcel?"

"It-it-it wasn't much," stuttered Teddy. "Nothing much at all."

Bessy dried her eyes and pushed Teddy's forearm from her shoulder. "You've gone this far, Teddy Jones. You may as well tell her the rest."

"I'm not sure I—"

"Leave it to me," snapped Bessy. "We unwrapped the parcel and found a bottle. Inside the bottle was a note."

Nancy felt a sudden rush of blood to her head. She stared at her mother with intent and exaggerated each word as it left her mouth: "What. Did. It. Say?"

"Your father struggled to unscrew the lid, so we smashed it open."

"What did it say?" repeated Nancy.

"It was a prophecy," replied Bessy.

"A what?"

"A warning," interjected Teddy.

Nancy's impatience spewed out: "What did it say?"

Her father's voice crept up in volume. "Calm down, Nanny Bo."

Nancy apologised and waited for her mother to continue. "At the time, we ignored it," mumbled Bessy. "It was just a scribbled note."

"We couldn't make sense of it," admitted Teddy.

"It was the first time we had met," explained Bessy. "It was all so very strange. Your father unrolled the sheet of paper..."

"And what did—?"

"It said that Teddy Jones and Bessy Hart would marry, have a baby girl, and on her eleventh birthday she would be taken to another world for safe-keeping." Bessy hesitated, then reached for her husband's hand, and whispered, "It was signed 'Z'."

The hairs on Nancy's skin stood to attention.

The family secret finally revealed. In the background, the sound of Elvis Presley's *One Night* crackled from the radio. Bessy waited for the song to finish and reached for her daughter's hand. "One of our neighbours said that a strange man came looking for you. They said he was very persistent and that he would search London from top to bottom to find you. We had to leave Weston Street. We *had* to cut and run."

Nancy's exterior was almost stone-like, but her insides housed a thousand fireworks. The first missing jigsaw piece now slotted into its rightful place. "What happened after you found the prophecy?"

Bessy blushed, gazed up at her husband, and sighed. "Well, over the course of time things just happened."

"What things?" asked Nancy, drawing an imaginary *Z* on the table top.

"Well, just, things. You know…"

"No."

"Let's just say we kept in touch and became friends."

Nancy giggled, her face crimson. "Oh, I get you."

"She couldn't resist me," said Teddy Jones, striking a catwalk pose.

Nancy gave her mother a kiss and whispered, "I love you."

They ate dinner in silence. Nancy picked at her fish fingers, excused herself, and left the kitchen. She climbed the stairs and fell face-first onto her pillow. Something sinister was controlling her family and her life. Something she had no control over. She grabbed her phone and thumbed her way through dozens of images – photos of her old life, her school, her friends. She enlarged a class photo – thirty-two children stared back at her. Tears rolled down her cheeks as she thought back to happier times.

The wardrobe door creaked open and Grizelda hopped onto the bed. "Let me catch a tear, Nanny Bo."

Nancy sat up and dabbed her eyes. "Are you mocking me?"

"No," clucked Grizelda. "If I catch a tear I share your woe and halve your troubles."

Nancy tilted her head. A single teardrop trickled down her cheek and rolled onto Grizelda's tongue. "I am your guardian from here on in. Your spirit is mine and mine is yours." Nancy hyperventilated as the parrot continued: "To love and protect is all we can ask of each other in this world. It is the teaching of the Great

One." Grizelda shuddered, then clucked two strange words: "*Lacrima Hirundo.*"

Nancy's tears dried as the bird absorbed her pain and frustration.

Grizelda waddled painfully back to the wardrobe and collapsed. "Good night," she clucked.

"Good night," whispered Nancy, then she set her alarm for eleven o'clock, pulled the covers to her neck, and let the weight of the day push down upon her eyelids. Within seconds she was asleep.

14
The Portal

It was 11.00pm. The buzz of Nancy's alarm startled her. She switched it off and pushed her duvet back. The sound of the wind rushing through the heavy boughs of Roebuck Woods was irresistible. She peered through her curtains and marvelled at the sea of treetops. Her lips curled into a smile as the reassuring tones of her father's snores were met by grunts of disapproval from her mother. Nancy opened the bedroom door, tiptoed across the landing into the bathroom, and pulled down the toilet seat. She sprung onto the lid and stared out at the rows of terraced houses. It was the ideal vantage point to spy on someone.

A three-way junction joined Oxon Road to Elsley Road. The streets were deserted – but for the local tomcat. After a couple of minutes, Nancy spotted her. *There you are, and you're early.*

Prema Sarkander appeared, her long black hair tied back, the hem of her pretty white dress protruding from her coat. She stopped beneath the glow of a lamp-post, pulled a note from her pocket, and began to read it. Moments later, she arrived at 145 Oxon Road. Nancy tapped the window and waved to her friend. Prema stood by the front door, unaware, swaying her torch up and down the street. Nancy tapped again, this time a little harder. She looked down at Prema and whispered her name. Prema looked at her watch, oblivious to her friend's efforts to gain her attention. Nancy climbed over the sink and pressed her face against the window. Her trailing leg caught the china cup housing three toothbrushes, it wobbled precariously on the edge of the basin, then crashed to the floor. She held her head in her hands and waited for her mother's footsteps.

They didn't come. Silence followed the smash.

Prema swung her torch to the side of the house. A narrow alleyway wove its way down to the garden gate. Nancy watched as Prema walked towards it. In one swift movement, she brushed past the overgrown shrubs and disappeared from view.

Nancy left the bathroom and darted back across the landing. Her bedroom curtains were tied back and the windows were wide open. A gentle breeze chilled the space around her as shafts of moonlight lit the room. She loaded her torch with four batteries, then placed *The First Book of Cosmo* into the leather holdall, its ornate calligraphy dazzling to the eye. She checked the time: 11.10pm, then opened the wardrobe door and cradled Grizelda in her hands, the bird's head lolling over her wrist as she lowered her into the rucksack.

"I need more sleep," groaned the parrot.

Nancy raised a finger to her lips. "Shh."

"I swallowed your tear, you ungrateful wretch."

"Please be quiet," said Nancy, pushing Grizelda's head back into the bag. The bird pushed back, and white feathers flew around the bedroom as the struggle continued. Nancy clasped the bird's beak with her thumb and forefinger. The thought of her mother waking petrified her. She was convinced she'd heard voices, so she raised a finger to her mouth and glared at the disgruntled parrot. Grizelda rolled her eyes, folded her wings, and nestled herself back into the rucksack.

Nancy pulled the zip and cupped her ear to the bedroom wall. "What's wrong with you, Teddy?" she heard her mother ask. "Go back to sleep."

"I thought I heard a parrot."

"A parrot?" replied Bessy. "Have you been drinking that dodgy rum?"

"Listen," said her father.

"I can't hear a thing, Teddy. Now go back to sleep, you big oaf."

A few moments later, she heard her father snoring once again. *Phew, that was close.* Nancy pulled three knotted sheets from beneath her bed. She tied one end to her bedpost, lowered the other from the window, and threw the leather holdall to the ground. She looped the rucksack over her shoulder and climbed down. With every descending jolt, she heard the muffled groans of Grizelda.

"Evening," said Prema, tapping her watch. "I've been waiting."

"I know," replied Nancy. "You were early. I said meet at eleven-thirty, and it's only twenty-past. Relax."

Prema inspected the leather holdall. "*The First Book of Cosmo*, spyglass, music box, Aero-Strazmicator, and compact mirror." She clapped her hands and congratulated Nancy. "Well done. All present and correct. Is Grizelda okay?"

"She swallowed my teardrop," replied Nancy, holding out her rucksack. "She hasn't been herself since."

Prema unzipped the backpack and peered inside. "Hello, Grizelda."

"I'm not allowed to speak," clucked the bird.

"Once Nanny Bo raises the portal, I'm sure you will feel better."

Grizelda tucked her head beneath a wing and muttered, "I hope so."

"Well, what do you think?" asked Nancy.

"It was an act of selflessness," answered Prema. "She will perk up as soon as you return the favour."

"How do I do that?"

"Simple," replied Prema, "put *her* needs before your own. I read it in the book – page seventy-two: 'Creatures and Ailments'."

Nancy arched her brow. "Really?"

"If you raise the portal and allow Grizelda back into Enerjiimass, you have returned the favour. She will be home, where she belongs."

Nancy smiled. "Oh, yeah, I never thought of that."

"It's important to feel like you belong," declared Prema.

Nancy nodded enthusiastically as she made her way towards the walnut tree that sat proudly in the middle of the garden. It rose up from the ground like a colossal wooden monument, branches sprawling like wooden tendrils, its leaves rustling against the wind. "Can you hear that?"

"What?" replied Prema, cupping her ears.

"The forest. It's alive, and it speaks."

"It's just the wind."

"It's calling me," said Nancy. She rested herself against the gnarled trunk and patted her rucksack. "Can I ask you something, Pre?"

"Of course you can – anything you want."

"What was that note you were reading outside my house?"

Prema's eyes widened. "You saw that?"

"Yes, I was looking out for you."

Prema checked her watch. "It was from my grandmother. I think she knows something."

"How can she?" asked Nancy. "I told you not to mention this to anyone."

"I haven't," said Prema, defensively.

"Well, what did it say?"

Prema pulled out the scrap of paper and read it. "Good luck, my child. Help others before yourself. I am with you. I love you now and always. Remember, *there is no end to love.*"

Nancy repeated, "*There's no end to love,*" under her breath.

Prema folded the note into her pocket. "My gran is special."

"Without doubt," said Nancy.

"And she's always been good with words," admitted Prema. "I want her to be proud of me."

Nancy nodded. "She will be."

Beneath the tree, in the haze of the moonlight, the two girls waited. Nancy picked at loose fragments of bark as Prema began to read *The First Book of Cosmo*. As time crept nearer to the midnight hour, the blank pages slowly began to reveal themselves. Luminous words and pictures appeared, as if written by an invisible quill. Prema remained quiet as she stared at maps, scribbled notes, and recipes for potions. Another page was thumbed. Scrawls of black ink ran across the parchment as if an ink pot had been upturned. Prema gasped, her hands pushing the sound back within her mouth. Then the dark blobs of liquid began to form shapes. Detail was added to the shapes, followed by intricate brushstrokes that created a vivid image. An image of depravity. A tortuous chair wired to a huge mechanical contraption. A machine of immense size and structure. Pistons moving back and forth, alive on the page.

"What's wrong?" asked Nancy.

"Nothing," said Prema, slamming the book shut.

"I can't stand waiting for people," complained Nancy. Then, without warning, she jumped up and pointed at the garden fence.

"What is it?" asked Prema.

Nancy's eyes widened. "I can hear footsteps."

"It's probably Eli and The Duke."

Two beams of light pierced Nancy's eyes. She turned her cheek. "Is that you, Eli?"

"Who else were you expecting – Saint Christopher?" replied Elijah, sarcastically.

"Turn the torch off, you idiot!"

Elijah flicked the switch and returned a contemptuous scowl. He entered the garden, penknife in hand, and torch dangling from his waistband. The Duke followed, his nails scratching the ends of two plasters above his bloody brow.

Nancy glared at the two boys and shook her head. "What's with the knives and searchlights?"

"We just wanted to be prepared," said The Duke. "We know what's in the woods and it didn't sound very friendly."

"What didn't?"

"You know, the Jagga—"

"Shut up," interrupted Elijah. "The knives will come in handy if we can't get through the wire fence. So, what's the plan, Nanny Bo?"

Nancy didn't answer. She paced around the garden in a figure of eight, deep in thought; then she stopped at the slatted fence. She peered over, but there was no sign of Jimmy James.

Prema tapped her wrist. "We have to leave."

"I know, but—"

"We have no time," interrupted Prema. "It's eleven thirty-five."

Nancy grabbed her torch, unzipped her backpack, and checked on Grizelda. The bird slept, both wings covering her yellow crest. Prema and The Duke grabbed the handles of the leather holdall at the same time. Their eyes met. Prema held her stare, then turned away as the blood rushed to The Duke's face.

"Eli can lead," instructed Nancy. "He knows where the portal is."

"Portal?" repeated Elijah. "What is this, some sort of space voyage?"

"No," said Nancy, sharply. "Am I right in thinking you know where the cellar doors are located?"

"Yes," replied Elijah.

"Lead the way, then." Nancy placed the rucksack carefully over her shoulder and pointed at The Duke and Prema. "You two can follow Eli. I'll bring up the rear."

Elijah puffed out his chest and grasped the lead role with pride. Within four paces he was over the wire fence that encircled Roebuck Woods. Nancy's eyes searched the alleyway for any sign of Jimmy James, but all she could see was a dark tunnel of weeds. She whispered, "Where are you?" from the side of her mouth, then skipped across the lawn and gazed up at her bedroom, where three white sheets hung like a giant knotted handkerchief.

Prema's tiny voice spilled out from the woods: "Hurry up. We need to leave."

"All right, I'm coming." Nancy clambered over the barbed fence and landed feet first on the sodden earth. The forest was colossal, an uncharted landscape of trees, shrubs, and nettles, all vying for space. Beneath the sprawling foliage the night appeared darker, like a thick black fog encapsulating the woodland. Nancy tied back her curls and barked her instructions: "Torches on."

Elijah flicked a switch and sniggered. "Here we go, Nanny Bo's magical, midnight mystery tour…"

The sound of splintering twigs crackled beneath their feet as they took their first tentative steps into Roebuck Woods. Nancy halted. "I can hear something."

"What?" asked The Duke, his hands already shaking.

"There's something behind us… it's in my garden." From the moonlit shadows, Nancy spied a small rotund figure lifting itself from its haunches and brushing the leaf mould from its torso. A cape ruffled in the wind, a bright yellow flag against the black of night. She shone her torch directly at the intruder.

"Nanny Bo, is that you?" said a familiar voice.

"Jim Jam!" shrieked Nancy, unable to contain her joy. She vaulted the fence, tumbled back onto the lawn, and hugged him beneath the walnut tree.

Elijah shook his head in disbelief. "Is there anything going on between those two?"

Nancy released Jimmy and tugged at his cape. "Why are you wearing Superman pyjamas?"

"I've just got out of bed."

"We need to leave," said Nancy, urgently.

"Time is running out," squealed Prema from the woodland.

"Who's that?" said Jimmy, looking around for the owner of the invisible voice.

"It's Prema," replied Nancy.

Jimmy spun three hundred and sixty degrees. "Where?"

Nancy pointed at the barbed fence. "Over there, in the woods."

"Come on, Nanny Bo," cried Prema. "We need to go!"

Nancy grabbed Jimmy's hand and sprinted back to the border of her garden. She helped him over the fence, holding his cloak as he scrambled up and over into Roebuck Woods. Then she vaulted the barrier and scarpered off into the bushes where her friends waited. Jimmy followed, puffing, panting, and cape-trailing. Elijah marched ahead, muttering his misgivings. Prema and The Duke followed in Elijah's footsteps, gripping the bag, pacing with military precision. As the torchlight cut through Roebuck Woods, nocturnal creatures darted from the invading light into the safety of the shadows.

"What's the time?" asked Nancy.

Elijah stopped and checked his watch. "Eleven forty-four."

"How much further?"

"Not far," replied Elijah. "About five minutes."

The children stopped in their tracks and huddled together, shielding themselves from the wind as it ripped the leaves from the trees. "Sounds like someone's crying," said The Duke, his eyes darting left and right.

"It's just the wind," replied Prema, trying her best to reassure him.

Nancy stared at the infinite sheet of black above her, then lowered her sights to the woodland – the trees, the leaves, the sprawling ivy, and the earthy scent of decaying leaf mould. Then she looked back up at the silver disc hanging in the sky, and the stars sparkling beside it. In that brief moment she felt miniscule, like a tiny grain of sand in a vast desert.

"Tick, tock," said Prema, rocking her head from side to side. "We haven't got time to rest."

Elijah sped off, ducking beneath every branch as if he had memorised them from his previous trip to Bymerstone Hall. Nancy and her friends did their best to keep up with his long, athletic strides. Within minutes he had led them to the arch that sat in front of the dilapidated mansion. One by one they walked through and huddled together on the lowered drawbridge, its charred link-chains clanking as they trundled across it.

Nancy pointed her torch at the remains of the stately home. "Wow, it's magnificent." She was absolutely dumbstruck, in awe of the mysterious building and its surroundings. Prema and Jimmy stood beside her, speechless.

"I go no further until you spill the beans," said Elijah. "I've come this far and I'm not going any further."

The Duke dropped the bag and nodded in agreement. "Me neither."

Nancy folded her arms into wings and laughed. "Are you chicken, Eli?"

"No," snapped Elijah. "I just want to know what's going on."

Nancy held her tongue, unflinching in the face of Elijah's quest for information. She nodded at Prema, who held up eight fingers, to indicate the remaining minutes before midnight.

Elijah raised his voice. "Is someone going to tell me what's happening?"

Nancy held out her palms and called for a circle of one. One by one, beneath the canopy of trees, they linked hands. They placed the torches in the centre, shining towards the heavens, their beams like white ropes hanging from the cavernous night sky. Nancy took a breath, before addressing her friends. "I would rather have done this alone, but circumstance has forced my hand." She paused and glanced over at the cellar doors. "Thanks for coming this far."

Elijah puffed his cheeks. "Get on with it."

"Behind that cellar door…" Nancy stopped and thought about the crazy statement she was about to make. It didn't deter her. She continued, suspending her disbelief. "Behind that door lies another world."

Elijah burst into a gut-wrenching fit of giggles. "This is mental."

"Carry on, Nanny Bo," said Jimmy, politely. "We are listening."

Nancy waited for Elijah's laughter to subside. "I have been asked to raise the portal at midnight and search for a precious stone. If we are unsuccessful, there is a chance we may never return." Nancy's eyes were now transfixed on the sky-bound beams of light. "I need your help, but I don't expect it. We have an ancient book of instructions and a guardian to give us safe passage. If you want to leave, I understand, but I need one favour before you go."

"Anything," said The Duke. "What can we do before we leave?" he asked, his mind already made up.

"Help me raise the portal and promise you won't mention this to anyone."

"I'm going with you," insisted Prema.

"Me, too," added Jimmy.

Elijah yanked his fingers from The Duke's. "Is this some kind of practical joke?"

An almighty bolt of lightning arced across the night sky, splitting the pitch black with geometric precision. Deep growls of thunder followed. Then there was more lightning: two white forks struck a rusty weather vane that swung from the mansion's gable. It fell to the ground. The four arrows of North, South, East, and West were now embedded in the mud.

From the depths of the forest came a voice – a cold, unforgiving hiss: "Sssstay away."

"It's that voice again," squealed The Duke.

Nancy ran across the drawbridge into the remains of Bymerstone Hall. Another rumble of thunder shook the sky, and the rain followed; within seconds, it has turned into hail. Jimmy and Prema trailed her, scurrying along like two drowned rats. Grizelda came to her senses and squawked, "Unzip this bag, let me out!"

Elijah panicked, his head shifting from side to side. "Who said that?"

Nancy straddled the cellar doors and yanked the handles. They were set rigid, weighed down by broken chains. Thunder echoed as the wind ripped the summer berries from the trees, catapulting them into the air like shrapnel.

"Let me help," yelled Jimmy.

Nancy refused. "What's that noise?"

Jimmy shrugged.

Prema raised the leather holdall to her chest. "It's coming from the bag."

Nancy rummaged through Mr Wuu's contraptions and found her compact mirror. Miraculously, it opened and closed like a dancing castanet, clip-clopping a frantic rhythm. Then an orb of light appeared and transmuted into the shape of a key. The sky continued to erupt, louder and louder—a cacophony of claps and bangs.

Prema screamed over the din of thunder and rain: "Put it in the lock!"

Nancy held the compact mirror and pointed the beam of light at the padlock that secured the doors. A deep, resonating boom shook her bones and the cellar doors burst open. Clouds of purple steam filled the air. Blood streamed from Nancy's nostrils as the airborne doors struck her in the face. Unconscious, she rolled head first into the open portal.

Jimmy and Prema didn't hesitate: they jumped, casting a final stare at The Duke and Elijah.

"What's the time, Eli?" asked The Duke.

"Eleven f-fifty-n-nine," stuttered Elijah.

The Duke tugged at Elijah's cuff. "They're our friends. Come on, they need our help."

Elijah was rooted to the spot, trembling. "Leave me alone. I want to go home..."

The Duke sped over the drawbridge, through the remains of Bymerstone Hall, and dived head first into the portal.

"Come back!" yelled Elijah. Against every instinct within him, he made his way towards the cellar doors, his feet slipping as he dashed over the muddy terrain. He checked his watch: 11.59pm and 58 seconds.

Mounds of loose earth began to slide over the black void. The portal was closing.

Elijah Lincoln cursed Nancy Bo Jones, then he jumped.

15
Enerjiimass

Nancy lay motionless, crushed beneath her friends, one on top of the other, her face pressed into the ground, nose bloodied, her body paralysed by the weight above. All she could hear was a gasping sound, as if someone or something needed to fill their lungs. The desperate inhalations intensified – a chorus of horrific breathlessness.

Something was wrong.

Elijah rolled down from the top of the pile, clutching his windpipe. The Duke, Jimmy, and Prema followed, their faces flushed as they struggled for breath.

Nancy stretched her crumpled limbs as the bodies rolled off her one by one. She had no time to think. Her friends were choking. She sat them up, opened their mouths, and attempted to blow air into their empty lungs. Prema clutched her throat with one hand and pointed at *The First Book of Cosmo* with the other, her pretty face creased in pain. Then the book began to vibrate. Its leather cover flew open: CHAPTER FIFTY-EIGHT: MIGRATION AND LITHONIA. New words appeared before Nancy's eyes. She read as quickly as she could, her finger trembling over every word:

Any individual bereft of dual-star status will be unable to withstand the bio-molecular atmosphere of Enerjiimass. The only suggested potion available is a small fruit known as 'air berry', grown on a tree close to the portal. It is anti-Lithonia, but not resistant to time.

Jimmy was the first to slump from his upright position, his head flopping to the side like a rag doll, the edges of his lips tinged blue. Nancy yelled, "No!" and cradled him in her arms, her voice faltering as she pleaded, "Wake up, Jim Jam, please, wake up." Four berries rolled out of Jimmy's pyjama pocket. Nancy didn't hesitate: she forced one of the berries into his mouth and crossed her fingers as it slid down his throat. Jimmy coughed and spluttered. Purple fluid spewed from his mouth, and between each vomit he reached for breath as his lungs began to inhale the new mix of atmospheric gases. Nancy force-fed the remaining berries to The Duke, Elijah, and Prema. Within minutes all four were gulping the new air of Enerjiimass. Nancy aided them one after the other, patting their backs and wiping the strange fluid from their lips. She whispered, "Thank you," at *The First Book of Cosmo* and expelled a huge sigh of relief. "Is everyone okay?"

Jimmy was the first to respond. "Absolutely." He wiped his mouth with the hem of his cape and burped. Prema nodded, then dabbed her lips. The Duke puffed his cheeks and returned a shaky thumbs up.

"I'm *not* okay," groaned Elijah. "I nearly choked to death and I've just puked purple water."

"No one forced you to come," snapped Nancy. "You're here now and part of our mission. We need to work together if we want to stay alive."

Elijah prodded his finger into Jimmy's midriff. "And what hope have I got of you lot keeping me alive? What am I supposed to do, call for Superman?"

"If it hadn't been for the berries in Jim Jam's pocket, you would be dead," countered Nancy.

Elijah raised his hand to his brow and viewed the new landscape. "Where the hell are we?"

It was only then that Nancy began to take stock of her surroundings. She couldn't answer Elijah's question: it was impossible. Only in her dreams had she witnessed such a strange and beautiful land. Behind her stood a copper tree, with a heart-shaped hole fashioned in the middle of its trunk. Beneath Nancy's pumps were masses of multi-coloured flowers; they smothered the ground as far as the eye could see, an infinite floral tapestry. Hundreds of zigzag paths cut the landscape into sections of mesmeric beauty, their cobbles a mosaic mish-mash of pinks, blues, reds, yellows and greens. Heavily clad fruit trees lined every one of them, their branches arching under the weight. Tiny stone huts resembling igloos dotted the vast landscape, and above each hut was a green flag emblazoned with the letter Z.

Nancy climbed the copper tree and gazed at the rolling hills and deep valleys. Distant fountains spewed jets of water into the air, miniature rainbows formed through the fine watery haze. The sky had a life of its own, fading from one colour to another. It was like looking through the world's greatest kaleidoscope. Clouds sparkled like jewels, and thousands of gigantic unmanned hot-air balloons hung in the air, their empty baskets bobbing against one another. In the distance, beyond the lush valleys, Nancy spied a castle perched on top of a craggy mountain. Dark clouds shrouded it from the neon sky – it was the only dismal blot on a beautiful landscape. The turrets reminded her of huge stone fingers pointing up at the heavens. She grimaced at the ugly gargoyles carved into the castle walls, their eyes looking up to an oversized chimney. She lowered her sights and followed the trail of steps chiselled into the side of the mountain – a rocky ladder to the forbidding castle.

Nancy closed her eyes and concentrated. She could hear something: the faint murmur of machinery, the turning of metal, steam hissing from valves as pistons churned, the grind of an industrious rhythm. She climbed down and gazed back to where she had crash-landed into this new world – the odd-looking copper tree and its heart-shaped hole replacing the cellar doors of Bymerstone Hall.

Jimmy pulled out a handful of berries. "I think these must be the Elixir of Life."

"I've heard it all now," said Elijah, waving his arms as if swatting a fly. "You lot are bonkers, absolutely crazy." He started to laugh. "And… hey, my phone has died."

"So has mine," replied The Duke. "It was fully charged before I left."

Nancy checked her phone. "No signal. It doesn't work."

Jimmy took a step closer to the Tree of Hearts. "Cynthia Leathwaite told me a story about the man who lived in that stately home." He stood up and looked through the copper heart, half-expecting to see Roebuck Woods. There was nothing but a black hole staring back at him. "She told me the gentleman who lived in Bymerstone Hall placed a curse on 145 Oxon Road."

Nancy gulped. "That's my house."

Jimmy held out a cluster of berries in his palm and continued with the tale. "Lord Bymerstone was a mixer of potions. He attempted to grow a magic tree. I think the berries it produced were supposed to give everlasting life. People tried to stop him meddling in witchcraft. They said it was not right to interfere with the gift of life."

There was a momentary silence, before Prema broke it. "It's a big mistake to alter the natural lifetime of man. My grandmother says that death is just as much a gift as life."

"Oh, yeah?" said Elijah, calmly. "What a fantastic present that would be. I think I'll put that on my Christmas list. Death, please, Santa Claus."

Prema sighed. "Death is what makes our life precious."

Nancy considered Prema's prophetic words, then placed her arm through the heart-shaped hole and wiggled her fingers. Pins and needles arrested her body; she winced and withdrew. "What else did Cynthia Leathwaite tell you, Jim Jam?"

Jimmy shrugged his shoulders, unsure if he should continue. Nancy wrapped an arm around him. "Come on, it's important – we need to know."

Reluctantly, Jimmy retold the story of Lord Bymerstone and the curse of 145 Oxon Road.

Elijah stretched and yawned. "So, a dead magician grew a tree, and its berries are the Elixir of Life... You lot are *so naïve*."

Nancy made one final attempt to get Elijah onside: "This could be your greatest ever summer holiday before you return to Oakwell."

"If I make it back to Oakwell," retaliated Elijah.

The Duke pushed his straggly hair to one side and marvelled at the stunning landscape. "I can't believe it, Eli. You were moaning yesterday that I didn't have a sense of adventure. And now you don't seem to have one when it matters. I trust Nanny Bo."

"You hardly know her, just because she's from London, you think—"

"Shut it, Eli!" Nancy took three paces forward and stood nose to nose with Elijah Lincoln. "I'm sick of your insecurities. I am who I am, and I can't change where I come from. My friends' lives are at risk and time is running out. Those berries that gave you your breath back won't last forever."

"I have some more," said Jimmy, quietly. "I thought they were cherries. I love cherries."

Nancy winked at her friend. "Nice one, Jim Jam. Keep them safe. We need to find what is missing and get out of here as quickly as possible." She pushed her finger into Elijah's chest. "Are you with us, or do you want to jump back through that trunk and go home?" She raised her palm high above her head. "Well, are you up for adventure?"

Elijah grunted, "Yes," then exchanged a half-hearted high-five with her.

"Nice one," said Nancy, with a satisfied grin. "Oh, there is one more thing, Eli…"

"What?"

"I've been invited here and you are my guests, so follow my lead."

Elijah peered down his nose at Nancy and shook his head. "I'm my own man."

The Duke pleaded with his friend, "Come on – drop the pretence, Eli. You know she's right. It's no big deal, Nanny Bo is our leader."

There was a momentary silence. A brief stand-off.

"All right," conceded Elijah.

Nancy unzipped her rucksack and tapped Grizelda's crest. The bird opened her eyes, crowed, and flew out of the bag. She landed on Nancy's shoulder and squawked triumphantly, *"I am home."*

Elijah struggled to take his eyes off Grizelda; every time she opened her beak and spoke, he laughed hysterically, repeating the bird's words in a squawky, high-pitched voice.

Order had been restored.

Nancy introduced Grizelda to her friends and motioned for everyone to sit beneath the Tree of Hearts. She leaned against the copper trunk, a gentle warmth bubbling within. She felt at ease. She was an eternal dreamer, always finding meaning in the idiosyncrasies of life. Her heart yearned for something different, and now she had actually found it. Something deep inside of her had been stirred, an awakening. The atmospheric pressure of Enerjiimass weighed in her favour. Her vision was sharper and her sense of smell more acute. The thoughts of her friends echoed randomly and uninvited in her head. It was a jumble, a barrage of information, white noise.

She tried to block out the sensory overload and focus on the task at hand. "How many air berries do we have, Jim Jam?"

"Eight."

"Eight," repeated Nancy. "That's two each between the four of you. I have no idea how long they will last."

"What about you?" enquired Jimmy.

"I'm okay." Nancy rocked her head back and forth, then she made three short sniffs. "Urgh..."

Jimmy tugged at her hoody. "What?"

"That smell. It pongs," replied Nancy, pinching her nose, "it's like rotten eggs."

"I can't smell a thing," said Jimmy, his nostrils tipped skyward.

"Me neither," added Prema.

Nancy crouched beside Jimmy and whispered, "Can you share out the air berries?"

Jimmy handed out the precious fruit to his friends, then straightened his cape. "There you go – that's two per person."

Nancy pranced around the Tree of Hearts, her thoughts darting through her mind. She stopped, held up her index finger, and declared, "Captain Carbunkle has—"

"Captain who?" interrupted Elijah.

"Not now, Eli," pleaded Nancy. "Save it for later. Captain Carbunkle has told us a precious stone is missing. We must return it to its rightful place."

"What place?" asked Elijah, disdainfully.

"I don't know," replied Nancy.

Elijah sighed. "This is getting worse by the minute."

Nancy's frustration unleashed itself. "Stop dragging us down, you oversized twit."

Elijah screwed his hands into fists.

Nancy winced as Grizelda's claws tightened on her shoulder. "We have *The First Book of Cosmo*, Prema's optical cards, and four mechanical contraptions to help us. We are going on an adventure,

Eli. Whether you like it or not!" Grizelda's clucks grew louder, her talons piercing Nancy's skin. "Ouch, that hurts."

"Jagganath!" crowed Grizelda.

Nancy climbed the tree. She placed her feet into the heart-shaped hole, shunted herself up the copper trunk and scrambled her way through the limbs of the tree. When she reached the highest supporting branch, she raised a hand to her brow and gazed incredulously at the rolling hills and deep valleys. In the distance, a foggy haze swirled around the castle, the clouds above split by forks of lightning, arcing against the huge chimney.

Prema unzipped the leather bag and threw Nancy the spyglass.

"Thanks," said Nancy. "Let's hope Mr Wuu comes good."

Nancy tugged at the concertinaed sections of the spyglass. The elongated lens twisted clockwise, then anti-clockwise, of its own accord. She peered into the eyelet. The magnification was strong. A dozen Jagganath were charging down the mountain steps, their red eyes gleaming like lasers. The bright, multi-coloured sky turned black in an instant. Night had fallen upon them like a curse against daylight. One by one the hot-air balloons flickered, flames burst from the burners, their coloured canvases glowing like effervescent light bulbs.

Nancy craned her neck and stared wondrously at the balloons. "Wow!"

"They look incredible," said The Duke. "There's millions of them…"

Nancy leaped down from the tree and landed flat-footed next to The Duke. "What did you see, Nanny Bo?"

"The Jagganath," whispered Nancy. "Grizelda, we need to hide."

"Follow me," crowed the bird. She flapped her wings and swooped off in a westerly direction. Nancy gave chase. Jimmy, Prema, The Duke, and Elijah followed. They ran for their lives, the foul smell of the Jagganath wafting through the air as they bolted through the fields of Enerjiimass. The spyglass shot a beam of light from its lens across the flower-strewn floor. Grizelda swooped from right to left and led them down a cobbled path. Soon, as they bobbed and weaved, the branches tangled like spiralled cord, then they joined, forming a knotted archway. Before they knew it, they were running single-file through a tree-lined tunnel, the bark walls growing narrower and narrower.

"I can't see," screamed Jimmy.

"We're here," cried Nancy. She turned the beam of light towards him. "Come on, keep running."

The twists of the tunnel were disorientating. Branches clawed at the children like wooden fingers as they ducked and dived their way through the arch of bark.

Nancy was the first to hear it: the distant sound of gushing water. Her eyes searched frantically for it. *It must be a way out.*

Grizelda flapped her way through the knotted treetops, clucking and squawking, "Keep up, children – just one more turn."

Nancy covered her ears, the immense sound of falling water unnerving her as she sped around another tight bend. Then, without warning, the tunnel of trees came to an abrupt end. Nancy fell to her knees, breathless and dumbfounded. A colossal waterfall stood before her. At its foot, an enormous whirlpool bubbled, vapour spewing from the foamy surface.

The Duke, Elijah, and Prema stumbled out of the tunnel. "Amazing," said Prema, between breaths. "It's huge. I can't see the top. It looks like the water is falling from the sky."

"Where's Jim Jam?" asked Nancy, in a sudden panic.

"Superman is lagging behind," replied Elijah, wiping the spray from his brow.

The Duke stretched out his arms, as if worshipping a higher force. "That is *unbelievable*. It's a wall of water."

Jimmy stumbled from the mouth of the tree-lined tunnel, his face scratched and his cape ripped to shreds. "I got caught on a branch. I couldn't untangle myself."

Grizelda disappeared behind the wall of water, crowing at the top of her voice, "Hurry, children. The Jagganath are closing in on us."

16
The Tunnel of Death

Nancy tiptoed across a narrow ledge into a dark cave. Moments later, her friends followed. They stood, petrified, behind the wall of water, a gushing curtain of aquatic noise. Grizelda didn't waste a second – she took flight and the children followed. Nancy fixed her sights on the flying white speck hurtling through the cave. She was running blind, as fast and as hard as she could. Grizelda spread her wings and landed on a huge boulder. "Be careful, we are going down. Down to the opening..."

"Down where?" asked Nancy, breathless.

"Be careful," squawked Grizelda. In a blink of an eye she had vanished behind a mass of marbled rock. Nancy lengthened her stride and vaulted the boulder, landing with her heart in her mouth.

She was teetering on the edge of a hundred-foot drop.

Her stomach gurgled at the dark vacuum of space staring back at her. It looked as if she was about to enter the jowls of hell.

Grizelda had all but disappeared, a tiny white speck hovering in the distance, then, she raised her crest and illuminated the space around her. It was just enough light for Nancy to navigate. She spied a steep, dusty, gravel-strewn slope disappearing into darkness. The distance between herself and Grizelda widened, but she knew she had to keep the bird in her sights. She placed one foot in front of the other and began her rapid descent. She felt her way, her fingertips outstretched, nails scraping sharp, craggy walls. The trailing footsteps of her friends scrambling down the slope resonated within the dark chamber. Nancy pressed on, bumping against rocks and stones, before finally reaching the bottom.

Grizelda darted left. "Follow," squawked the bird.

Nancy hollered back, "Slow down." She spun on her heels and waited for her friends. "Is everyone okay?"

Jimmy brushed the dust from his face and answered for all. "Yes."

Nancy sprinted off, her long, skinny legs striding after Grizelda. As she made her way through the rocky labyrinth, droplets of fine, white, crystallised water began to ooze from the walls and swirl around her. She felt as if she was running through an almighty snow-globe. She swiped her arms wildly, her vision blurred, her heart pounding. She continued in a straight line until, finally, in the distance, tiny specks of light twinkled. She narrowed her eyes and focused, running full pelt until the source of the light was visible. "They're lanterns!"

Dozens of rusted oil lamps swung from the jagged walls, their wicks flickering through the mist. Nancy stepped closer to the lights, then crouched down and inspected the shadowy figure below.

A high-pitched scream followed.

A skeleton was manacled to the wall. Rats crawled out from the eye sockets and scampered off into the abyss.

Then she noticed another. And another. There were hundreds of them: skeletons all around her, each one chained against the next. She raced on, trying to keep up with Grizelda. Beyond the skeletal remains, a circular opening appeared, light spilling into the cave as the sound of gushing water faded to nothing.

Grizelda flapped and fluttered, squawking with jubilation, "We've made it." The children stumbled towards the opening and made their way out into the bright skies of Enerjiimass. "Rest here," instructed Grizelda. "The Jagganath will not enter the tunnel. They will have to go around it. They have contaminated souls."

Nancy and her friends collapsed onto the lush grass, puffing and panting. The sky was radiant, the clouds fizzed with colour, and the hills rolled into oblivion. Prema removed the optical cards from her pocket and placed one on her lap. She glanced at the image and shrilled, "It's the Tunnel of Death!"

"Yes," chirped Grizelda, with pride, "and we made it."

"W-what's the Tunnel of Death?" asked The Duke, nervously.

Grizelda stretched her wings and perched on a low-lying branch. "The Tunnel of Death is an outdated way of checking one's soul." She swooped down from the branch and landed on Nancy's shoulder. "There was a time when a certain family was able to cross the threshold and enter Enerjiimass. Each generation was told that a forbidden treasure lay beyond the portal. Decade after decade, a new member of the family couldn't resist the temptation to open the portal and search for it. Unfortunately, they all died terrible deaths in that tunnel."

Nancy glared at the parrot.

Grizelda twitched her beak. "The Great One cast a spell on the tunnel. It checks the purity of one's soul."

Elijah rolled his eyes and exaggerated a loud yawn. "Can someone show me the way home? I'm bored with these ridiculous stories. You're mad, the lot of you."

Grizelda continued, undeterred by the interruption. "If you entered the tunnel and were free from greed or hatred, you could claim the treasure of Enerjiimass."

Nancy felt a sharp stabbing pain in her heart – a warning from her senses.

"Due to the nature of their efforts, no one ever made it through that tunnel," proclaimed Grizelda. "That's why it got named the Tunnel of Death."

Nancy wrinkled her brow. She had a question, but was unsure if she needed the answer. "Are the skeletons from the same family?"

Grizelda turned her head, refusing to acknowledge the question.

Nancy pushed the bird from her shoulder and asked again. "Are the skeletons of the same bloodline?"

"Yes," clucked Grizelda. "To make it through the tunnel indicates a pure soul."

Elijah smiled, without humour. "You took us through that tunnel and risked our lives, you selfish—"

"You have not yet lived a dozen years, young man," replied Grizelda. "Your soul has had no time to become tarnished."

An uncomfortable silence passed. The children lay flat on their backs, staring up at the sky, where one colour faded into the next: pink, green, purple, blue, yellow, red, gold, silver, then, finally, morphing into a dull, murky grey. Without warning, the sky flickered and had the last of the light sucked from it.

To remind them of their plight, Grizelda squawked one word, "Jagganath."

"Where's the daylight gone?" asked The Duke.

"Run," crowed Grizelda.

Elijah got to his feet and moved his weary legs. "I'm sick of this blasted parrot."

The race through the Tunnel of Death had taken its toll on everyone. Grizelda flew off at half-speed, clucking, "They're close."

Nancy sniffed the air and bolted, arms flailing, lungs burning. The rest followed. Running without destination was debilitating. The fear of losing sight of Grizelda was the only thing that kept the children going. One field led into another, and all the while their limbs grew tired and their hearts heavy. The sight of a steep hill smothered in igloo huts was the final straw for Jimmy's tired legs. When he reached the top, he paused for breath, then tripped on his cape and rolled down, tumbling past his friends and bumping into half a dozen igloo huts, like a human pinball.

Nancy and Grizelda waited at the foot of the hill, where seven cobbled paths left a stone-clad circle. In the centre of the circle an iron arrow spun like a magical weather vane. Grizelda whizzed around the junction, waiting for it to point the way.

Nancy watched the spinning arrowhead, her eyes circling around and around, giddiness giving way to nausea. "Which path, Grizelda?"

"It's been such a long time since I was here," trilled the parrot.

Nancy gagged, the putrid scent of the chasing monsters churning her guts. "They are close, so close."

The arrow spun rapidly. There was no sign of it stopping. With every revolution, the Jagganath were gaining ground.

"I'm not sure which path to follow," chirped Grizelda.

"Hurry up and decide, or I will pull your feathers out," yelled Elijah.

"Shut up, big nose, or I will claw your eyes out," retorted the bird.

Prema and The Duke dropped the leather holdall and fell to the floor. Nancy raised the spyglass and twisted the lens: the Jagganath appeared, marching over the brow of the hill, salivating at the sight of the children.

Finally, the rotating arrow stopped and pointed to a path that snaked its way towards a white cliff. "It's this one," crowed Grizelda. "Quickly, we need to find the Invisible Valley." She took to the sky, flying way above the chosen path, her crest emanating white light.

"I can't run," confessed Jimmy. "Go without me."

Nancy refused. "No way!"

"What shall we do?" asked Prema.

"The rest of you follow Grizelda. I'll walk with Jim Jam."

Prema stared at Nancy, shaking her head. "What about the Jagganath?"

Nancy swiped her arm towards the cliff and yelled, "Just go!"

Prema, The Duke, and Elijah fled.

The Jagganath were gaining ground, their hooves tapping out a regimented rhythm. Nancy's throat tightened as she watched her friends run off, their flailing limbs heading for the safety of the cliff. Her stomach cramped; then a deep, painful, plunging sensation filled her with dread. The haunting sound of the Jagganath tormented her inner ear, hissing a repetitive chant as each slimy hoof fell in front of another: "Zay-Ock. Zay-Ock. Zay-Ock. Zay-Ock."

"Leave me," pleaded Jimmy.

"No!" screamed Nancy, ignoring the invasive chants.

Jimmy had surrendered. "They need you, Nanny Bo. Leave me. I'm finished."

"I won't leave you. We are in this together."

The distance between Nancy, Jimmy, and the Jagganath reduced with every laboured step. Then, the white noise clogging her headspace cleared, as if a channel or frequency had opened for help. Grizelda's voice permeated her mind: "Do you need me?" The bird was nowhere to be seen, but the squawk came again. Nancy raised her arms to the sky and screamed, "Yes!"

Grizelda swooped down from the safety of the cliff-top. "Wait here, children. The Chosen One calls…"

Elijah scrambled up the cliff, his fingertips embedded in the chalky face. "What's that stupid bird doing now?"

"It looks like she's going back," replied The Duke, as he pushed himself up onto the cliff-top.

Grizelda flew through the air like a white dart. When she reached Nancy and Jimmy, she lowered her talons, glided to the ground, and lifted the children up into the foreboding sky. Nancy's eyes watered as the cold air pushed against her pupils. She wrapped her arm around Jimmy and shrilled, "*Awesome*," at the top of her voice. "This bird is so strong."

Grizelda swayed effortlessly between the glowing hot-air balloons, the weight of her passengers forcing her to fly below the clouds.

"I love it here," screamed Jimmy. "I'm on top of the world."

"You are in between worlds," cackled Grizelda. "And we are heading for the Invisible Valley."

"Yeah, to the Invisible Valleeeeeeeeeey," cried Jimmy, unaware what or where the Invisible Valley was.

Grizelda approached the cliff-top and released her grip. Nancy and Jimmy tumbled head over heels and crash-landed into their friends.

"Glad you could make it," grumbled Elijah, his face ashen, as he edged away from the precipice. Nancy didn't need the spyglass to see how close the Jagganath were. The largest of the beasts was now halfway up the cliff, its claws making light work of the rock face. She stepped away from the edge. The menacing howls of the Jagganath grew louder and louder as they clawed their way up the cliff.

"What are we going to do?" asked The Duke. "They're gonna eat us alive!"

Nancy looked up at the crowded sky – hundreds of balloons bobbed on the prevailing wind. A bright yellow canvas floated towards her. She was convinced someone was inside the basket. She glanced over her shoulder just as the Jagganath's claws ripped at the grassy verge. The slimy beast stood on the cliff-top, translucent slime seeping from its grey, leathery skin and large webbed hands. A thunderous growl revealed two rows of serrated teeth.

The Duke fell to his knees and pleaded, "Don't hurt us!"

The yellow balloon landed. In the passenger basket stood a small Chinese man. "Mr Wuu!" yelled Nancy, in a state of shock.

He gave a broad smile and waved his arms, beckoning them. The children scampered over and clambered aboard the vessel.

The Jagganath let out a collective roar, teeth glistening, eyes flashing.

The balloon left the cliff-top and floated high up into the coloured sky. Nancy and her friends embraced one another, the gift of life now truly appreciated. Mr Wuu was dressed just as Nancy remembered him: a formal, navy-blue pinstripe suit, bow-tie, and shiny ox-blood brogues. "Let's get you to the Invisible Valley," he said.

"Where is the Invisible Valley?" asked Nancy, unsure if she should shake his hand or kiss him. Mr Wuu gave a customary bow of his head and Nancy returned the gesture.

Jimmy bowed out of courtesy, accidentally butting Elijah.

"Ouch," groaned Elijah.

Jimmy rubbed his forehead and apologised, "Sorry, Eli."

Mr Wuu straightened his bow-tie and beamed. "We are very close to the border."

Nancy's blank expression tickled Mr Wuu. Beads of sweat trickled down his temples, as his stumpy legs pedalled a circular wheel at the bottom of the basket. "The Invisible Valley is a safe haven from Zayock and his smoke."

Nancy winced as a rod of pain shot through her. "Who. Is. Zay-ock?"

"Too much information can distract someone so young," replied Mr Wuu. "The Jagganath will not be able to find you when we land."

The balloon climbed up into the sky and beyond the darkness that had shrouded them. Daylight reappeared as if someone had flicked a switch, the coloured clouds reappearing like magic. Soon the balloon began its descent, coasting towards a coppice of trees. Sprawling branches scratched and clawed the bright yellow canvas. Jimmy reached for a fruit and yanked it from its branch. He held it aloft and looked at Mr Wuu for permission. Mr Wuu smiled and nodded his approval. Within two gulps, the fruit was inside his stomach. Laughter erupted as the basket hit the floor with a thud, forcing a thunderous burp from the pit of Jimmy's stomach.

Mr Wuu lifted them out one by one, shooing away Grizelda as she flapped around his head in a frenzy of excitement. He passed the leather holdall to Prema and smiled as he caught sight of its contents: his hand-made toys.

Nancy lost count of the igloo huts dotted around her. They were everywhere: a stony village waiting to be explored. The landscape was just as beautiful. Nothing had changed. She clapped her hands in appreciation of the incredible scenery. "It looks like the same place we just left."

"You are still within Enerjiimass," replied Mr Wuu. "The circle of love surrounding the Invisible Valley is impenetrable to Zayock."

Nancy flinched. "Who is Zayock?"

"An evil sorcerer," admitted Mr Wuu, shuffling nervously from side to side, "and he is poisoning our beautiful world."

A sharp stabbing pain disabled Nancy. She held her stomach and groaned.

Prema raced to her side. "Are you okay?"

Another raft of cramps brought Nancy to her knees. "Er, yeah. I think so."

Elijah addressed Mr Wuu. "What's wrong with her?"

"It's that name," replied Prema. "Whenever she hears Z—"

"Shh," hushed Mr Wuu. "There is no time to explain." He pulled Nancy to her feet and patted her on the back. "Make sure you stay within the border of the Invisible Valley."

"Where is the border?" asked Nancy. "All I can see are hills and stone-huts."

Mr Wuu's expression clouded. "Do not cross the line of Black Poppies."

Nancy shielded her face from the sunshine. "Okay. Night and day follow each other so quickly around here."

"Ah, the joys of an interactive atmosphere," said Mr Wuu with delight. "The closer you are to the Jagganath, the darker it becomes. Enerjiimass is an amazing place. If you have sombre thoughts, the sky will reflect them. If you think positively, your day will be bright, and you will have a better chance of… escape."

"I want to escape right now," confessed Elijah. "I've had enough."

Mr Wuu fiddled with his cufflinks and continued: "Enerjiimass absorbs every bit of energy that we emit, both good and bad. Before Zayock arrived with his machinery, we lived in a world where all our thoughts and feelings were positive. Sadly, that has changed. Now we are stuck in a tumultuous battle with dark thought and negative emotion."

"Sounds ominous," declared Prema.

Mr Wuu nodded. "Negativity is destroying the creatures of Enerjiimass."

Nancy shuddered, her thoughts returning to home and how her mother always expected the worst in life, and her father's eternal struggle to realign her perspective. Their relationship was a constant battle between conflicting attitudes. Mr Wuu placed his hand on her shoulder, her thoughts momentarily shared with the toy-maker. "It is regretful that your own kind dwell so much on the negatives of life. If they changed their perspective, their world and their lives would dramatically improve." He paused, then concluded, "It is vital that you remain positive within Enerjiimass. It will give you the light that you require."

Nancy turned to Elijah. "Did you hear that?"

Elijah frowned.

"Let's sit down and eat," said Mr Wuu. They rolled out a blanket on the floral carpet and unpacked a hamper. "I don't have

159

much time," confessed the toy-maker. "I leave for The Home For The Incurably Curious within the hour."

Nancy shot him a disapproving look. "But, we need you here."

"I am requested by the High Priest. I will return, you have my word."

The children feasted on an assortment of cakes and scones, while Mr Wuu riffled through the leather bag. "You have chosen wisely," he said, inspecting the Aero-Strazmicator. "You should keep this tuned at all times."

The Duke pulled the aerial and looped the leather strap over his shoulder. "Why's that?"

"It will pick up any change in atmosphere and help you find a path back to the Tree of Hearts. When the sky is dark you will know the Jagganath are close. The Aero-Strazmicator will scan every inch of Enerjiimass and find the safest place for shelter."

"Like a radar?" enquired The Duke.

"Sort of," replied Mr Wuu. He checked his watch and sighed. "It could save someone's life."

"S-s-someone's… life…?" stuttered The Duke. He attempted to swallow, but coughed up a mouthful of cake – it flew through the air and splattered against Prema's legs.

"You must stay here, children, and find the Great One," instructed Mr Wuu. "He will waken only at the call of Zayock or The Chosen One. He has been cursed."

Prema wiped the food from her leg and fluttered her lashes. "Who is the Great One?"

Mr Wuu kissed his hand, then touched his heart. "He is the only force of true love in our universe. Unfortunately, he has been sedated by Zayock."

Nancy groaned at the sound of the name, a repetitive dull thud clunking in her stomach. Mr Wuu apologised and went on, "Without the Great One, we will perish. I must leave now."

"No!" exclaimed Nancy. "What about the stone?" She threw down her food as Mr Wuu checked his watch and climbed into the whicker basket. "Aunt Elma told me a precious stone is missing."

"One thing at a time, Nanny Bo," replied Mr Wuu, calmly. "Find the Great One. He is the Path and the Light. It is unfortunate that time is our enemy. His Highness, Captain Carbunkle, summons me." He twisted a valve and fired up the balloon. "Captain Carbunkle has given you the book. It informs us you are The Chosen One. You must read more to find the Great One. When the Great One aligns himself with The Chosen One, the search for the stone can begin." For the first time, a hint of desperation crept into Mr Wuu's voice. "The Great One sleeps here, and he alone can guide you. Only you can waken him – the rest of us are just helpers in the passing of time."

Nancy bit her lip, emotions simmering beneath her calm exterior. She fought back her tears as the balloon left the ground and floated up into the multi-coloured sky. "Why do you have to go?" she asked.

Mr Wuu cupped his hands to his mouth. "Zayock's plan is working. We creatures of Enerjiimass are more sensitive than you." He sprung up from the basket and dangled precariously over the ledge, yelling at the top of his voice, "I cannot survive here. I must join Aunt Elma and Captain Carbunkle." He pointed at the stone igloos scattered over the hills, then blew Nancy a kiss. "Trust the Mooyats. They will help you." Within seconds he was above a purple cloud and out of sight.

Elijah took a swig of milkshake and sighed. "We're doomed."

17
The Great One

The afternoon sun warmed Nancy's back. She sat alone on the crest of the hill; it offered her a splendid view of the Invisible Valley. She studied the silver horizon: it reminded her of a David Hockney print hanging in her father's shed. A magnificent camelback rainbow pierced the clouds, the entire skyscape a work of art. Time was suspended: there didn't seem to be a beginning or an end to the day. Nancy cocked her head and marvelled at the cluster of balloons, their empty baskets rocking against the gentle breeze. She sat perfectly still, at one with herself, safe in the splendour of her surroundings. The thrill of Enerjiimass gave her a purpose and the sense of belonging that she craved. For the first time, her old life in London was a distant memory, not a painful reminder of unattainable happiness.

She closed her eyes and slipped into a whimsical daydream.

Every August she would board the train at Fenchurch Street station, arriving sixty minutes later in Leigh-on-Sea. Aunt Nora offered free accommodation and evening meals. It was a welcome break from the high-rise estates and smog of Bermondsey. Two weeks at 38 Sea View Road were treasured memories for the Joneses. The sun always seemed to shine. Their days were spent on the beach, throwing stones into the surf, swimming, wave-diving, and eating freshly shelled cockles. After dinner, her father would buy ice creams on the promenade, line up three deckchairs, and insist they watched the sun setting. Just as the last of the sun's rays were dissolving into the sea, Teddy Jones would ask his daughter the same question: "Nanny Bo, did you know that the horizon is only the limitation of our sight?" His mysterious words sparked Nancy's imagination – she'd often dreamed that there was a secret world her eyes couldn't see. Now she actually believed it, and wondered if her father had known more than he was letting on.

At the foot of the hill, Prema held *The First Book of Cosmo*. On page 172, a new chapter appeared. She whispered the words, "Guidance and Senses."

"What?" replied Jimmy, who lay flat on his back, admiring the neon sky.

"Nothing," murmured Prema.

Jimmy lifted his head and pointed at the grassy mound. "What's Nanny Bo doing up there?"

"Thinking," replied Prema.

Nancy waved at Jimmy, then she spotted The Duke and Elijah, who were walking in a figure-of-eight, arguing and gesticulating. They reminded her of lost tourists at London Bridge, stomping around aimlessly in search of the Tower of London. Then a sudden, loud hiss startled her. She turned and watched as jets of water spurted from the ground. Dozens of springs arced across the sky, their droplets raining down upon the floral carpet like Christmas glitter. She enjoyed the moment, and what a moment it was – the permanent camelback rainbow dancing in the sky like a serpent, its tail connecting with the horizon. Her mind was energised as images of her parents flashed before her, magnifying her mood, lifting her spirit.

Nancy knew that the Invisible Valley only offered a temporary place of sanctuary. Beyond it, Enerjiimass had to be explored. She had to find the Great One, and she needed to call upon her friends and formulate a plan. She raced down the hill, her legs buckling under the sharp decline. Then the soft, delicate voice of Prema Sarkander crept inside Nancy's ear. She looked down at her friend, reading *The First Book of Cosmo* silently to herself. Her sensory gifts were growing stronger. She focused on the voice:

"The Chosen One is a dual-star, a leader of the land. Emotional and physical senses will guide the soul."

"They certainly will," said Nancy with a cheeky grin, as she reached Prema.

"Hey," said Prema, astonished, "can you hear me reading?"

Nancy nodded. "Yeah."

"You can hear my thoughts! Now I have no internal privacy."

"I wouldn't worry too much, Pre," admitted Nancy. "It's all a bit of a jumble."

"But I'm not sure I like that," said Prema, turning another page of the ancient volume. "You must be acclimatising. You belong here."

Nancy felt giddy in a sea of conflicting emotions, her mind clouded by a life of unanswered questions. "Where's the music box?"

Prema reached for the leather holdall. "It's here."

"Get it out."

"A *please* would be nice," clucked Grizelda. She swooped down from a branch and landed on Nancy's shoulder.

"*Please*," repeated Nancy; then she shooed the parrot away.

Prema unzipped the bag, grabbed the music box, and passed it to her friend. Nancy stared at the ornate musical carvings, flipped it over, and read the inscription: *There's a place the music plays.*

Prema lowered her voice. "What are you thinking?"

Nancy spun the box on its side and squinted. "I wonder how this thing works?"

"Look," Prema exclaimed. "There's a handle."

Nancy's eyes shone, electric. "I've never seen that before."

"Go on," urged Prema. "Wind it."

Nancy wound the handle. With each turn there was a faint murmur from within. Jimmy gawped as the box opened. Shaanue appeared, wrapped in her bronze cape. She raised her tiny arms and unfolded her wings. The Night Fairy fluttered over to Nancy like a humming bird. "I am Shaanue, your Fairy of the Night."

"I know," said Nancy, softly.

"You are The Chosen One."

Nancy nodded.

"I am here to help you," chimed the fairy.

Nancy whispered, "*Amazing*," and waited for Shaanue to continue.

"The sun burns my wings, Nanny Bo. Please, let me back into the box. I will return when you need me most and the light is no more."

Nancy held out her hands. "But I need you now."

"Help comes when you need it most," replied the fairy. "The sun burns. I am your Fairy of the Night."

"Sorry," said Nancy, holding out the box. Shaanue disappeared into it, a trail of light sparkling behind her. The lid slammed shut, just as The Duke and Elijah returned.

"What's the plan, Nanny Bo?" asked Elijah, his hands placed either side of his hips. "I'm bored of walking around trying to find a way out of here. It's like a maze, and we're lost."

Nancy pointed at the igloo huts. "Mr Wuu told us to ask the Mooyats for help. They must live in these stone houses."

Elijah shook his head. "I've walked around and around and I haven't seen a soul. They must be empty, every last one of them."

"Did you try to enter any of them?"

"Er, no, we—"

"You were scared," interrupted Nancy.

Elijah puffed his chest. "No!"

"It didn't seem right walking into someone's house," added The Duke.

"Well, you're right, it doesn't look like there are any Mooyats around here," proclaimed Nancy. She bobbed her head from side to side, narrowed her eyes and gestured to a far-away dwelling. "Let's try over there."

"Why?" quizzed Elijah. "That's a very long walk and there are hundreds of stone huts all around us."

"Instincts," admitted Nancy. "I must follow them." She winked at Prema and gave a thumbs-up. She grabbed *The First Book of Cosmo* and trudged off, head down, flicking through the tatty pages. Grizelda flapped her wings in anticipation of flight. The Duke followed, flinging the Aero-Strazmicator over his shoulder like a guitar. Jimmy took a breath and prepared himself for another long hike. Prema grabbed the music box and zipped it in the holdall. Elijah's moans and groans fell upon deaf ears.

The Invisible Valley wasn't the easiest of places to navigate – most of the igloo huts were congregated on the hilltops. The constant up-and-down slowed their progress. Nancy focused on a distant mound, a small gathering of igloo huts surrounded by dozens of spindly willow trees. Her instincts were strong. She felt as if there was a compass within her, as if something or someone was guiding her. Finally, they approached the small hamlet. Nancy brushed through the coppice of trees, passed the book to Prema and counted nine huts. A sandy track led to the largest hut, whose door sported a rusty knocker resembling an elephant's head. A circular window was ajar, its handle rattling against the ledge. The remaining igloo huts were identical – whitewashed, with small green doors, but no windows. There was no sign of life, not a murmur.

Jimmy pointed to a set of paw prints. "Look."

Nancy winced. "What are they?"

"Looks like rats to me."

"No rats here," chirped Grizelda. "They are Mooyat tracks. They used to roam the hills of Enerjiimass. Disciples of the Great One."

"Doesn't look like anyone's home," said The Duke. "Maybe we should leave."

The children huddled together at the edge of the path, but, after a brief discussion, they decided to leave. Nancy's eyes searched the sky, desperately hoping Mr Wuu's balloon would miraculously reappear. Then there was a grinding noise, a rusty bolt sliding from its keeper. She grabbed Elijah's collar. "Stop!"

"Take your hands off me."

"There's someone inside. Look – the lights are on."

"That's just a reflection," replied Elijah, angrily.

"It's not," insisted Nancy. "Let's knock on the door."

"No way," replied Elijah. "I want to leave."

Nancy walked up the path, her steps cautious and measured. She pinched the rusty elephant trunk and rattled the knocker.

There was no answer.

She turned to her friends, then knocked again, this time louder. Nancy shrugged her shoulders and walked back down the path, ignoring the smug grin on Elijah's face. The sound of a lock turning and the creaking of hinges stopped her in her tracks.

Standing in the doorway was a small creature that resembled a monkey, its tail a furry corkscrew as long as its body. Twelve long, tentacle-like fingers twisted in different directions on each hand.

"Who knocks on my door?" asked the strange creature.

"I do," cried Nancy.

"And you are?" came the creature's high-pitched response.

"Nancy Bo Jones."

"Ah, why on earth didn't you say?"

"I just did," replied Nancy.

"Welcome to the Invisible Valley," squeaked the odd-looking animal. He bowed before Nancy and grinned. "You are protected by a magical charm. Please wipe your feet and enter."

The creature held the door open, his wide smile revealing three buck-teeth that protruded from his top lip. "Yes, you are all welcome here," said the furry animal, his rubbery fingers wriggling like worms.

Grizelda didn't wait. She flew into the hut, clucking and crowing.

Nancy crawled into the lowered passageway of the igloo and stood when she reached the dome. Her friends followed suit, squeezing into the cramped room, nudging and elbowing one another for space. Several pictures of Captain Carbunkle and Aunt Elma were hung on the walls and framed with holly. A large mosaic of a strange beast adorned the far wall, and clusters of tiny hearts and musical notes edged the impressive mural. The oval-shaped room was pristine. Small bunches of dried lavender hung from the ceiling and two logs sizzled and spat in the grate of a fire. In the centre of the floor was a brass hatch. Nancy's heart swooned every time she gazed at the mural. She bent down to greet the creature and offered her hand. "Hello."

The creature stared at Nancy, then back at the mural on the far wall, as if comparing two family members in a portrait.

The silence was unnerving.

Nancy coughed for attention.

"Oh, good afternoon. I'm Cortillian, chief of the Mooyats."

"I'm Nancy Bo Jones, but my friends call me Nanny Bo."

Cortillian nodded, licked his lips, then pulled a small trumpet from his belt. He blew into the mouthpiece. The sound of a hundred foghorns left the brass instrument. The walls shook, the ceiling trembled, and the floor vibrated. Then he lowered the trumpet from his mouth and stared disapprovingly at Jimmy. "You stand on Gateway Number Three, young man."

Jimmy peered down at his slippers. Beneath them, the brass hatch shook violently on its hinges.

"Stand aside, please, stand aside," ordered Cortillian.

Jimmy squeezed himself against the dome of the igloo. Then the hatch burst open. Hundreds of Mooyats appeared, each one a different shade of grey. Their oversized eyes on their miniscule heads were fixed upon Nancy. One of the creatures pointed at the mural, then back at her. It bristled with excitement, unable to remain still for more than a second. In a shrill helium pitch, it said, "Follow…," then repeated, more insistently, "Follow… Follow…"

Another Mooyat squeaked and gestured for Nancy to get closer to Gateway Number Three.

One after the other, they chanted, "Follow…"

Cortillian counted. "A one, a two, a one, two, three, four," then he blew through one of his rubbery fingers. The children were gobsmacked as a plethora of notes oozed from his limbs – it was beautiful, Cortillian played his fingers like an oboe. Within seconds, a chorus of Mooyats sang their hearts out, producing layers of harmonies at different melodic interludes, their heads swaying in time with the tune.

Nancy was mesmerised, seduced by sweet harmony.

Cortillian was lost in the music, his eyes rolling, his body pulsing to the rhythm. The sound waves bounced from one wall to the next, and the igloo hut was filled with musical energy. The Duke sang along, pitch-perfect, moving his fingers over an imaginary keyboard. Cortillian played with consummate ease, a musical maestro in control of his talent. He clicked two of his twenty-four fingers and the Mooyats stopped right on cue.

The Duke continued, oblivious of the conductor's instruction. "Oops, sorry."

"That's okay, Master Duke," smiled Cortillian. "You have music in your veins."

The Duke offered a sheepish grin.

"A gift from the Great One," mused Cortillian. "Now then, are you ready, Nanny Bo?"

"I was born ready," admitted Nancy. She stared down the hatch, where the Mooyats were congregated. One after the other, they disappeared within, leaving nothing but a dark vacant space. Cortillian clicked his heels and jumped.

Nancy took one last look at her friends, clicked her heels, and followed.

Elijah scowled with discontent. "There is no way I'm jumping into the unknown."

"You already have," said Prema, calmly. "Remember Roebuck Woods?"

Elijah huffed, then looked at The Duke for moral support. "This is one step too far. I need to get out of here and go home."

The Duke tried to reason with Elijah. "We should follow Nanny Bo, she needs our help, Eli. Safety in numbers."

"You must be mad! I'm getting out of here." Elijah crawled through the narrow entrance of the igloo hut, kicked the door from its hinges and sprinted off into the distance.

Prema linked fingers with Jimmy. "I think they call this a leap of faith."

"I'm ready when you are," replied Jimmy. "On the count of three…"

Prema nodded, then began to count. "One, two, three…"

Jimmy and Prema jumped.

"Ouch!" cried Prema, as she crash-landed on her backside. She yelped again as Jimmy tumbled onto her lap. "Goodness me, you're heavy."

"Sorry," squealed Jimmy. "I can't see a thing. It's pitch black down here."

Nancy reached out and felt the back of Jimmy's head. "Is that you, Jim Jam?"

"Yes," whispered Jimmy. "Where are we?"

"I don't know. Where's Pre?"

"I'm here," answered Prema, "right beside you."

There was a loud bang as the trap door closed from above. They linked arms and shuffled closer to one another. The sound of dripping water echoed through the veil of darkness. It unnerved Nancy. She had no idea where it was coming from. The *drip-splash-drip-splash* aggravated her senses.

"What's that noise?" asked Jimmy.

"Sounds like a leaking tap," replied Nancy. Her voice returned seconds later: "I think we're in another cave." The echo returned again.

"It sounds like there are two of you."

"Well, there's only one of me, Jim Jam. I can assure you of that."

Jimmy chuckled. "Yeah, I suppose so. One's enough."

Nancy giggled, then called for help. "Cortillian, where are you? Cortillian…"

Prema fumbled with the bag and began to wind the music box. The soft murmurings of Shaanue reverberated within the dark chamber.

"Well done," said Nancy, her voice bouncing off the walls and returning once more.

Sparks of light spilled from the music box, the lid popped open, and white light filled the cave. Shaanue appeared, waving her wand like a flag of honour. "Help comes when you need it most," cried the Night Fairy.

The children cheered with delight, their voices rushing through the wide-open space before them. They were sitting inside a rocky basement, its flinted walls crammed with beautiful paintings, each one a different image of the same creature: a stone-age art gallery with one subject.

"It's the same *thing* as the mural in Cortillian's igloo hut," said Nancy.

"That *thing* you refer to," said Cortillian, appearing from nowhere, "is Ergonwold." He bowed after mentioning the name. "Otherwise known as… the Great One."

"I need to find him," whispered Nancy. She was overcome with emotion. There wasn't a single patch of the wall without paint. Even the ceiling was smothered with images of the creature. In the far corner, hundreds of Mooyats surrounded a dripping tap, and with each drip its echo returned. *Drip-splash-drip-splash.*

Nancy felt the eyes of every painting follow her as she made her way towards the tap. Cortillian skipped behind her. "Your instincts are strong, young lady."

All that mattered to Nancy was finding Ergonwold. Butterflies circulated within the lining of her stomach as she tip-toed towards the tap. A strange magnetic force pulled her closer and closer. Her eyes became glazed, her words groggy: "I need to find him."

Cortillian's fingers wriggled, his voice furnished with childish excitement. "Follow your heart…"

As Nancy approached the huddle of Mooyats, they purred with delight and parted at her feet, forming a pathway to the leaking tap.

She reached out and grasped it.

Sparks of electrical current ignited her body. She flew twenty metres through the air and landed on her back. Her hands scalded, her expression frozen by the electric shock. Her limbs twitched, but there was no sign of life. Jimmy and Prema raced to her side. Shaanue flew through the air and landed on the tip of Nancy's nose. Cortillian clicked his fingers and the Mooyats began to sing a slow, mournful tune, each note hanging in the air for an age. *"Sleep not, The Chosen One. Breathe, dream, awaken, the Great One."*

Prema glared at Cortillian conducting his vocal orchestra. "Help us!" she cried. "Stop singing. She's dying."

Cortillian ignored her desperate pleas and continued conducting with his elasticated fingers. Prema turned her attention to the Night Fairy. "Shaanue, please help us."

The tap continued to drip. Beneath it, a porcelain bowl rested on a large rectangular slab of granite. Water seeped over its edges, running off the stone and trickling into an abyss of darkness. Shaanue pointed her wand at the bowl. Jimmy scrambled over and grabbed it with both hands. He waddled back, trying his best not to spill a drop.

"Drink," instructed Shaanue.

Jimmy lifted the bowl to his mouth.

"No, not you," cried Prema. She snatched the bowl, raised Nancy's head from the floor, and poured some water into her open mouth.

The Mooyats continued to fill the basement with their sombre vocals. "*Sleep not, The Chosen One. Breathe, dream, awaken, the Great One.*"

They held hands and formed a circle around Nancy's body. She was lifeless, her head resting on Prema's lap. The Mooyat ensemble continued. Cortillian gesticulated wildly, eyes spinning and tail flapping.

Jimmy stood over Nancy and steepled his fingers. All he could do was pray.

Then the incessant sound of continual dripping stopped.

Shaanue whizzed past the choir of Mooyats and hovered above the slab of granite. Her eyes sparkled as the rectangular slab began to vibrate. Slowly, with every passing second, the rock became translucent, morphing into a formidable lump of ice. Staring back at the Night Fairy were two enormous green eyes.

Shaanue shed a silent tear and flew back to Nancy. "He is with us," she proclaimed.

The Mooyats stopped singing.

Cortillian saluted and stood to attention.

Jimmy and Prema stared agonisingly at their unconscious friend. "Do something," screamed Prema, hysterically.

"He is with us," repeated Shaanue. "The slab is disintegrating."

"Wake up, Nanny Bo," sobbed Jimmy.

The Night Fairy flew back to the tap and hovered above the lump of ice. A large, grey, wrinkly creature was housed within. It stared back at her, its beautiful emerald eyes blinking. With great effort, the creature smiled. It looked as if it had just awoken from an extended hibernation, its movements slow and cumbersome.

"Stand back," instructed Shaanue. "Give him space to re-enter our world."

Finally, the slab of ice cracked, pinging shards of icicles up into the air like miniature javelins. The creature mustered enough strength to shake the last of the frost from its body, and climbed out from its chilly slumber.

Cortillian fainted.

The Mooyats dropped to one knee and saluted.

Prema glared at Jimmy, then dropped gracefully to one knee. Jimmy walked towards the creature, his slippers gliding over the icy surface. He lowered one leg, then slipped as he attempted to pay his respects.

The gigantic beast resembled a strange-looking elephant. Long, feathery lashes framed its green eyes. Three glass vials dangled from a studded dog collar that wrapped itself around a heavily creased neck. A white stone shimmered in one. The remaining two were empty. The creature stood momentarily on its hind legs. Its grey skin appeared too large for its frame, giving way to a multitude of wrinkles and creases. Floppy ears hung either side of its face, while a miniature tusk protruded either side of its mouth. There was no sign of a trunk, just an elongated snout and a large white heart painted on its chest.

"Who lies there?" asked the creature.

"My friend," sobbed Prema.

"Can you help us?" begged Jimmy.

"What... happened... to... her?" asked the creature, its words slow and laboured.

Shaanue flew towards it, nestling herself between its tusks. "The Chosen One is here," she said. The creature nodded and thanked the Night Fairy. The wrinkly beast ambled towards Nancy and placed one of its domed paws on her chest.

Jimmy covered his face with his hands. "Please don't hurt her."

"I can only heal," replied the creature in a rich, deep, velvety tone. "No harm will come to her." It rocked its head from side to side. "I am Ergonwold. You have woken me from my frozen prison. Now let me waken you. It is my duty."

Ergonwold lifted his paw. The colour returned to Nancy's cheeks. She coughed, opened one eye, and rubbed the other. "Who are you?"

"I am Ergonwold. You must be Nancy Bo Jones?"

"Y-yes, I am," stuttered Nancy. She pushed Ergonwold's paw from her chest and sprung to her feet.

Ergonwold lowered his neck until his oval eyes were only centimetres from Nancy's. Nancy shuffled back on her heels. "Do not be alarmed, young lady," advised the creature. "Deep down, you know the truth. It is me that you seek." Ergonwold curled his snout and beckoned Nancy.

Nancy stared into the emerald eyes, her nerves momentarily subdued. They were the same as in the dream: the vision in the courtyard. Then, in one swift, lunging movement, she leaped forward and grabbed Ergonwold's collar. The glass vials chimed as her feet nestled into one of the many creases in his neck. She arched her back and dangled one-handed from an ivory tusk. "My friends call me Nanny Bo."

"I know," grunted Ergonwold.

"What happened to me?" asked Nancy.

"You turned the tap of Tu-Nahh," replied Ergonwold.

Nancy let go of the tusk and landed with a thud. "What on earth is that?"

"It's an old curse," answered Ergonwold. He looked down at her, his white heart flickering as if it was running out of power. "If anyone but the person who is last invited to Enerjiimass turns that tap—"

"Yes?" interrupted Nancy, unaware of the creature's dismay.

Ergonwold's ears flapped open. Their span was so great, Nancy thought he was about to take flight. He ruffled his snout and continued: "If an uninvited individual turned that tap, the ancient gremlins of Tu-Nahh would return and feed on every living thing within Enerjiimass. And nothing would stop their desire for flesh." Nancy pushed out her charred palms and presented them to Ergonwold the Great. "You took the full force of the ancient curse, young lady."

Nancy blew onto her fingertips. "I know."

"But you were invited," added Ergonwold. "The gentle shock you experienced was the de-magnetisation of the spell."

"Gentle shock," repeated Nancy. "It felt like a bolt of lightning."

Ergonwold dipped his snout into the porcelain bowl and sucked up a mouthful of water. "Ah, that's better." His eyes sparkled and his chest expanded with an intake of air. "I need you to do something for me."

"Anything," said Nancy, with a subservient bow.

"Please remove one of the empty vials from my neck."

Nancy stared at the studded collar.

Ergonwold drew another deep, elongated breath and continued: "Fill it with the water from the bowl." The Great One lowered his enormous head. Nancy unclipped a vial and submerged it in the porcelain bowl. "Keep that safe. It will ward off the darkness and keep your mind bright."

"How?" asked Nancy.

"That water is healing liquid," boomed Ergonwold. "It is precious – a real tonic, something to perk up the most troubled of minds. It is the liquid that counterbalances Tantibus."

"What's Tantibus?"

"Zayock's evil fluid."

Nancy flinched, then she placed the vial of liquid in the leather holdall and patted Ergonwold's snout. She felt inextricably connected to the strange creature. There was peace and tranquillity in his presence. Ergonwold glanced around the cave, acknowledging all who paid homage to him. Cortillian regained consciousness, bowed with reverence, then gave a hearty cheer. His congregation followed suit.

Ergonwold spied *The First Book of Cosmo* and ruffled his ears. "The book of all knowledge. Who keeps this for me?"

"I do," answered Nancy.

"Then you *must* be The Chosen One. I am here to serve you. We must leave the Invisible Valley and search for the missing stone."

"What stone?" asked Nancy, excitedly.

"The Bloodstone," replied Ergonwold, shaking the empty vial on his collar. "It belongs in here, next to the Wisdom Stone."

Nancy couldn't take her eyes off the beast and his collar. "Where is it?"

"It's been stolen," replied Ergonwold. "We must leave. The smoke is rising."

Nancy wrinkled her nose and sniffed.

"Time is precious," insisted Ergonwold.

"Follow me," instructed Cortillian. "I will lead us back to my igloo hut. You can begin your journey from there."

The chief of the Mooyats played a merry tune on his instrumental fingers, jigging and giggling through the cave. Nancy skipped behind him, her worries now evaporated in the presence of Ergonwold the Great. Cortillian pointed to a mural at the highest point in the flinted basement. Miraculously, a door slid open, splitting the ornate oil painting of Ergonwold in two.

"Wow!" said Nancy. "I love magic."

Ergonwold reared up and placed his front legs between the opening and onto a ledge. One by one they grabbed his tail and clambered up his back, using it as a makeshift ladder. Cortillian ran along Ergonwold's spine, jumped over his collar, onto his head, tiptoed across his tusks, then perched precariously on the tip of Ergonwold's snout.

"Geronimo," shrilled Cortillian, as he leaped onto the ledge.

Nancy was next in line.

"Don't look down," advised Cortillian from the safety of the ledge.

Nancy swallowed hard, then sprang one-legged from Ergonwold's snout. "Geronimooooooo…"

She landed, flat-footed, wobbled, then steadied herself.

"Follow me," enthused the chief of the Mooyats.

Nancy ruffled Cortillian's fur and accepted his invitation, trailing the creature up two short flights of steps, where they were met by a revolving door. Cortillian placed a paw over his heart and purred, "*Home.*"

Nancy placed one foot into the spinning door and disappeared. The revolutions were so fast she was sucked in, her stomach springing into her mouth as she was spun around like a rag-doll.

A sudden blast of Cortillian's trumpet and the doors stopped.

She was thrown out and landed in a dizzy, incoherent heap. Her friends followed, landing next to her, dazed and confused. The aromatic smell of lavender was a welcome reminder that they were now back inside Cortillian's igloo hut.

"Welcome back," squawked Grizelda.

"That was weird," said Nancy, in a fit of dizzy giggles. She had no idea of time, but was conscious of it. She pulled Prema and Jimmy to their feet and took three short steps towards the door of the stone hut. Cortillian placed a finger into his mouth and played a descending scale of notes. Nancy spun around and hugged him, unintentionally muting the music. The chief of the Mooyats nestled his furry face into her neck and whispered, "There is no end to love."

Nancy, Jimmy, and Prema crawled out of the igloo hut into the bright sunshine of the Invisible Valley. They sat beneath the shade of a willow tree and waited for Ergonwold. "I'm starting to enjoy this," said Nancy, staring at the silver line where the sky met the land. "Did you know that the horizon is only the limitation of our sight?"

No one answered her.

Jimmy and Prema writhed in agony, arms flapping, mouths open, gulping desperately for air.

18
Black Poppies

T he Duke chased Elijah as fast as his legs would carry him. The frustration of leaving Nancy to follow after his friend grated with every step. Soon, his lungs began to burn and his strides deteriorated to a laboured walk. With slow, painful progress, he approached a field of ripe sunflowers, their heavy heads hanging wearily, soaking up the sun. He stepped forward and began to brush aside the stems that blocked his route. One after the other, he forced the flowers to the ground, clearing a pathway for himself, his hands now tinged with a fine yellowy powder. Finally, in the middle of the flower-strewn field, the last of his energy left him. He collapsed into a dejected heap.

All he could think of was home. He longed to be sitting at the piano with his mother. He would play for hours on end for her, losing himself in an ocean of musical bliss. When the final note sounded, she would embrace him and declare: "Where words fail, music speaks."

The Duke got to his feet and trampled through the endless rows of sunflowers, and with every flower head that he punched, he visualised Elijah's face. He kicked the last of the stems to one side and traipsed back into the open expanse of the Invisible Valley. He continued to walk, arms swinging, hair flowing, oblivious of direction, his mind a blur. His calves tightened and his heart thumped as he crawled up another hill. The view was magnificent – the Invisible Valley in all its glory.

The Duke raised his hand to his brow and squinted. There, less than a few hundred feet away, was Elijah Lincoln, perched on a small, grassy mound. The sense of relief was overwhelming. He ran the short distance, dropped to his knees, and confronted his friend. "Why did you run away?"

"Because I want to go home," confessed Elijah.

"Don't you think I do, too?"

"No," replied Elijah, angrily. "You wanted to follow *her* down that hatch."

"They are our friends, Eli. We should have followed Nanny Bo."

"We can find our own way back."

"That's a stupid idea."

Elijah clenched his fists. "Don't you call me stupid."

"Why don't you come down here and punch me, then? That'll solve everything." The Duke trudged cautiously up the slope, sat beside his friend, and offered a forgiving smile. "We have to stick together, Eli. Let's go back and find Nanny Bo."

Elijah shrugged him off. "Leave me alone. I've had enough of this place. It's weird; like a freaky dream."

"We have no chance of making it on our own. We need to go back…"

Elijah's eyes darted to the dense undergrowth. "Something's moving…"

"Where?" asked The Duke, spinning full circle.

Elijah stared at the hedgerow intently, shifting his head one way, then the other. "There's something in the bushes, and it's moving."

The Duke followed Elijah down the hill towards the hedge. "Can you see anything?"

"Not sure," whispered Elijah. He rolled onto his stomach and prodded the undergrowth. "It must be a bird caught in the bramble. I think I can reach it with this stick."

"Leave it alone," said The Duke. "Let's go and find—"

"I've got it," cried Elijah. "It's a compass." Elijah grabbed the compass and rubbed the dirt from its face. "It's gold. I've never seen anything like this before."

The Duke craned his neck over Elijah's shoulder. "Show me."

"Look!" said Elijah, enthusiastically, "it has three hands."

The Duke pulled a face. "That's *strange*. Three hands." He watched, as Elijah spun the compass over and inspected it. A green button marked 'Home' protruded above an intricately engraved *Z*. The Duke arched his brow, then looped the Aero-Strazmicator over his shoulder and extended the aerial. As soon as it reached its maximum length, a high-pitched horn screeched from the speaker.

"Turn that thing off," barked Elijah.

"I don't know how to," replied The Duke. He smothered the speaker and stared at the display screen. Green lights flashed intermittently: D-A-N-G-E-R. D-A-N-G-E-R.

Elijah's face turned to thunder. "Turn it off!"

The Duke held the Aero-Strazmicator aloft and yelled over the din of the siren, "It's a warning."

Elijah was interested only in the compass. "This will lead us home. All I have to do is press the 'Home' button."

"Eli!" cried The Duke.

"What?"

"The machine spells D-A-N-G-E-R."

Elijah crossed his fingers and pressed the 'Home' button. Miraculously, two wings appeared, flapping and humming like a bumble-bee. Then the face of the compass revealed an alphabetic dial, the minute letters rising up from the ivory surface, shimmering like diamanté braille. The three hands spun in opposite directions, and every time they stopped on a letter, there was a loud click.

"Sounds like dolphins chattering," said Elijah, cheerfully. With every click and clack, Elijah drifted deeper and deeper into a trance. The compass was buzzing and whirring as it hovered above him. The hands clicked on five letters: N-O-I-S-Y. It was only then that Elijah realised it was communicating. "Stop that blasted siren, Duke."

The colour drained from The Duke's face. "I don't know how to."

"You're scaring it," complained Elijah. The three golden hands of the compass continued to whizz around the alphabetic face, clicking and clacking. Another word was spelt: A-E-R-I-A-L.

Elijah yanked the Aero-Strazmicator from The Duke and forced the aerial down.

The siren stopped.

"Phew," said The Duke. He removed his fingers from his ears and grinned.

Elijah punched the air and jumped for joy. "We are going home, my friend! This compass will lead us back to where we belong. And we don't belong here."

"We have to go back and find Nanny Bo. It's only fair."

"No way," said Elijah, he turned his back on his friend and kissed the compass. "Nanny Bo has led us into nothing but trouble."

The Duke's smile turned to a frown. "We followed *her*, Eli. Do you remember?"

Elijah was transfixed by the magical instrument. The hands spun so fast, he struggled to decipher the words. He searched his pockets for a pen, but all he found was a tissue. "Do you have a biro?"

The Duke threw a pen from his pocket. Elijah snatched it mid-air and, with every click of the compass's hands, he wrote the corresponding letter onto the tissue. The humming of its wings stoked his excitement. He placed the pen behind his ear and read the message:

'*Cross the Black Poppies and find the path marked Z. Follow it to the castle and your home will lie in wait.*'

"What are we waiting for, Duke? Let's get going." Elijah ran off, with the compass whirring above his head.

The Duke picked the Aero-Strazmicator up and grunted, "Wait for me."

"Hurry up," replied Elijah, skipping towards a wooden stile.

"I said *wait*!"

Elijah stopped in his tracks and raised a hand. The compass fell obediently into his palm. Then the alphabetic dial clicked on fourteen letters:

D-O-N-T W-A-I-T F-O-R H-I-M.

The Duke switched the Aero-Strazmicator on and pulled the aerial. The loud siren ruptured the tranquil air. Elijah covered his ears and fell to the ground. The compass retracted its wings and landed next to him. "Turn it off. Please, stop that noise. I'll do anything – it's hurting."

"Anything?" hollered The Duke.

"Yes."

"I want you to listen to me, Eli. Then, and only then, will I turn it off."

"All right, hurry up. It's hurting."

The Duke raised his voice as loud as he could. "Nanny Bo brought this machine here for a reason, and I think it's trying to tell us something."

"It's just an old radio," groaned Elijah. "A piece of junk. It can't tell us anything. Turn it off."

The Duke held out his arms and enveloped his surroundings. "Look around you. We're in a strange land and you are following a flying compass. Don't try and tell me this is just a radio."

"Turn it off," pleaded Elijah. "Please."

"No!" screamed The Duke over the tumultuous din.

"Why?"

"Because I've remembered what Mr Wuu said."

Elijah curled up into a ball and squealed, "Turn it off!"

The Duke ignored Elijah's pleas, desperate to make his point. "Mr Wuu told us not to cross the Black Poppies, and your stupid compass is leading us right into a field of the things."

"Okay. Now, turn it off."

The Duke watched his friend writhing uncontrollably on the floor. He switched the machine off and retracted the aerial. Elijah let out a huge sigh of relief. Then, a single, loud click emanated from the compass. It began to hum, followed by a continuous clicking and clacking. Elijah wiped a tear from his eye. "I just want to go home."

"So do I," replied The Duke. "But we need to think before we act."

Elijah held out his hand. The compass levitated, its two gold wings reflecting the sunlight. It buzzed, clicked and hummed, then it landed in his palm. Elijah smiled, then declared: "Our home lies in wait."

The Duke shook his head. "You're bewitched, Eli." He studied the Aero-Strazmicator and pressed one of the buttons. "Before we follow that compass, let me fiddle with this machine. If I can fathom how it works, it might lead us back to the others."

"You must be mad," replied Elijah. "This magic compass will lead us home. That stupid Chinese man didn't have a clue what he was talking about."

"That compass will lead us into trouble."

Elijah shook his head furiously. "You're wrong, we are heading home. You go your way, and I'll go mine…"

The Duke had to surrender: the last thing he wanted was to be left alone. It was his biggest fear. Whenever he was alone, he played music to mask the silence. "The first sign of trouble and I'm turning back."

Elijah released the compass into the air like a carrier pigeon. "Okay, let's go home, Duke..."

The boys walked side by side, following the faint hum of the compass. Gradually, the sky faded from bright yellow to a slate grey. The Duke studied the reactive sky: it was a colour-coded atmosphere that reflected his mood. He had to use every ounce of concentration to banish the negative thoughts from his mind. They continued through glades, streams and woodland. Finally, they approached a gate that creaked on a single hinge, bumping against a crooked post. Beyond it was a field of Black Poppies, stretching as far as the eye could see. Elijah pushed the gate. He stood at the edge of the field and stared out at the sea of poppies, then he placed his right foot into the field.

A row of cobbles rose miraculously from beneath the earth, creating a pathway through the mass of black. "It's magic – the path home."

The Duke shook his head and reluctantly stepped onto the cobbled path. His tired eyes were drawn to the letter *Z* that was scored on each individual cobble stone. The compass whizzed up and down, performing loop-the-loop, as they made their way through the field. It wasn't long before they reached a slatted fence smothered in bramble. The compass flew over, out of sight, but audible.

"We have to climb over," instructed Elijah, his excitement at fever pitch. The Duke looked up at the darkening sky and sniffed. A musty smell wafted through his nasal cavity. Elijah scrambled over the fence. The Duke knew something was wrong, so he reached out and grabbed Elijah's ankle. "Let go of me," squealed Elijah, "we have to follow the—"

"Eli, I *have* to tell you something."

"What?"

"This doesn't feel right."

"Stop fretting!"

"It's that smell, Eli. It's like rotten eggs."

Elijah sniffed. "What smell?"

"Don't you remember that awful smell in Roebuck Woods?"

"No." Elijah climbed the fence and vaulted over.

The Duke waited with baited breath. There was no sound of his friend landing on the other side, only the distant buzz of the compass. His call was a dry, nervous rasp: "Are you okay, Eli?" He waited for a reply, but there wasn't one. Then he placed one foot on the bottom rung of the fence and began to climb. He made slow, tentative progress, constantly calling out to his friend. But Elijah wasn't responding. The Duke continued to climb, his body rocking from side to side with every nervous step. He reached for the next timber and squashed his thumb on a thorn. A trickle of blood seeped out just as the last of the light faded.

Darkness had returned in an instant.

The foul odour clung to The Duke's lungs and his breathing became difficult. Something was affecting his psyche. When he reached the top of the fence, he swung himself over and landed on his backside. He got to his feet and faced a slimy nightmare.

Twelve Jagganath stood in two rows of six, their red eyes gleaming in the darkness. The largest was holding Elijah, who appeared unconscious. Through mucus-drenched teeth, the creature held out a webbed hand and grunted, "Come."

"Leave me alone," whimpered The Duke.

Piercing red eyes bore down on him and a forked tongue licked the air, tasting the scent of the atmosphere. The Duke flinched as two leathery arms scooped him up. Within seconds, he was carried deep into the forest. The vile stench of the Jagganath's breath forced his stomach into sporadic cramps. The compass dangled from a chain around its neck like a precious locket, its sporadic clicks and hums an unwanted metronome in The Duke's ears. He wriggled incessantly in a vain attempt to free himself, but the beast forced him back into the crook of its arm with ease.

The Jagganath marched like soldiers. The creature clutching The Duke was the leader. He occasionally nodded or grunted at the ensuing pack. They marched in rhythm, breathing through their nostril slits, blowing jets of air with every second footstep. The compass clicks grew louder, its wings beating as the chain tightened around the Jagganath's neck. The beast pulled against it. The compass flapped harder, straining on the link-chain. Then it broke free, clicking and clacking as it wove its way through the tangled forest towards a collection of tree-stumps protruding from the ground like wooden thrones. One by one, the Jagganath chose their respective stumps and rested their slimy limbs. The Duke and Elijah were thrown to the floor like discarded litter. Elijah came to and embraced The Duke. "I'm so sorry. I was convinced the compass would lead us home."

"You were bewitched," whispered The Duke. "The compass must have hypnotised you."

Elijah studied the pack of Jagganath pulling leaves and berries from nearby trees. "Do you think they're vegetarians?"

The Duke opened his mouth as wide as he could and attempted to fill his lungs. He began to wheeze, his body convulsing, his throat constricting. "Berry…" He clenched his neck. "Air berries, air berries."

Elijah was grief-stricken. He momentarily froze, then checked The Duke's pockets and found two red berries. He placed one in The Duke's mouth and swallowed the other. They vomited a purple watery substance and expelled a gutful of loud burps. The Duke wiped his mouth and spat out the last of the bile. "Where do you think they are taking us?"

"No idea," confessed Elijah. He pointed at the snow-capped mountains in the distance. "The compass was leading us towards that castle."

"Forget the compass. It can't be trusted."

Elijah bowed his head. "I know."

The golden compass shimmered in the dark sky like a tiny star, circling above the tree tops, then it zoomed off towards the mountains. The Jagganath roared, stood to attention and grabbed the boys. The Duke and Elijah were carried like babies as the slimy monsters followed the clicks and clacks of the compass.

As the forest thinned, they approached an open field enclosed by rows of yew trees, their gnarled branches devoid of life: there wasn't a single fleck of green in sight. Beyond the field was the mountain range: six impressive peaks, the highest point mutating into the foundations of a gothic castle. Gargoyles peered down from the turrets, their eyes hollowed out by the weather, their backs smothered in moss. The Duke was convinced he could hear the faint chug of machinery, then, through the crook of the Jagganath's arm, he noticed clouds of smoke puffing from a monstrous chimney, the vapour contaminating the sky like a poisonous fog.

The twelve Jagganath marched towards the foot of the mountain and threw the boys to the ground. The Duke brushed himself down and looked Elijah in the eye. "What are we going to do?"

"Be grateful these monsters haven't killed us," replied Elijah. He glanced up at the frosted peak. "And pray whoever is in that castle can help us."

"You're crazy," said The Duke, his gaze shifting from Elijah to the Jagganath, then back up to the summit of the mountain. "We are being led to evil by these creatures. We need to find Nanny Bo."

"Oh, really?" said Elijah. "Why don't you ask that seven-foot monster with the sharp teeth if we can go back and find our precious Nanny Bo?" He grabbed The Duke and pulled him close. "We are at a dead end."

The Duke didn't flinch, his stare fixed upon his friend. "I won't give in to negativity."

The Jagganath gathered around the boys, their laser eyes flashing, and their webbed hands gesturing wildly at the castle. The

Duke peered up at the mountain. A light mist swirled around the castle. It seemed a world away, like a tiny black speck hanging in the clouds. "I think they want us to climb the steps."

Elijah was beaten. "We won't make it up there, it's a mountain."

A slimy arm shunted The Duke in the back. He stumbled forward and placed one foot on the first step. Elijah stayed close to his friend.

The long ascent was now underway.

The Duke's strides fell into a laboured rhythm, his thighs swinging in time with each breath. The wind lashed at his garments and the rumble of thunder grew louder and louder. He made slow but steady progress, constantly looking down at the Jagganath, who stood like sentinels at the foot of the mountain.

"How much further?" moaned Elijah. "My legs are giving way."

"Don't look down," replied The Duke. "Just keep going. I have a plan."

"What is it?" asked Elijah, his pace slowing to a standstill.

The Duke disappeared behind another flight of steps. "I'll tell you at the top..."

Elijah continued his relentless climb, complaining non-stop. Falling was now almost a preferred option. He staggered around another narrow flight of steps and appeared before The Duke, pale, withdrawn and exhausted. The Duke pushed his face into Elijah's, their sweaty brows colliding. "I'm not prepared to lie down and surrender just because you think it's all over, Eli. I miss my home as much as you do. We can get out of this mess if we believe in one another."

Elijah gave a lacklustre nod. All he wanted was food and shelter, and the comfort of home. The Duke peered over the mountain edge and realised just how high they had climbed. "It's all we have left – faith in one another. We *must* remain positive."

"What's the plan?" asked Elijah.

The Duke shrugged. "I'm not sure."

"But you said you had a plan!"

The Duke presented the Aero-Strazmicator to Elijah. "I'm convinced this thing will be able to help us. Let's get to the top and re-group." He pulled Elijah by the arm and tiptoed along a narrow ledge. Side by side, they climbed the last turn of flinted steps, the gigantic castle looming over them like a stone-clad beast. "Come on, Eli – one more step and we've made it."

A black ironclad door greeted them. It was wider than a house. Twisted horns protruded from a skull that hung over the threshold. Sparks shot across the gravel from two fires that crackled in grates either side of the door. The Duke warmed himself and gestured to his bedraggled friend to join him. He studied a row of buttons on the Aero-Strazmicator. Two were marked 'Entrance' and 'Exit'. The remaining knobs were labelled 'Mute' and 'Flare'. Then he extended the aerial, pressed 'Mute', and switched the machine on. He braced himself in anticipation of the screeching horn.

Silence.

The LED screen pixelated, then a triangle appeared, followed by twelve green dots. The Duke realised in an instant that the triangle represented the mountain and the dots were the Jagganath. There were two larger dots at the top of the triangle. *That's us*, he thought. Then he noticed a third, unrecognisable dot. He pressed the 'Exit' button and a map flashed intermittently. The Duke's face was radiant. "Can you believe it?"

"What?" asked Elijah, puzzled.

"This little beauty is a map."

Elijah's lips curled.

The Duke twisted the volume button and released the mute setting. A soft female voice gave directions to the Tree of Hearts. "It's talking to us, telling us how to find the Tree of Hearts." He shuffled closer to Elijah and said, "Listen!"

The sound of three bolts sliding alerted The Duke. He switched the Aero-Strazmicator off and retracted the aerial.

The door creaked open.

A skinny man appeared. He was dressed in a purple suit with a black velvet cape. His face was pimpled, his bug-like eyes framed by a heavy brow. In one hand he clutched a wand, in the other a green stone. He stepped theatrically into the forecourt, strode past the boys, and stopped at the mountain's edge. Then he screamed at the heavens, "The Bloodstone will stay with me. I will destroy its seeker. *Destroy!*"

The wind lifted his cape like a black sail as he roared with sardonic laughter, spittle clinging between his lips. He spun on his heels and glared at the shivering juveniles.

The Duke and Elijah were set rigid. Their lives in the balance.

A loud clap of thunder was followed by a bolt of lightning; it struck the top of the castle, dislodging a gargoyle's head. The boys curled up and shielded themselves in anticipation of the falling rock. The cloaked man sprinkled the tip of his wand with a grey powdery substance and waved his arm. Wisps of purple smoke left his wand, forming the letter *Z*.

The Duke watched as it rose to the sky like a gigantic mauve kite. The scrawny man looked down dismissively at the boys and hissed through a set of decaying teeth. "I am Zayock, Keeper of the Bloodstone, and Lord of Enerjiimass."

19
The Bloodstone

Nancy rummaged around Jimmy's pyjama pocket and pulled out two air berries. She dropped one onto his tongue, and crossed her fingers. A gutful of purple vomit was followed by a loud burp. Within three breaths, Jimmy was smiling again.

Nancy raced to Prema's side. As she accelerated, she tripped, stumbled, and fell agonisingly to her knees. The remaining berry fell from her hand and disappeared into the dense floral carpet.

Prema groaned heavily, her body jerking as she tried frantically to inhale.

Nancy scoured the undergrowth, her fingers jittering as she pushed the flowers back and searched the earth for the precious fruit. Petals flew through the air as she riffled through the undergrowth. Then, just as Prema's desperate groans faded, she saw it. Hidden beneath a violet bloom. She grabbed the berry and forced it down Prema's throat. After several short-lived spasms, Prema smiled, wobbled to her feet, and hugged Nancy.

"Look," yelped Jimmy, pointing to a patch of earth.

Ergonwold's snout popped out like a periscope. He sucked at the air, then pushed himself from the muddy hole. Nancy marvelled at the parting of earth, waving at the emerging beast in a state of shock.

Ergonwold trumpeted his arrival, the deep resonating hoots a rallying call to the creatures of Enerjiimass. He walked towards the children, the glass vials chiming like bells on his collar. Grizelda swooped down and landed on his back, her crest glowing and her head bowing in reverence to the wrinkly beast. Ergonwold's eyelids flickered as he acclimatised to the bright sky. He flapped his ears and arched his back. "This small corner of Enerjiimass is known as the Invisible Valley. It has been protected for centuries. We must venture out beyond this place of refuge and find the Bloodstone." Two large fangs were revealed as he yawned. "Young lady of the cards…"

"Me?" asked Prema.

"Yes, you, the young Sarkander of Bhopal." Ergonwold's oval eyes were now glued on the leather holdall. "I see you are entrusted with the toys of Shen Wuu."

Prema clasped the bag with pride. "Yes, O' Great One," she answered. "I read in *The First Book of Cosmo* that these artefacts are of exceptional value."

"This is true," replied the Great One.

Prema pulled the zip. "One of them is missing."

"So I see, Miss Sarkander." Ergonwold sighed heavily. "I believe the boys who have it may need it more than us."

Nancy's stomach knotted. "The Duke and Eli."

"They have crossed the field of Black Poppies," said Ergonwold. He lowered his snout and sniffed the earth. "My heart is heavy for them, but I cannot help. I am weak and I need my nest."

"We need to find our friends," said Nancy in a low voice.

Ergonwold circled the children. "I can offer you the best guide for this magical land. Your friends have the finest navigational toy Shen Wuu ever invented. The Aero-Strazmicator will serve them well… if they use it wisely."

"Will they be okay?" asked Jimmy.

"That I do not know," admitted Ergonwold. Then he inspected Jimmy with his emerald eyes, as if he was reading the boy. "You possess a heart of gold, young man, and a loyalty to your friends that I admire."

Nancy placed her arm on Jimmy's shoulder and winked.

"Jimmy James..." snorted Ergonwold.

Jimmy stepped forward. "My friends call me Jim Jam."

"My sincerest apologies," replied Ergonwold. "Jim Jam, you possess two things that most people in your own world lack." Jimmy held up two fingers and stared directly at them. Ergonwold relieved Jimmy's curiosity. "Optimism and belief, young man. They are two fantastic qualities." He stretched up onto his rear legs, towering above the children like a majestic dinosaur. "Climb upon my back, Jim Jam."

Nancy elbowed Jimmy. "Go on, Jim Jam. Do as you're told."

Jimmy didn't hesitate. He pulled Ergonwold's tail, raced up his hindquarters, and leaped onto his back. Nancy laughed as Jimmy clung on for dear life. He placed his feet between the layers of loose skin and made his way up to the crown of Ergonwold's head. "I can see everything."

Ergonwold coiled his snout as he inspected the vivid scenery. "Take a look at this enchanted landscape, Jim Jam."

Jimmy raised a hand to his brow. "It's incredible! I've never seen so many colours."

"Enerjiimass has been the keeper of all the positive energy people like you emit."

"Me?"

"Yes, you," answered Ergonwold emphatically. "It is an invisible energy. More precious than any treasure your own kind can possibly imagine. If only humans realised that the greatest commodity is produced by the kindness of one's heart."

Nancy gazed up at the towering beast and cupped both hands to her mouth. "So, if we are in a good mood, it creates energy?"

"Of course," replied Ergonwold.

"And it gets stored in Enerjiimass?"

"Yes, Nanny Bo," confirmed Ergonwold. "Think of Enerjiimass as a place where all your happiness is kept for a rainy day."

"Really?" queried Nancy. "It's all here?"

"Well, it should be," said Ergonwold, grimly. He fluttered his lashes and continued, "unfortunately, since my enforced spell of hibernation, there has been a problem. Our reserves of positive energy are depleted."

Nancy arched a brow. "How come?"

"Smoke," replied Ergonwold. "Someone is releasing poisonous fumes throughout Enerjiimass. Our positive atmosphere is turning into a negative one. There is a by-product of the smoke. It is called Tantibus." The Great One flapped his ears, aggravated by his own words. "Once Tantibus is swallowed, it will turn the most optimistic and positive thought into one of pure negativity. It controls the dark side of one's mind and even has the power to kill."

"How is Tan-ti-bus made?" asked Nancy.

"Machinery and magic," muttered Ergonwold. "Machines of another land, your land, combined with the magic of my land, and the Bloodstone. And that precious stone is in the wrong hands."

Nancy's stomach plunged. Her world blurred, then snapped back into focus. She refused to hide from the name she could hardly pronounce, and braced herself as the word trickled off her tongue: "*Zayock.*"

"Correct," replied Ergonwold, his leathery snout caressing her face. He sucked away her pain and flushed it out of his jaw, coughing up translucent phlegm. "Your inner-radar is strong, young lady."

"Who is he?" asked Nancy, amazed by the healing powers of the Great One.

Ergonwold didn't reply.

She tried again. "Who is he?"

"A man too close to home," declared Ergonwold, his voice bereft of spirit.

Nancy racked her brains. Then the penny dropped. "Lord Bymerstone!" Ergonwold nodded, his emerald eyes shrouded by a grey mist. It all made sense – the prophecy, the sudden move, the curse on 145 Oxon Road, Bymerstone Hall; and, of course, the invitation to Enerjiimass.

"You are a victim of circumstance and historical timelines," Ergonwold said. "Zayock has stolen the Bloodstone. It belonged to my forefathers. It has the power to heal, protect, and circulate all the positive energy within our shared universe." Nancy reached out to stroke him, as his voice waned. Ergonwold nestled his snout into the crook of Nancy's neck and sighed. "The Bloodstone is one-part ingredient to the Elixir of Life. Without it, we will perish."

"I know," confirmed Nancy. "Aunt Elma told me, and she is so worried. How can we get it back?"

"Defeat Zayock, and we can reclaim the stone."

Nancy felt a sudden rush of adrenaline. "Let's go! Where can we find this thief?"

"Your spirit is strong," said Ergonwold, cheerfully. "We need to prepare. Zayock is a dangerous man. He imprisoned me in a tomb of ice for nearly twelve years. If it wasn't for you, I wouldn't be here."

Nancy raised her fists. "I'm prepared."

Ergonwold peered down at Nancy. "I'm glad you are ready. There is not another with the required sensory gifts."

"There must be *someone*?"

"No," replied Ergonwold. "You are our only hope, Nanny Bo. You are of the chosen bloodline. We *must* begin our quest." He paused momentarily, then gazed up at the sky. "If we are to stop Zayock's smoke poisoning the bright souls of Enerjiimass, we must head for the mountains." Ergonwold shook his head, sending Jimmy flying through the air into a field of irises.

"Whoops," said Ergonwold. "I forgot you were up there."

"I'm okay," said Jimmy. "It was a soft landing."

"Are you sure?" asked Nancy, giving in to a fit of hysterical giggles.

Jimmy nodded and brushed a handful of petals from his face. "Of course I am."

Ergonwold raised his snout and inhaled. Long, razor-sharp claws extended from his paws. He scratched the earth several times and declared, "I smell the smoke of Zayock."

Nancy sniffed. "I thought the Invisible Valley was protected."

"His machinery is getting the better of us."

"We can do this," said Jimmy, passionately.

"Your enthusiasm will help us in our quest for victory, Jim Jam," replied Ergonwold. "We need the ancient book, Shen Wuu's toys, and, most importantly, we need every ounce of positivity you can muster."

"Let's do it," screamed Nancy.

"Climb onto my back, children," instructed Ergonwold. "We are ready. It is time to leave."

Nancy attached the leather holdall to Ergonwold's collar and scrambled up his back. She pulled her friends up and patted the Great One's neck. "Giddy up!" The glass vials clanged as Ergonwold broke into a canter, while Grizelda whizzed up and down as if she was performing for him, fanning her wings above his tusks, then swooping around his wide frame, her yellow crest gleaming. Nancy gawped at the hot-air balloons flickering in the sky – it was as if they were welcoming the Great One back from hibernation. Ergonwold strode effortlessly across the countless hills of the Invisible Valley, his domed paw prints embedding themselves in the lush floral carpet. They marched on for what seemed like hours, and spoke hardly a word.

In the distance, Nancy spied a bright archway, a white curl punctuating the green and pleasant land. As they drew near, she felt the warmth of its rays. The light was intense, so bright that she shielded her eyes with one hand and grasped Ergonwold's collar with the other.

"The Archway of Love burns brightly," squawked Grizelda.

Ergonwold stopped without warning, and his passengers tumbled over his head, landing in a tangled heap beside a millpond. The Great One lowered his neck, extended his tongue and began to lap. While he was satisfying his thirst, Prema pulled the optical cards from her pocket and dealt three onto *The First Book of Cosmo.*

"Turn them over," said Nancy, urgently.

Prema revealed the cards: the first, a castle sitting high on top of a mountain, its smoke clogging the sky; the second, a portrait of a middle-aged gentleman dressed in parliamentary robes; the third, a chilling image of Captain Carbunkle and Aunt Elma lying dead within The Home For The Incurably Curious. Nancy's smile vanished. She watched as Prema placed her hand on *The First Book of Cosmo* and fell into a deep hypnotic state. Her mouth opened as another voice spoke through her. It sounded familiar to Nancy: older, full of wisdom.

"The cards illustrate past, present and future. Be strong, children. The gentleman in his robes represents the past."

"Lord Bymerstone," whispered Nancy, through clenched teeth.

"Yes," replied Prema's grandmother. "The castle is the present and the death of—"

"My loved ones could be the future," interrupted Ergonwold.

Nancy shook her head. "No. That can't be true…"

Prema came to, unaware of the invasive spirit.

"If we do not find the Bloodstone, the optical cards will ring true," admitted Ergonwold. Nancy was crestfallen, suddenly consumed by a sense of hopelessness. "Your mood changes so quickly," complained Ergonwold, his ears flapping back and forth. "Take a look at the sky, young lady."

Nancy stared at a dark mist swirling high above her. "Where did *that* come from?"

"It's your energy," replied Ergonwold. He curled his snout and gestured at the gathering cloud. "When will you take heed? Every moment of weakness strengthens Zayock's cause. The darkness above you is a beacon for him."

Nancy felt the blood rush to her cheeks. "I'm sorry."

"The cards of Bhopal are accurate, but we have it within us to change the outcome. We are about to leave the safety of the Invisible Valley, when we walk through the Archway of Love…" Ergonwold let out an exasperated sigh. "Once we are on the other side of the arch, Zayock will be alerted. His senses are strong."

Grizelda clucked and crowed, "Can we rely on The Chosen One to be strong within her mind?"

"Yes," snapped Nancy.

"Control your anger," pleaded Prema.

Nancy cocked her head. The cloud had expanded into a large black mass, a dark thought manifesting way above her, its roots invisible, but somehow connecting body and sky. "I'm ready," she said. "I *will* control my feelings."

"All is well," said Ergonwold, softly. "I suggest we speak plainly prior to walking through the archway." The Great One paced up and down, beams of white light forming an angelic glow behind his enormous frame. "Once there was a wonderful human being by the name of Lord Bymerstone—"

"We know this story," interrupted Nancy.

"Manners," squawked Grizelda.

"Sorry."

Ergonwold continued. "Lord Bymerstone was blessed with the gift of crossing freely between the two realms of Earth and Enerjiimass. Unfortunately, he took a wrong turn on the road of life." He looked Nancy in the eye. "It can happen to anyone at any time. We are all vulnerable."

"Some people follow family traits," clucked the parrot.

"What is *that* supposed to mean?" asked Nancy.

Ergonwold intervened. "Enough, Grizelda."

The children sat in the glare of the arch as Ergonwold continued: "Lord Bymerstone had a precious stone given to him."

"By whom?" asked Nancy.

"I think we both know the answer to that, Nanny Bo, don't we?"

Nancy gave a reluctant nod.

Prema and Jimmy exchanged an empty stare.

"It was me," admitted the Great One. "I gave it to him. It is my biggest regret. My personal failing." Then he shook himself and listened to the vials jangle on his collar. "These glass tubes should encase the vital ingredients of Enerjiimass and aid my magical powers. Zayock stole the Bloodstone, emptied the bottle of healing liquid, then sent me to my frozen slumber."

Nancy pointed at the tube containing the white stone. "Why didn't he take that one?"

"Ah, the Wisdom Stone," sighed Ergonwold. "Removing the Wisdom Stone from my neck is almost impossible. It can only be released when all wisdom and knowledge is passed over to the next guardian of Enerjiimass. A regeneration."

There was a moment's silence as Nancy digested the information. "What's a regeneration?"

Ergonwold ignored her. "Zayock wants to live forever. He craves the Elixir of Life. He tried to remove the Wisdom Stone, but failed – the protection charm scorched him. He escaped with the healing liquid and the Bloodstone. He keeps them under lock and key. Without the Bloodstone, my power to wrestle Enerjiimass back from Zayock will be impossible."

"Imagine," exclaimed Jimmy, "a man that evil living forever."

"A sobering thought, Jim Jam," mused Ergonwold. "The Elixir of Life is a complex potion to make, but if he is successful—"

"He won't be," interjected Nancy. "We will find the Bloodstone."

"Thank you," said Ergonwold. "I appreciate your optimism."

Nancy inclined her head and smiled. "Who gave *you* the Bloodstone?"

"Patrem," replied Ergonwold.

"Who?"

Ergonwold raised his snout and proudly repeated the word. "*Patrem.*" Nancy echoed the name internally and waited for the Great One to continue. "I am the third keeper of the Bloodstone, Nanny Bo. I am of a bloodline that had no say in the matter. I, like you, am The Chosen One of my realm. Unlike you, Nanny Bo, I can only exist within this world and no other. I possess no hate, greed, or malevolence. All I desire is the well-being of others. I can only rest when good outweighs evil."

Nancy stared at Ergonwold's heaving chest. "Where has it gone?" she asked, puzzled.

"You do not miss a trick, young lady," chuckled Ergonwold. "My white heart will return if we locate the Bloodstone. If we do not…" Ergonwold paused, trying not to affect the atmosphere with his words. "If we fail in our attempt to regain the Bloodstone, I will die within three of your Earth days."

Nancy's bottom lip quivered. "No…" As the word left her mouth, the cloud above her magnified.

"Look," crowed Grizelda. "Her mood returns to haunt us. The dark clouds grow – she may as well call out to Zayock."

Shame rained down upon Nancy. Controlling her emotions was a battle she often lost. And this was one defeat too many. She covered her face and stewed in her sorrow.

"You are a selfish fool," squawked Grizelda. "Be off with you. Let us find the Bloodstone alone. Go back to Cortillian and await your fate. Cross your fingers, say a prayer, go find a four-leaf clover – you are of no use to us."

"Enough!" roared Ergonwold. He stood resolute in front of the gleaming archway. "Nanny Bo, you need to confront your weaknesses and master them before you pass through this archway." Nancy peered at Ergonwold between the gaps of her fingers. "Show yourself," instructed the Great One. "We are on the brink of a perilous journey. It will be wasted if you cannot control your thoughts and feelings."

Nancy slid her hands down and faced the creature. "I understand. I *will* try harder. I promise."

Ergonwold's oval eyes shimmered. He expelled a jet of air through his snout and boomed, "A promise is an oath, Nanny Bo."

Nancy raised her arm and presented Ergonwold with two crossed fingers. "I know."

"You succumb too quickly to the worst possible imaginings. I know that it's your way of coping – maybe a family trait – but shake this weakness from yourself. Let it go."

This moment defined Nancy's short life. Her upbringing had not prepared her for this. She had always relied on her parents to discern right and wrong. Now, something inside was speaking to her, an unrecognisable voice, one that had faith in the future. From her birth, her mother had only instilled cynicism and continual warnings: "Something will go wrong, so be prepared for it," or, "Someone will let you down, so trust no one." To top it all, Bessy Jones would crush any hopes and dreams her daughter dared to mention. Nancy knew it was time to free herself from her mother's failings. She sat down, closed her eyes and focused. The radiant heat of the archway strengthening her resolve. *I love you, Mum, but I want to be different. I am different.*

When she opened her eyes, it was to a whole new world.

Ergonwold waddled through the Archway of Love, his rich, velvet voice calling out to The Chosen One, "You are strong in spirit – now walk free..."

Nancy watched as the dark clouds of negativity fizzled from the sky. She felt lighter, as if she could float – an emotional weight removed from within. She raised her forearm and waited for Grizelda to land.

The parrot clawed herself up onto Nancy's shoulder and clucked, "Is The Chosen One ready?"

"I was born ready," beamed Nancy. Then she linked fingers with Jimmy and Prema and pulled them through the Archway of Love.

20
The Engine Room

An icy hand grabbed The Duke and Elijah. Long, sharp fingernails scratched their necks as they were pulled to their feet. Fragments of the gargoyle's head lay scattered amongst the gravel. At the foot of the mountain, a dozen slimy Jagganath were bowing before their master. Rain teemed down from the heavens as forks of lightning sparked the darkness into brief moments of light. The Duke opened his mouth, but the howling wind drowned out his feeble voice.

Zayock dragged the boys inside the castle and bolted the doors.

They stood within a large rectangular lobby that ran the entire width of the mountain. Narrow flights of steps were carved into the four corners. The tip of the mountain had been hollowed out, creating a strange, vaulted, angular ceiling. Burning tallows hung from the walls, their flames dancing as the wind blew through rows of slatted windows. A twisted snake was chiselled into the flagstone floor, its green-jewelled pupil glistening in the firelight. The Duke was convinced he could hear structural groans from below, as if a wounded monster were imprisoned in a far-off dungeon. On the wall opposite him was a velvet tapestry, its golden embroidery and tassles dazzling to the eye. It was enormous, impossible to ignore. A statement of intent that read: *Forever is not long enough.*

The Duke thought briefly about the prospect of eternity, a never-ending path of routine and monotony. His eyes shifted from the elaborate material to the flying compass buzzing around Zayock's shoulder. "What do you want with us?" he asked.

Zayock's evil eye devoured the boy from top to bottom.

The Duke tried again. "Why have you brought us here?"

Zayock opened his pocket and clicked his fingers. The wings of the compass retracted and fell within. The Duke stood firm, maintaining eye contact with the sorcerer. Zayock rolled his eyes and tutted. "Welcome to Enerjiimass. I placed a message in a bottle many years ago to warn that girl off." The Duke remained tight-lipped as the sorcerer paced up and down, the sound of his boots reverberating around the lofty hallway. "She comes to undo what I have done," said Zayock, "but the stone was given to me. It is mine. All mine!"

"What stone?" asked The Duke, confused.

Zayock circled the boys, his stride widening. "No one can say I didn't warn them. I have done all I can to stop bloodshed, but no one listened. How dare she come here uninvited." Zayock slammed his fist on a large table in the centre of the room. "The Bloodstone belongs to me. I will destroy her bloodline. And you are the greatest bait any fisherman could have."

The Duke shrugged and repeated, "Bait?"

"Quiet!" barked Zayock. "My magic compass brought you here. Now, you will bring her to me. She will come and I will strike."

Zayock spun on his heels, his cape trailing behind him as he made his way down a flight of stairs.

Elijah turned to his friend. "Let's run."

"No point," replied The Duke. "We're surrounded. I'm starting to think we are just tiny cogs in a machine that's serving something we know nothing about."

"I don't know what you mean."

The Duke's lips hardly moved. "He wants to kill Nanny Bo."

"Don't be silly," replied Elijah. "She's probably found her way home by now."

The clapping of Zayock's soles as he entered the lobby hushed the boys. He placed two bowls of soup in the middle of the table and grunted, "Eat. I need you alive. For the time being, anyway."

The Duke's momentary smile at the mention of being kept alive morphed into a look of horror. He froze, mouth open, clutching his spoon as if his life depended on it.

Zayock barked his orders once more. "I said eat!"

The boys frantically slurped their dinner. Zayock threw a loaf onto the table. "Here, have some bread. You need energy for your work."

The boys tore into the bread like savages.

Zayock twitched with nervous anxiety, clawing at his pimples and mumbling a strange, incoherent dialect. The Duke shovelled the soup into his mouth. With every gulp, the churning of machinery from the foot of the mountain grew louder. The walls began to shake. He nudged Elijah and pointed to the corner of the lobby, where wisps of vapour were wafting up the stairwell, creeping into the castle lobby like an autumn fog.

The Duke and Elijah placed their spoons inside their empty bowls and waited for the sorcerer to address them. "I will put you to work in the engine room. One more bottle of Tantibus and my dream will be complete."

"And what if we don't want to work?" asked The Duke.

Elijah closed his eyes.

Zayock grabbed The Duke's throat and lifted him from the floor. "You are in my land and you are my prisoners. Do you really think you have a choice?"

The Duke tried desperately to speak, but his vocal chords were constricted by the hand of the sorcerer. Zayock released his grip and sniggered, his attention drawn to the Aero-Strazmicator. "What is this strange contraption?"

"Our radio," said Elijah, cautiously. "We love music."

Zayock huffed as he walked across the hallway towards a flight of spiral steps. "Music is the language of artists," he spat, "and most of them are weak-willed fools. Ambition will always bite the nails of success."

"Music is what feelings sound like," retaliated The Duke.

Zayock laughed out loud. "Idiot!" Then he pulled a wand from his cloak and muttered, "*Luxous, imperia.*" A bright sphere of light emanated from the tip of his wand. The magician disappeared down the stairwell and roared, "Follow me!"

The boys shuffled across the lobby and peered down the stairwell. The Duke gripped an ivory handrail and descended countless flights of steps. Reluctantly, Elijah followed. The heat and pungent smell of mechanical fumes clogged their lungs. The stairs spiralled further and further into the belly of the mountain; skulls of ancient goats greeted them at every intersection. The Duke stared at a set of twisted horns as he passed Level Seven. He was convinced there was a light flickering behind the skull. They descended another three floors before Elijah paused for breath. The Duke pulled him along, fearful of Zayock's impatience. They continued, step after step, passing dozens of hollowed skulls, the craggy walls splicing their garments. The lower they descended, the noisier it became – grinding, churning, steam valves hissing. As they approached the final flight, The Duke retched, the industrial emissions and gases stimulating his nausea. He gripped the handrail and stumbled down the last three steps.

Two purple doors greeted them at the foot of the stairwell. They were joined by a magnificent golden crested Z. Zayock tapped the lock with his wand and smiled with satisfaction as the bolts released themselves.

Slowly, the doors creaked open and a great chamber was revealed.

A machine large enough to power a steamship took centre stage. The noise was deafening. Chrome pipes ran up, down, sideways, and looped back on each other like metallic spaghetti. Four huge pistons jumped in and out of time with one another as jets of black smoke were pumped into an extractor that propelled it to the far corner of the room and into a spherical glass bowl. Droplets of water turned the fumes into a sticky black liquid. The remainder was funnelled off into two separate chambers. The chamber on the left processed the black mist into rows of glass vials, while the chamber opposite was full of scientific instrumentation. A small vent was positioned on the right side of the glass bowl where the smoke escaped, wafting its way up a colossal chimney.

A leather chair sat beside the pistons, its restraining straps dangling, awaiting its next victim. Wires connected the chair to an electronic circuit board that crackled and fizzed.

The Duke was aghast, fear and confusion rooting him to the spot. He fanned his hands and stared misty-eyed at the sorcerer. Zayock looked through The Duke as if he didn't exist and pointed at Elijah. Then he jabbed his finger ominously at the chair.

The mechanical din drowned Elijah's protests. Zayock flicked his wand at the chair and mouthed, "Sit down."

Elijah turned away.

Zayock stepped forward and pushed his wand onto Elijah's temple, communicating silently through the nib of the baton: "If you do as I ask, Elijah Lincoln, no harm will come to you." Elijah returned a tight smile, unable to fathom how he could hear Zayock's voice. "If you want to go home, all you need to do is co-operate."

The Duke yanked Zayock's cape. "Don't hurt him."

Zayock lashed out with the wand. Sparks fizzed past The Duke and scolded the centre console. "Do as you're told, Elijah Lincoln."

Elijah swallowed hard and nodded.

Zayock softened his tone and coaxed Elijah: "Just sit in this chair, and my machine will take away your pain, remove your fears. You will feel free. When your friends arrive, my compass will guide you back to the Tree of Hearts."

Elijah relaxed as he sat submissively in the chair. The Duke tried to gain Elijah's attention, but it was too late. His friend was trapped, and he seemed to want to be. He watched helplessly as Zayock placed a metal skullcap on Elijah and connected a cable to the control panel where the pistons chugged and churned. He strapped his wrists and ankles, then tapped his wand on the buckles.

They locked immediately.

Zayock left Elijah and prodded The Duke's forehead with his wand. "When your friend's troubles are gone, it will be your turn to release your nightmares."

The Duke steepled his fingers and pleaded desperately. "We mean you no harm, sir. Please, leave us be, I beg you."

Zayock pointed his wand at the stricken Elijah. "Soon all of his fear and loathing will be turned into smoke and inhaled by the creatures of Enerjiimass." He spun three hundred and sixty degrees and thrust his wand forward. A white rod of light left the nib and illuminated a dark corner. "Behind this machine is a well, the pistons require water. Pour it into the pipe next to the pressure gauge. And don't spend time trying to free your friend. If you do, your efforts will be wasted and he will die of energy overload. Understood?"

The Duke returned a stiff nod.

"My servant will keep an eye on you. I will return when the moon rests." Zayock retracted the wand and slammed the door behind him.

The Duke pinched sponge from the rim of his pumps and placed it in his ears. Elijah howled in a fit of pain, his negativity now fuelling the machine into a high-pitched mechanical wail. The Duke hugged Elijah in an act of solidarity; he could feel his friend's body being attacked by the surge of electrical current. His muscles were taut, his cropped hair wet with perspiration, and the veins in his neck inflamed against his skin. The pistons bobbed up and down. The quicker they moved, the hotter they became. As the temperature increased, a high-pitched alarm rang out.

The Duke panicked. He sprinted to the pool of water at the rear of the room.

A small bucket was attached to a coil of rope. He threw it in and yanked it up. Water lapped over the edges as he rushed back to the centre of the room where the machine shuddered and smoked. He searched for the pressure gauge. He couldn't see it for looking. Wafts of steam and smoke scalded his face.

"I can do this," hollered The Duke, his eyes darting in every direction as he searched for the elusive pressure gauge. An array of levers, buttons, and switches confronted him. His fingertips danced frantically across them. There, just above the last piston, was the gauge. The tiny arrow within the concealed glass unit pointed at the red section marked 'Overload'. Beside it was a short, plastic pipe.

The Duke poured the water in, stood back, and held his breath. The alarm stopped and the machine returned to its regular speed and momentum. He punched the air and wailed out a triumphant, "Yes!"

From the corner of his eye, he noticed the glass bowl was full to bursting point with a sticky substance. It bubbled and boiled like black porridge. Whatever Elijah was thinking somehow stimulated the machine into making the liquid. The Duke glanced across to his manacled friend, who was now slumped unconscious in the chair, unaware that his fears were halfway up Zayock's chimney and liquidised in the bowl. The Duke walked the perimeter of the engine room, inspecting the intricate workings of the machinery. He passed two white domes marked 'Positive' and 'Negative'. Then, just past a row of transistors, he came to an electronic keyboard plugged into a visual display unit. A piano stool and music stand stood beside it.

He couldn't believe what he saw. *What's a musical instrument doing in here?*

He squeezed past it and ran his fingers across the keys. Finally, he came to a dead end. He had reached the furthest point from the entrance. He squatted, leaned against the wall, and yawned. The Duke's tired limbs ached for rest, but the screaming pistons forced him back to his feet. They churned at full pelt. The valves struggled to keep pace and pressure was building.

Then the alarm sounded.

The room was a violent capsule of noise and fumes. The Duke sprinted to the well, filled the bucket, and poured as much water as he could into the pipe. He sighed with relief as the machine shuddered, then slowed to a respectable rumble. The sudden stillness was beautiful. He pulled the sponge from his ears and sighed.

A gentle prod in his back startled him. "You're new around here."

"Who are you?" yelped The Duke.

"Arnus Pilkus," a gigantic bald man replied. Arnus Pilkus extended his arm to greet The Duke. "Do you not shake hands in your world?" enquired the giant.

The Duke shook the man's little finger with his right hand.

"I mean you no harm," replied the giant, his enormous frame somehow squashed within the confines of the engine room.

"H-h-how on earth did you get in here?" stuttered The Duke.

Arnus Pilkus pointed at the door. "There."

"No way," replied The Duke. "You're too big to fit through that."

"If I crawl through on my hands and knees, I can just about manage it," replied Arnus Pilkus. He ruffled his dungarees and sneezed.

Elijah's eyes split open. "Where am I? What's going on?"

Arnus Pilkus turned his head and smiled. "Your friend is awake." The giant crawled on his stomach from one side of the engine room to the other and found Elijah.

"Aaaagggh! Who-the-heck-are-you?"

The giant's kind smile turned to a shameful wince.

"Please don't hurt me," squealed Elijah.

"It's okay, Eli," said The Duke. "He's friendly."

Elijah wriggled and squirmed in the chair, the restraining buckles tearing his skin. The giant pointed at two pistons rising up from the centre console of the machine. "Calm down. You're making it worse. Zayock's machinery has taken part of you. You need rest."

The Duke stepped closer to his friend. "The more you fret, the more this machine will take from you. It's powered by fear, Eli."

"He's right," added Arnus Pilkus.

"Be calm," pleaded The Duke. "Try to think positive."

"Think positive!" snapped Elijah. "You're not strapped in this chair with a bald giant staring at you."

The Duke tried desperately to convince his friend of the machine's intentions. "The fuel that drives this contraption is your fear. You need to stay up-beat, Eli."

"Correct," interjected Arnus Pilkus. "Shall I release the shut-off valve for you?"

Elijah nodded.

Arnus Pilkus leaned across the control panel and pulled a lever. A jet of steam hissed from the pistons and the machine was disabled. The Duke, satisfied that Arnus Pilkus wasn't going to kill them, thanked the giant and introduced himself at the top of his voice.

"I'm The Duke, and this is my friend Eli."

"No need to shout, Master Duke," replied the giant. "It's nice and quiet now."

The Duke laughed. "Oh, yeah. Sorry."

"That's okay," replied Arnus Pilkus. The giant gave a toothless smile and clapped his hands. "We should be left alone for a while now. Mind you, once the master comes back, I will have to turn that beastly machine back on."

Elijah attempted to free himself from the straps that bound him. "No, not again. It fills my head with darkness."

"When the master returns, I will have to," said Arnus Pilkus. "I will be severely punished if I do not."

"Can you release my friend?" asked The Duke, with a whimsical grin.

"No. I'm sorry. Zayock's magic is incredibly powerful." The giant began to weep, his tears splashing onto the floor, saturating The Duke's feet. "I'm sorry," sniffled Arnus, wiping his nose on the back of his hand. "I'm a traitor, that's what I am – nothing more, nothing less."

The Duke shook the water from his feet and addressed the blubbering giant, "What do you mean, you're a traitor?"

Arnus began to slap himself across the face, his cheeks turning blood red from the violent smacks.

"What are you doing?" cried The Duke. "Stop it at once."

Arnus ignored The Duke and pointed to a slab beneath the chair. The Duke's eyes followed the giant's finger. "What do you want?"

"That," mumbled Arnus. He pointed once more at the slab beneath Elijah's feet. "Lift it up," sobbed the giant. "I'm nothing but a traitor."

The Duke squeezed his nails between the mortar and lifted the slab. "You're no traitor, Arnus." Then he removed a wooden box, and held it aloft.

Arnus Pilkus cowered like a frightened animal, convulsing in a curled-up ball, wailing and whimpering.

"What's the matter?" asked The Duke.

"I am ashamed," replied the giant, sniffing back his tears.

The Duke opened the box and stared at two scrolls of paper.

"What's happening?" asked Elijah. "I can't see a thing. What have you got?"

The Duke unrolled one of the scrolls and held the paper at arm's length. "Wow. It's *beautiful*."

"What is?" replied Elijah. "Let me have a look."

The Duke stared wide-eyed at an oil painting. Large gold-leafed letters edged the margins: 'Ergonwold the Great'. Intricate brushstrokes filled every inch of the parchment, the colours fading into one another, creating a collage of natural beauty. Ergonwold's emerald eyes were at the heart of the picture, and in the background was a tall, skinny blonde girl with corkscrew curls holding a sign: 'Is the power of love worth the pain of loss?'

"She's asking a question," whispered The Duke.

"The teachings of Ergonwold," replied Arnus. The giant struggled to maintain eye contact. "To open up and love someone enriches the soul, but the pain when they pass is excruciating." Arnus paused, wiped his eyes, and added: "Is the power of love worth the pain of loss?"

"Of course it is," replied The Duke. He glanced from Ergonwold to Nancy. "It's Nanny Bo."

"Where?" asked Elijah, his head twisting beneath the metal cap.

The Duke held the artwork in front of his friend. Elijah smiled, his expression momentarily alight with hope.

"You know her?" asked the giant, unable to contain his excitement.

"Yes," replied Elijah.

Arnus Pilkus was astonished. He pursed his lips, kissed his palm and blew it towards the girl in the painting. "She is part of our folklore. Some of the creatures within Enerjimass do not believe she exists. I do. I knew it."

"She is our school friend," said The Duke.

"She is our saviour," enthused the giant. "For the past eleven years every creature in Enerjiimass has been forced into hiding. Zayock's smoke has turned thousands of joyful souls into dejected ones."

"I saw the chimney," exclaimed The Duke. "It's massive."

Arnus went on: "Years ago, *The First Book of Cosmo*—"

"What's that?" interrupted The Duke.

"Our holy scroll, Master Duke," replied Arnus. "It is braided in pure gold and holds the secrets of the universe."

The Duke listened intently, arching his brow as the giant went on: "*The First Book of Cosmo* foretold the coming of The Chosen One. Many didn't believe it. Captain Carbunkle instructed every mother to read the tale of *Ergonwold's Golden Girl* to their newborns." The giant blew his nose and continued: "That painting you hold is stolen from the holy scroll. It is a drawing attached to the fable. Do you know of it?"

"No, sorry," replied The Duke.

Elijah exaggerated a loud yawn. "*Ergonwold's Golden Girl* and The Chosen One? That's just a load of old tosh."

"It is not," countered Arnus, "it is a tale that gives us hope."

"Who is Er-gon-wold?" asked The Duke.

"He was our teacher, our king, the light of the world." The Duke nodded, gesturing for the giant to continue. "He has not been seen alive for more than eleven years, presumed dead by the hand of Zayock."

"Oh, I'm really sorry," said The Duke.

Arnus bowed his head. "So am I, Master Duke. I am the traitor that turned my back on him. I now serve Zayock. I hope and pray for the arrival of The Chosen One." Tears began to well in the corners of the giant's eyes. "Maybe you bring The Chosen One to us?"

The Duke shook his head.

The giant sighed. "Maybe you know where The Chosen One hides?"

The Duke shrugged, uncertain of Nancy's exact whereabouts.

"Maybe the spirit of Ergonwold will return?" Arnus Pilkus raised his brow briefly in expectation, then screwed his face up in defeat.

"Arnus," whispered The Duke.

"Yes."

"We stumbled into this world accidentally. We followed our friend, and that friend just happens to be Nanny Bo. We're lost. We shouldn't even be here."

The giant's thick brow creased.

The Duke busied himself by the centre console, flicking switches and pulling levers. "We have no idea what is happening or why it's happening." Then he kicked the machine as hard as he could, a hot rod of pain arresting his left toe. He hobbled around the room one-legged, cursing Zayock and his machinery until the discomfort finally waned. "We just want to find our friends and go home."

"I could help you find her," said the giant. "Zayock told me Ergonwold was dead, frozen in ice somewhere. That was after he stole something very precious and placed a spell on it."

The Duke pressed a button on the machine and listened to a faint hiss of steam escaping from a valve. "Have you any friends or family, Arnus?"

"I was one of thirteen forest dwellers known as the Giants of Nilpor."

The Duke turned to face the giant, a brief plan of attack forming in his mind. "There are more of you?"

"There were," admitted Arnus. He pulled his knees to his chest and tightened one of his bootlaces. "But now they are gone."

"Oh," said The Duke, his plan defeated in a nanosecond.

Elijah wriggled in the chair, trying desperately to free his limbs. "What happened to them?"

There was an awkward silence before the giant continued. "When Zayock entered Enerjiimass, he was a good man, a respected magician from the Earth realm. He wanted to do good. He wanted to create healing potions. He was a physician. He knew the Elixir of Life could be made within Enerjiimass."

"So, what happened?" enquired The Duke.

"Ergonwold refused to help him. He said it was wrong to search for the everlasting." Arnus paused, his words choking him into a shameful confession. "It was me who convinced Ergonwold to loan Zayock the Bloodstone."

"The what?" asked The Duke.

"A stone so precious it should only be kept around the neck of Ergonwold. It has magical powers and can be used for many things."

"Magical powers?" repeated The Duke, "sounds interesting."

"There is a recipe in *The First Book of Cosmo*. The Elixir of Life. It is Zayock's dream, his never-ending quest," explained Arnus. "Have you seen the tapestry in the lobby?"

"Forever is not long enough," whispered The Duke.

"Precisely," replied the giant. "The recipe is missing. Many Earth-dwellers have crossed the threshold in search of it."

"And no one has found it?" asked Elijah.

"No. They normally perish in the Tunnel of Death. Their hearts are not pure. They seek it for the wrong reasons."

The Duke and Elijah stared at one another. Then the giant pointed to the glass bowl in the corner of the room.

"What is it?" asked The Duke.

"That liquid is the by-product of Zayock's smoke, a cruel substance gleaned from one's darker side." Arnus stared at Elijah. "Let's just say there is a piece of you in there, young man."

"Me?" replied Elijah, startled.

"Yes. Zayock bottles it up. He needs a certain amount to make the—"

"Elixir of life?" interrupted The Duke.

"Correct," replied the giant. "Ergonwold agreed to loan Zayock the Bloodstone because of my lies. It's all my fault."

"Don't be so hard on yourself, Arnus."

"It's true," howled the giant. "Zayock lied to Ergonwold to obtain the stone, and so did I. Zayock said he needed the stone to create an antidote for an incurable disease."

The Duke tilted his head. "And Ergonwold believed him?"

The giant gurgled and sniffed away streams of tears. "Ergonwold had faith in Zayock. He wanted him to return to his own world and help others, but he stayed in Enerjiimass and continued his search for the Elixir of Life."

"He's crazy," said The Duke.

"Yes," confessed Arnus. "He is possessed. Countless years of searching for eternity will do that to a man. It is an obsession that has strangled the life out of him. Some say the Bloodstone sucked away his kindness."

"Kindness? That's got to be some kind of joke," replied The Duke. "He's evil, through and through."

"Ergonwold believes that we are all born as good souls," said Arnus, quietly. "Zayock tried all sorts of dark magic in an attempt to make his own everlasting potion. He tested various concoctions on the Giants of Nilpor. Soon they became ill and eventually died slow and miserable deaths."

"There you go," exclaimed The Duke. "Evil, through and through. And how come you escaped the potions of Zayock?"

The giant looked down at the floor. "I was offered a deal. Help Zayock overturn Ergonwold and live a pain-free life, or die like the others. If I died, who would pass on our story? The Giants of Nilpor would be extinct."

"Oh, I see…"

"I had to serve the new master of Enerjiimass," confessed Arnus. "So, it's obvious. I am a traitor."

The Duke patted the giant's leg. "You were only trying to stay alive."

"I signed a contract with Zayock," the giant continued, his meaty voice now a childish whimper. "My blood was taken and I made an oath."

Arnus pointed to the second scroll in the wooden box.

The Duke unravelled it and read the contract.

I (Arnus Pilkus), forest-dweller of Enerjiimass, hereby agree to serve Zayock. I will obediently maintain all mechanical duties within the engine room and take it upon myself to ensure a constant supply of negative energy is circulated throughout the land on a daily basis. Any optimism within Enerjiimass will be distilled and re-energised through the electric chair.

Any existing Enerjiimass creature found to be following the teachings of the deceased Ergonwold will be brought to 'the chair' and de-energised by me (Arnus Pilkus).

Refusal of duties will be punished by my swallowing a spoonful of Tantibus.

Signed in blood,
Arnus Pilkus.

The Duke shuffled closer to the giant and lowered his voice: "You have put your own people in this chair?"

Arnus nodded, shame forcing his head into his hands. "I witnessed Zayock kill my twelve brothers. The creatures of Enerjiimass were reduced to miserable, soul-less beings, their hopes and dreams drained by a single whiff of Zayock's smoke."

The Duke sat and stewed, his head bowed, his heart heavy. "Why didn't you seek help?"

"Every living soul went to ground," murmured Arnus. "I was petrified. I thought only of myself and, because of my selfishness, I am responsible for the mess we are in today."

The Duke shook his head. "No, you're not."

"Yes, I am," hollered the giant. "And now I'm responsible for you being trapped here."

"You're not to blame," insisted The Duke.

Arnus smiled, revealing the only tooth in his mouth. His eyes glazed over and the lids closed. A protracted silence followed as the giant mumbled and gurgled.

The Duke exaggerated a cough. "Arnus, are you okay?"

"I have a dream," confessed the giant.

"A dream?" repeated Elijah.

"Yes, a dream that will release me from my guilt and captivity. Can I share it with you?"

"Yes, please do," replied Elijah, sarcastically. "I'm not going anywhere."

"I have a dream that our king is still alive."

"Ergonwold," confirmed The Duke.

"Yes," replied Arnus. "Sometimes I can actually feel his energy within me. If I believe it, I actually feel it. In my dream I am forgiven for my lies and The Chosen One is triumphant." Arnus lashed out at the apparatus. "If it came true, this wicked machine would be destroyed."

The giant crawled to the doorway and punched the golden *Z* emblazoned on it. The door was smashed into smithereens, flying off its hinges, and crashing against the mountain wall. He kissed the painting of Ergonwold and held it ceremoniously over his heart.

"Look at the girl in the painting," insisted The Duke. "That's our friend. She will help us. We followed her here. She *does* exist and you *will* be freed. You just have to believe."

"I am ashamed," admitted the giant.

"Why?" asked The Duke.

"I reassured Ergonwold that Zayock wanted to cure the sick. I told him I had witnessed Zayock's new wonder drug, but I hadn't. I lied to Ergonwold the Great." The giant struggled to get the words from his blubbering mouth, then he rubbed his eyes and bawled, "I love Ergonwold."

"And I'm sure he loves you," countered The Duke.

"He is dead because of me."

"And you're certain of that?" asked The Duke.

Arnus nodded. "Yes, Zayock said so."

"Do you trust him?"

A cold draught blew in from the open doorway. The sound of footsteps sent a shiver of fear through The Duke.

Arnus panicked. "The machine needs to be switched on."

"No!" screamed Elijah.

"Yes," growled Zayock, as he entered the room. He brushed past The Duke, kicked his way through the splintered doors, marched towards the back of the room and tapped the glass orb with his finger. "My beautiful *Tantibus*!" Then he twisted a tap and whistled nonchalantly as droplets of the sticky black liquid drizzled into an empty vial. He corked it, held it aloft, and began to laugh. "One more of these and my dream of immortality will be fulfilled."

21
Ergonwold's Nest

Nancy emerged from the Archway of Love and gawped at the sky. Every imaginable colour was stacked on top of the other, layer upon layer: a multi-coloured sandwich of light floating high above her. Her fingertips tingled as she brushed through rows of silvery grasses and her nostrils thrilled to the honeydew scent of Enerjiimass. A broad smile spread across her face as she strolled down a pathway to a derelict shack: four walls constructed from earth and stone supported a half-thatched roof. Strands of hay were sprinkled haphazardly around its outer edges. There was no door, just a wide circular opening.

Inside, the mood changed.

Grizelda's talons were wrapped around Ergonwold's tusks. "It's gone!" cried the parrot.

"What has?" asked Nancy, kicking away mounds of straw as she entered.

"Ergonwold's Nest."

Nancy ignored the angry parrot and inspected the shack. "Is this where you slept, Ergonwold – in a muddy hut?"

"Sort of," yawned the Great One.

"It's gone," shrilled the bird. "It's gone…"

Nancy's interest was now drawn to a circle of stones embedded in the soil. "So you keep saying, Grizelda."

Ergonwold let out another loud yawn as he struggled to stay awake after eleven nestless years in ice. Grizelda fluttered from one tusk to the other, her beady eyes fixed upon Nancy. "If you had taken the time to read the book, maybe you would realise the severity of the situation."

Nancy's hackles were up. "Taken. The. *Time?*"

Prema intervened. "I have taken responsibility for *The First Book of Cosmo.*" She turned to Grizelda, her voice calm and measured. "Nanny Bo has much to think about. She has to remain positive. For all our sakes."

"She needs to try harder," squawked Grizelda.

"I am trying!" screamed Nancy.

Prema gestured for silence. "Stay calm, Nanny Bo."

"That's impossible," said Nancy, her eyes boring into Grizelda's.

"*Please,* Grizelda," begged Prema, clapping her hands to her chest, "be patient with Nanny Bo. *The First Book of Cosmo* was practically invisible prior to crossing over. Since our arrival, she has had little time to read it."

Nancy smirked at the parrot, then blew Prema a kiss and watched as her friend flicked her way through the ancient text, the gilded pages of *The First Book of Cosmo* sparkling as they fanned open. Prema's finger landed on page 565. Letters appeared, one by one, forming words, then sentences. Within seconds an entire page was filled, topped by a new and glistening chapter: 'ERGONWOLD'S NEST AND THE POWER OF RECHARGING'.

Nancy peered over Prema's shoulder as she read the chapter, it was a silent observation of a magical moment. Prema lifted her chin over the book and pointed to the circle of stones. "It was there, wasn't it?"

"Yes," squawked Grizelda.

"What was?" asked Nancy, glancing from the book to Ergonwold and back again.

"Ergonwold's Nest," replied Prema. She walked towards the Great One and stroked his snout. "Your heart must ache."

Ergonwold nodded. "I have two hearts, Miss Sarkander, but my white heart has vanished. If we can put a stop to Zayock's machinery, it will return."

"I understand," whispered Prema.

Ergonwold ambled towards the circle of stones and laid himself within the border. He curled up like a gigantic cat and closed his eyes, a look of contentment spreading from one tusk to the other.

Grizelda flapped her wings and landed beside him. "The Great One is weak. He has led us to this sacred resting place. If he cannot recharge, we must continue without him."

"Why?" asked Nancy. "We've come all the way from The Home For The Incurably Curious." She kneeled beside Ergonwold and rubbed his back. "Ergonwold said he would lead us. He said he would show us the way through Enerjiimass."

"It's all in the book," explained Prema. "This is where Ergonwold was born. His mother and many generations gave birth here. It's a spiritual place."

Nancy stared glassy-eyed at the sleeping beast. "I can feel the love."

"Since time began, there has been a nest here," Prema added. "The book says that beneath the nest a map was buried. It was ripped from *The First Book of Cosmo* for safekeeping. The nest gives Ergonwold his energy and magical powers. If he doesn't sleep on it at the end of each day, he will—"

"What?" gasped Nancy.

"Patience," clucked Grizelda.

Prema turned back to page 565. "Sleeping on the nest at the end of each moon cycle recharges the Great One for the next day." She closed the book and zipped it in the holdall.

"Recharge?" quizzed Nancy. "Like a battery? Come on then, we haven't got all day."

Prema chose her words carefully: "Ergonwold was frozen beneath Cortillian's igloo hut for eleven years."

Nancy scratched her head, unable to fathom the situation. "But if he was sleeping, how can he be tired?"

"It's not about how long he was sleeping, Nanny Bo, but how long it has been since he last recharged his magical powers through the maternal nest."

"You read *The First Book of Cosmo* well," crowed Grizelda. "A scholar."

Nancy rested her head upon Ergonwold's and lifted his ear. "We will find the Bloodstone and your nest. Then you will rise again and live your life like a king. I promise."

"Kind words, young lady," chirped Grizelda. "Now, it is time for you to make the ultimate sacrifice. You know what to do."

Nancy stared at the bird, her pupils dilating as Grizelda left the stony circle and flew in a clockwise direction around the shack. White rays shone from the bird's crest, bathing the muddy hut in a glorious light.

"I am the Reader of Hearts and Minds," sang Grizelda, her yellow crest unfurling. "You know what needs to be done, Nancy Bo Jones. Search your soul."

Nancy's words fell effortlessly from her lips. "A tear-drop removes an ocean of pain."

Handfuls of straw fell from above as the roof yielded to the wind. "It is time," Grizelda cried. "Make your sacrifice and take away Ergonwold's fatigue. Swallow his tear."

Nancy's heart thumped as she watched Grizelda swirl around the shack.

"What shall it be, little girl?" goaded the parrot. "Travel alone or make the sacrifice?"

Nancy placed her right index finger beneath Ergonwold's feathery lashes and whispered, "There is no end to love."

Then a teardrop formed in the Great One's left eye and trickled onto her finger. Nancy raised her hand and opened her mouth. The tear hung like a dewdrop, glistening like a jewel.

Prema dropped the ancient book and raced towards Nancy. She fell to her knees, her mouth wide open beneath Nancy's finger.

"What are you doing?" asked Nancy.

But it was too late. Prema had swallowed the tear. Foam spewed from her mouth, saliva bubbling over her lips as she coughed and gagged.

Nancy embraced her friend. "She's having a fit!"

"Do something!" Jimmy yelled.

But there was nothing they could do. The fit was over as quickly as it had come. Prema fell from Nancy's arms and collapsed next to Ergonwold, her eyes closed, her body paralysed.

"Ergonwold needs to recharge," trilled Grizelda. "This sacrifice will aid his recovery. Let him sleep."

"It should've been me," cried Nancy. "Why did she—"

"You are loved, Nanny Bo," interrupted Grizelda. She flew to Ergonwold's side and clawed herself up onto his enormous back. "Your friends lay their lives down for you. Young Prema wanted to protect The Chosen One."

"Why?"

"So *you* can continue the journey. That is of the utmost importance, all of our futures depend upon that. And Prema knew it."

Nancy placed her hands on Prema's face and kissed her forehead. "But why did you ask *me* to do it?"

"I had to," replied the parrot. "I am forbidden to put the lives of the uninvited at risk. You must overcome this grief. Find the map – it is our only hope."

"What about Pre?" asked Jimmy, anxiously.

Grizelda hopped onto his lap. "Your friend has risked herself for the greater good. The ancient book has enlightened her, Jim Jam. She knows more than she shows. If we are to stop Zayock and his machinery, we need The Chosen One to be with us. If my plan works, Ergonwold and Prema will waken from their slumber."

Jimmy stared at the circle of stones that encased Prema and Ergonwold. "How?"

"Ergonwold's fatigue has been transferred to Prema," explained Grizelda. "It will buy us some precious time. We need to find Ergonwold's Nest and allow him to recharge properly." The white parrot gazed through the rafters, her beady eyes locked on a dark, foreboding cloud. "Prema's body is smaller than Ergonwold's, but if we can wake her, Ergonwold The Great will rise again."

22

The Serpent

Zayock prepared to unleash his fury upon the colossus of Arnus Pilkus. He fumbled within the lining of his cape, pinched a small mound of powder, and sprinkled it on the tip of his wand. With one zap, he sent the toothless giant sprawling across the floor like a rag doll.

"No!" screamed The Duke.

Zayock reached for the lever to engage the machine.

The Duke lunged forward and grabbed the hem of his cape. "Stop! Eli's had enough."

"Get. Your. Hands. Off. Me."

"I feel sick," whimpered Elijah. "Please, I beg you. Not again."

The sight of Elijah begging for mercy troubled The Duke deeply. He had always viewed his friend as the tough guy in school. Now, with the wrath of Zayock bearing down upon him, Elijah was reduced to a gibbering wreck.

"I will do anything," pleaded Elijah. "I just want to go home."

Zayock pulled the lever.

A loud clunking sound echoed and the pistons fired into motion. The room began to shake. The noise was deafening – the hissing of steam and the churning of cogs reminiscent of a mechanical monster coming to life.

Elijah's sobs didn't deter the sorcerer.

"Fantastic," said Zayock. "A crying soul emits so much more sadness. And more sadness means more *Tantibus.*"

The Duke covered his face as Elijah's body shuddered in the chair. He was ashamed of himself, helpless, set aside as a morbid spectator in a game of torture, his will to fight evaporating by the second, his mind now dark and sorrowful.

"Just a few minutes of extraction will give me enough smoke to smother Berringer Hill," squealed Zayock. "Finally, I'll have done with those interfering Night Fairies." He strutted towards a map of Enerjiimass and marked a cross over Berringer Hill. He was about to infect the entire landscape in a cloud of smoky negativity. Beside him, Arnus Pilkus lay flat on his back, twitching, coughing, and spluttering, struggling to fill his lungs with air, his body singed by the wand, his eyes fixed on a sheet of paper beneath Zayock's sole. He reached agonisingly for it.

Zayock lifted his boot. "What is this, you pathetic creature?" He grabbed the parchment, his bug eyes glaring at the painting as he held it to the light, his tongue skimming over his lips, his nostrils flaring at the sight of Ergonwold and Nancy Bo Jones.

The Duke slumped against the machine as Zayock inspected the painting. It was as if someone had disturbed a nest of vipers. Zayock cleared his throat and spat at the artwork. Then he ripped it in two. "I can't think with this noise!" He flicked a switch, pushed a button, and pulled a lever.

The pistons stopped and Elijah slumped forward as the machine faltered.

"How dare you worship this filth?" growled the sorcerer. "After all I have done for you, Arnus Pilkus." He paced frantically between the machinery, scratching his chin, his sharp fingernails drawing blood from a wart. "My search for the everlasting will not stop. You, Arnus Pilkus, have a light in your heart for my enemy. For this reason, I no longer trust you."

The Duke winced as Zayock kneeled beside the trembling giant and pulled a glass vial from his pocket. He popped the cork and sniggered as a thick black substance oozed from the tube.

Arnus Pilkus closed his eyes and covered his mouth. "No. Not that."

"Leave him alone," pleaded The Duke. He crawled towards the giant and begged for mercy: "Please, Mr Zayock. He is a troubled soul. Leave him be."

Zayock raised his wand. "Stay where you are," instructed the sorcerer. Then he climbed onto the giant's chest and pushed his thumb and forefinger into his mouth. "Do you remember our contract?"

Arnus nodded.

"You signed it in blood," declared the sorcerer. He forced the giant's mouth open and lowered his voice. "A spoonful of Tantibus – that's your punishment." Zayock tapped the bottle with his wand. "Open wide, Arnus. Be a good boy."

Droplets of the black liquid trickled into the giant's mouth.

"Swallow!" ordered Zayock.

Arnus writhed and groaned in a final attempt to free himself, but the nib of the wand forced him into submission. He raised his head and swallowed the Tantibus. A wild and uncontrollable convulsion followed.

The Duke choked back tears as he witnessed the defenceless giant shudder and jerk. Foam spewed from his mouth, his huge face now blood red, veins popping from beneath his skin, his body contorting in muscular spasms as the Tantibus filled his gut and poisoned his soul.

Then it was over. Arnus Pilkus lay perfectly still.

"It is done," whispered Zayock. "Punishment inflicted. Life over."

Then, with a final burst of energy, Arnus lifted himself.

Zayock stepped back, dumbfounded by the giant's resilience. "Impossible…"

"I love Ergonwold!" screamed Arnus at the top of his voice. He wobbled, pushed the palms of his hands together, then collapsed next to The Duke. Zayock breathed a huge sigh of relief, kissed his wand, then skipped towards the electric chair. He unbuckled the restraining straps and released Elijah.

The Duke cradled the massive head of Arnus Pilkus. He was overcome with emotion, lost in a sea without a sail, tears rolling down his cheeks and falling onto the giant's face. He was beaten, ready to surrender his last morsel of hope. He stroked the giant's heavy brow and prepared himself for the end.

Arnus opened one eye and then the other.

The Duke's lips curled, a flicker of hope sparking his heavy heart. He pinched the giant's cheeks and winked. Arnus shivered in The Duke's arms. His limbs twitched, his words were faint, nothing more than a breathless whisper. "The Bloodstone, tonic, and key are beneath the serpent," groaned the giant. "Use them wisely, Master Duke, and drink the liquid if your mind is troubled. It will help."

The giant's chest expanded, before he stuttered, "Break the curse. Break the curse."

"What do you mean?" asked The Duke, quietly.

"You must break the curse before you touch them. *Incanta, Malouchia.*"

Arnus Pilkus closed his eyes for the last time.

The Duke screamed at Zayock, "What have you done to him?"

Zayock spun on his heels and faced the crying boy. "Given him what he deserved – death." He placed his wand in the lining of his cape, lifted the half-conscious Elijah from the chair, and traipsed out of the engine room.

The Duke stared at Arnus Pilkus. It was the first dead person he had ever seen. He grabbed the Aero-Strazmicator and followed Zayock up the cold, damp stairwell, not wanting to lose sight of his friend. A long, arduous, painful climb was interspersed by the sorcerer's growls of fury and frustration – a sermon of anger and pain. When they reached the lobby, Zayock threw Elijah to the floor.

The Duke sat beside his friend and prayed it wasn't the second dead person he'd see that day. Zayock hauled The Duke from Elijah's side and dragged him towards the table. "Eat. My machine needs you alive." He swiped his wand, sparks bouncing off the mountain walls, fizzing around the castle like fireworks. The Duke shielded himself from the bolts. Finally, the rods of light fizzled to nothing. "Your friend served me well today," announced Zayock. "And you are next. When the sun rises, you will be strapped into the chair." He squeezed his head through a window and peered down at the army of Jagganath at the foot of the mountain. The tallest and slimiest of the beasts howled at the sight of its master. A satisfied grin lit Zayock's face. "My children – trustworthy, adoring beasts that serve me well. My Centurion and his foot soldiers patrol the entire landscape around this mountain range. There is no escape."

The Duke stuffed two lumps of bread into his mouth. All he wanted was to sleep, and to wake from this living nightmare. He watched helplessly as Zayock dragged Elijah up a short flight of steps to a spherical room where a balcony overlooked the castle lobby.

"Come here," shouted the sorcerer.

The Duke continued to fill his stomach.

Zayock stepped out onto the balcony and peered down at the boy. "You!"

"What?" replied The Duke, between mouthfuls of bread and glugs of water.

"I said *get up here.*"

This time, The Duke obeyed. He sprinted up the steps, leaped onto the balcony, and gazed down at the lofty hallway.

From here, it was a formidable yet majestic view, a natural extension of the mountain with no visible join, the impressive castle doors glaring at him: his gateway to freedom. Then he lowered his sights. He couldn't believe what he saw. A huge snake carved into the flagstones, its emerald eyes dazzling in the glare of the burning tallows. The Duke's heart sprung into his mouth, his head giddy with excitement. He left the balcony and entered the concave room, where a small fire crackled in an iron grate.

Zayock ruffled his cape and pointed at two crumpled rugs. The Duke sat on one. "If your breathing stops…" muttered the magician.

"Y-yes?" stuttered The Duke.

Zayock reached for a jar of red berries. "Take one of these."

The Duke nodded his appreciation. "Thank you."

"You can't escape," said Zayock, forcefully. "So don't waste your energy trying. I will return at dawn." He trotted back down the steps, slammed the castle doors shut and slid three bolts into position.

The Duke curled up and closed his eyes, while visions of Arnus Pilkus kept him company as the firewood spat and crackled. Moments later, his sleep was interrupted by the sound of Elijah's strains. His friend was attempting to squeeze his head through the angular windows. "What are you doing, Eli?"

"Looking at the chimney. I've never seen anything like it. It's huge."

The Duke nodded. "I know."

"There's tons of smoke," said Elijah, between coughs. "It's clogging the sky."

"He's poisoning every soul with his own woe."

Elijah puckered his face. "I don't understand. It's only smoke."

"Oh, it doesn't matter," replied The Duke, mindful of Elijah's fragile spirit.

Within seconds, they were both sound asleep. Dreams flooded The Duke's headspace, he tossed and turned as a familiar voice came to him. "*The Bloodstone and key are beneath the serpent. If your mind is troubled, drink the tonic.*"

"Arnus, is that you?" asked The Duke, rubbing his blood-shot eyes. "Arnus, are you there?"

Elijah's eyelids flickered. "What did you say?"

The Duke sat up. "I heard a voice."

"You must be dreaming," said Elijah. "Go back to sleep."

"But I just heard Arnus!"

Elijah sat up, his fingers pointing to the depths of the engine room. "Impossible, Duke. He's down there."

"Yes, you're right, Eli. It is impossible… Arnus is dead."

Elijah's eyes widened. "What did you say?"

"Zayock killed him. You were out cold. Unconscious."

"Dead?" whispered Elijah. "Are you sure?"

"I'm afraid so."

"Oh my—"

"We have to find the Bloodstone and key," interrupted The Duke.

"What do you mean?"

"There is a serpent carved into the lobby floor."

"A what?"

"A serpent.

"What's a serpent?"

The Duke wriggled his forearm and hissed. "It's a snake, you dimwit. Arnus told me I would find a key, a stone, and some sort of tonic beneath it."

"Nonsense," replied Elijah. "I'm not roaming around down there. If we're caught, Zayock will kill us."

The Duke held the Aero-Strazmicator aloft and shook it. "Eli, we have this box to lead us back to our own world. If we can get out of this castle, we're home and dry." He pressed two buttons and held his breath in anticipation of sound.

Silence.

"That machine is rubbish," grumbled Elijah. "There's no escape. No hope. I can't sit in that chair again."

"All the more reason to try and get out of here," replied The Duke, prodding his temples. "Once my mind is as negative as yours, we may as well join the Jagganath."

Elijah laughed. "You already look like one of them."

The Duke smiled. He pulled his friend to his feet, grabbed a handful of air berries and bellowed, "Come on, let's take a look. Zayock won't be back till dawn."

Elijah glared at The Duke. "If I hear anything, I'm coming right back."

"Of course," said The Duke, with a bright smile, his reassuring tone soothing Elijah's nerves. He threw Elijah an air berry, stood on tiptoes, and looked out of the window. The Jagganath circled the castle grounds, grunting and groaning like hungry pigs. In the distance were the multi-coloured hills of Enerjiimass. They looked beautiful – a neon feast for The Duke's eyes. The mountain range was the polar opposite: cold, ugly, and surrounded by ribbons of smoke. He stepped back and sighed audibly. "She's out there somewhere."

"Who?" asked Elijah.

"Nanny Bo. Who did you think I meant?"

"Oh, yeah, sorry," replied Elijah. He hopped out onto the balcony and gripped the handrail. "Nanny Bo and the others seem like another time and another place. I can't help but think of the here and now."

"Think positive," said The Duke; "it's the only way."

Elijah peered down at the chiselled serpent. "The trouble is," he said, "I can only think positively when everything is okay."

"That's easy," laughed The Duke. "To be optimistic when things are going against you is the real challenge. If you can do that, it'll make you a great man." He paused, placed an arm on Elijah's shoulder and went on. "You *must* stop thinking the worst, Eli."

"I know."

"Nanny Bo is out there, and I'm certain she is looking for us. I'm absolutely convinced of it."

"It's my fault we're here," admitted Elijah. "I knew we should have followed Nanny Bo. Maybe they are safe. Maybe they're already home and dry."

The Duke rolled his eyes. "Maybe this, maybe that. The truth is, we don't actually know. Try not to think the worst of Nanny Bo. Sometimes I think you hate her."

"Well, not really," Elijah confessed. "I think she is quite nice."

"Quite nice?" said The Duke, in a state of shock. Then, as the silence passed, he nudged Elijah and winked.

Elijah blushed, his words sticking in his throat: "Well… you know… she's very…"

"What?" asked The Duke, holding back a smile.

"Pretty," whispered Elijah. "She's different. I like that."

"I don't get you, Elijah Lincoln."

"What?"

"You know what," said The Duke, gesturing furiously at his friend. "If you like her, why are you so nasty to her?"

"I don't know. Maybe I'm jealous of her."

The Duke stared at Elijah and waited for him to continue.

"When she turned up at Oakwell, everyone was fascinated by her. It annoyed me."

"Why?"

"She was new. And she got all the attention. Her clothes were different – her accent, her attitude, everything about her was different. I wanted to be with her, but I didn't know how to tell her. Whenever I spoke, what I said wasn't what I meant."

The Duke held his head in his hands. "That's a shame."

"Yeah, it is," replied Elijah. "I always get it wrong, don't I?"

"You're not that bad," said The Duke, softly. He peered down at the serpent and sighed. The snake stared back, its green eyes

237

sparkling like mysterious gems. The Duke didn't hesitate: he left the balcony and scampered down the stairs into the lobby, his thoughts returning to the dying words of Arnus Pilkus.

The Bloodstone is beneath the serpent. If your mind is troubled, drink the tonic.

"What are you doing?" hollered Elijah, from the safety of the balcony.

"Searching," replied The Duke, his finger prodding the air as he counted the heavy slabs on which the serpent was carved. Each one was mortared to the next, creating a grid from one end of the lobby to the other. "I might need some help lifting these slabs." The Duke placed the Aero-Strazmicator on the floor and curled a finger. "Come and help me…"

Elijah stepped forward, then hesitated.

"Come on, it's all right," insisted The Duke. Elijah tiptoed reluctantly down the steps, his body rigid with fear, his eyes flitting from side to side. The Duke summoned his friend once more. "Hurry up, we haven't got all night."

Elijah shuffled across the lobby floor and stood shoulder to shoulder with his friend. "This castle spooks me…"

"And me," whispered The Duke. He pushed his fingers between the solid mortar that joined two slabs. "It has to be here somewhere. Come on, Eli, lend a hand."

Elijah used all his might as he tried to lift one of the flagstones. He groaned with frustration as his fingers searched for a loose edge. Every slab seemed fixed, set rigid. "We don't have a hope in hell of lifting one of these."

The Duke's cheeks ballooned as he tried another slab. "Typical," he puffed. "We've only tried five and you've already given up."

Elijah attempted to lift another. There was no movement. He tried the next one. Nothing. The entire floor appeared to be one solid mass. Then The Duke shuffled himself over to the slab adjacent to the serpent's emerald eye. He wedged his thumb and forefinger between the slabs and strained. "Argh, it's fixed solid."

Elijah ran his thumb along a line of mortar and found a crack. He pushed his fingers in and lifted. "It's. Stuck. Duke. I. Can't. Move. It." He fell back, spreading his hands to cushion the fall. Something sharp nestled against his palm. Elijah lifted his hand and stared inquisitively at the green-eyed jewel.

"Press it," said The Duke, enthusiastically. "Go on. Press the eye…"

Elijah placed his finger on the jewel and pushed it down.

There was a dull clunk, followed by a loud grinding noise.

"Amazing," hollered The Duke. "The eye is the access button." He punched the air as four slabs slid open, revealing a sunken chamber. He leaned over and peered into a dark recess. "Maybe it's a way out."

Elijah edged closer to the opening, his teeth chattering with anxiety. The Duke was unable to contain his excitement. "Come on, this is our chance. It looks like a way out of here. Our way home."

"What happens if Zayock comes back?" asked Elijah, his eyes darting to the castle doors, then back to the subterranean chamber.

The Duke eyeballed his friend. "Are you joking? Do you want to stay here and wait for him?"

"Well, maybe it's best—"

"Are you mental?" interjected The Duke. He peered down into the dark void, his imagination running wild. "We need to investigate." Then he grabbed Elijah's wrist and yanked him forward. "When I count to three, we jump down. Okay…"

Elijah had little choice. "Okay."

The Duke drew breath, "One, two…"

"What if there's no ground beneath us?" interrupted Elijah. "We could be jumping to our death."

"Do you remember Cortillian's igloo hut?" asked The Duke with a sardonic grin. He raised a hand to his brow and squinted. "I can see a tiled floor. We won't die jumping down a few feet."

Elijah threw his arms up and conceded. "All right, I'm game."

"Get ready," said The Duke. He squeezed Elijah's fingers and counted: "One, two, three."

They jumped into the darkness. The four slabs slid back into position and an eerie silence returned to the castle lobby.

23
The Floral Stretcher

Nancy stood over Prema's lifeless body. She swept away a tear and fell into Jimmy's arms. "She's dead."

"She sleeps," retorted Grizelda, "and she will be safe here, but we must leave. Your anxiety is strong. The dark clouds are gathering. Your mood will alert Zayock."

"I'll carry her," said Jimmy, cradling his arms.

"Stop," squawked Grizelda. "Prema needs to be moved with caution. She carries the tear of the Great One within her. And the Great One carries the weight of the world within him. She is fragile. She has removed Ergonwold's fatigue and needs rest."

"What are we going to do?" asked Jimmy, his nerves at breaking point.

Grizelda perched herself on Ergonwold's tusk. "There is a young man who lives in the hills of Sanitatum. He was trained by Zayock in the art of potion-making."

Nancy recoiled in pain. "Zayock's an evil so and so."

"Maybe," conceded Grizelda. "But there has never been one so brilliant at concocting a potion. Zayock is the finest, and his young apprentice is our only hope. He alone has the skill of making a potion strong enough to wake Prema."

"We need to find him," exclaimed Jimmy.

"Yes," clucked Grizelda. "If we find him we can wake Prema. Her new energy will transmit to Ergonwold and then—"

"Then we can find the Bloodstone and Ergonwold's Nest," interrupted Jimmy. His round face flushed red as his excitement got the better of him.

"But we need the map," added Nancy. "If we find it…," she trailed off, her vision glued to the text of the ancient book.

"Yes?" crowed Grizelda.

"We can use it to navigate to Sanitatum."

"Correct," replied the parrot. "We need to dig beneath the stolen nest and retrieve the map. If we find the potion-maker, Ergonwold will rise." Grizelda paused. "For a while, anyway."

Nancy narrowed her eyes. "What do you mean?"

"We have little time," clucked Grizelda. "Energy transfer is old magic. I'm confident Ergonwold will wake if Prema does."

"Why do we need to waste time digging for a map when you can fly us to Sanitatum?" asked Nancy, flapping her arms like makeshift wings.

"Just dig," snapped Grizelda.

Nancy crossed her arms and persisted: "But you carried us up onto that cliff. Remember?"

"Dig!"

Nancy refused. "Why?"

"Because I said so."

Jimmy mediated: "Prema is our friend. We can't leave her behind."

"Yes," said Nancy, resolutely. She stood firm, her anger simmering, her eyes following Grizelda as she hopped off Ergonwold's tusk and clawed her way around the circle of stones.

"We are short of time," said the parrot. "If we do not find the Bloodstone, Ergonwold only has three days to live."

Nancy moved closer to the parrot. "If you don't care for Prema, do this for Ergonwold."

"Not care for Prema?" cheeped Grizelda. "Quite the opposite. She is a rare breed, and I do not plan on leaving her here. She is a perfectly good soul."

Nancy whispered, "I know," then raised her forearm.

Grizelda landed and brushed her crest against the tip of her nose. "I was a young chick when I left Enerjiimass, Nanny Bo. I know this land well, but not as well as you would like. My inner strength comes from Ergonwold. He sleeps, and because of this, I am weak." Grizelda ruffled her feathers and let out a great sigh. "Without him, I am as lost as you. He is my energy. My light. Enerjiimass is a vast place; we need the map. It is my responsibility to read hearts and minds – that is all."

"I understand," said Nancy. She stroked Grizelda's chest and murmured, "You are hurting."

Grizelda lowered her bill. "Yes, and you are so young. I worry that your mood is fragile. The dark clouds above are a terrible sign." Grizelda left Nancy's arm and landed within the circle of stones. "Zayock will see us before we see him."

"No, he won't," said Nancy. "We are in this together, so let's dig together. You should be proud of yourself, Grizelda. Without you, we would have had no hope." She gave a sideways glance at Jimmy and winked.

Jimmy marked a cross in the earth and yelled, "Let's dig!"

"Let me start," insisted Grizelda. "My talons are sharp."

Nancy and Jimmy stood back and watched as the parrot made light work of the earth. Her legs moved furiously as clumps of earth flew through the air. Soon, Grizelda had dug down beyond the depth of her body.

Jimmy stepped forward. "Take a break." He cupped his hands and began to spoon the loose earth. Faster and faster he moved his arms, puffing, panting, and dripping with perspiration. Just as he began to tire, Nancy peered down at the crater. "I can see it."

"I can feel it," Jimmy added, his fingertips scratching against crumpled paper. He pulled out a tatty, mud-stained map.

Grizelda flapped and chirped, "We can continue our journey."

Jimmy rubbed the dirt from his hands. "I knew we would find it."

"We need to transport Prema to Sanitatum," said Grizelda. "We have far to travel. We need to make a stretcher."

"How?" asked Jimmy, wiping his muddy brow.

"Branches and leaves," crowed the bird.

Nancy and Jimmy sprinted out of the hut and began pulling branches from nearby shrubs and trees. They placed layers of leaves upon a lattice of branches. Grizelda wove them together with a combination of willow and vine. It didn't take long before a bed of leaves was assembled.

Nancy lifted the makeshift stretcher and ran back inside the shack. "Be very careful," instructed Grizelda. "If we wake Prema, she will not have the energy to live. She is safe and well protected within her coma."

Nancy stroked the parrot. "What shall we do?"

"When I say so, roll Prema onto the stretcher."

"Okay," replied the children. Nancy placed her hands on Prema's back, while Jimmy cushioned her head.

"Easy does it," crowed Grizelda. "Now, be gentle; roll her forward."

As Nancy pushed against Prema's spine, Jimmy guided her body onto the stretcher. Twigs and branches supported her slender frame, and bundles of lush green leaves cushioned her head.

Nancy grabbed the leather holdall. "What about the bag? We might need it."

"Leave it for the Great One. If he wakes, he will bring it."

"What if he doesn't?"

"Put it down, Nannny Bo," instructed Grizelda. "The bag is of no use unless Ergonwold rises. Our lives depend upon his second coming."

Nancy dropped the bag and strained as she lifted the leafy stretcher. "One step at a time, Jim Jam."

Slowly and very carefully they carried the stretcher out of the shack. Nancy cocked her head and observed the turbulent sky. A warm, comforting sensation tickled her insides as cracks of light pierced the dark clouds like spikes of hope. Grizelda swooped off into the distance, looping, clucking, and crowing. Their journey to Sanitatum had begun.

Nancy's steps were measured and cautious; occasionally her long strides would force Jimmy to break into a trot. Soon they found a rhythm and pace that ensured their sleeping passenger remained undisturbed. Nancy couldn't help but laugh as the eccentric parrot, with the map dangling from her claws, performed in the neon sky like a feathered acrobat, weaving her way through dozens of hot-air balloons. She let out a high-pitched squawk as a trail of white dots appeared on the tatty paper: it was a dot-to-dot magical guide of their environment.

Reading the map was easy. Finding the energy to walk was hard. Nancy's legs cramped just as Jimmy's arms began to wane. They lowered the stretcher gently to the ground. "Where are we?" asked Nancy.

Grizelda landed on the stretcher. "Take a look."

Nancy pinched the map from the bird's beak and placed her finger on the last dot. "Right here," she beamed. "That's exactly where we are."

"Where?" asked Jimmy, straining his neck to see the map.

"To our left, beyond the silver lake, is Berringer Hill," explained Nancy. "Behind us is the forest. To the north of that is a place called Tu-Nahh, and next to that is the village of Sanitatum."

"Yippee," cried Jimmy.

Nancy tucked the map into her pocket. "Not far now." She skipped up onto a small mound of earth and marvelled at the impressive peak of Berringer Hill gleaming in the distance. It was huge – a large green dome surrounded by a silver lake. A beacon had been lit and the flames roared in the iron basket, the magnificent peak illuminated by the roaring firelight. Trails of light whizzed around the summit. Nancy squinted, her eyes unable to fathom the source of energy. She was too tired to focus. She spun around to see what lay in the other direction. Beyond the forest, the mountains loomed, their triangular tops piercing the sky like arrowheads. She needed rest, so she dragged her heels back to the stretcher, curled herself up into a ball, muttered a silent good night to her parents, and closed her eyes.

Jimmy shuffled up to Nancy and drifted off.

As the children and Grizelda slept, the stretcher's twigs, leaves and branches began to produce tiny buds. Petals sprung from the buds and the foliage thickened, swaddling Prema from head to toe.

Grizelda swooped down from her perch, crowing at the top of her voice, "Wake up! Wake up! We have a sign of good fortune."

Jimmy stirred. "Leave me, mum. I'm too tired for school." Then his eyes split open. "Uh, where am I?"

"Enerjiimass," trilled Grizelda. "Wake up!"

Nancy remained in the foetal position. She yawned, then rubbed her eyes and stared at the stretcher. "Wow! Look at Pre. She looks like a bouquet of flowers."

"It is a sign," crowed Grizelda. "A glorious sign of life."

Nancy raised her head. "What's happened to her?"

"It's a sign," repeated Grizelda.

"I wonder what the book would say?" mused Jimmy.

"Worry not. I know what this is," clucked Grizelda. "A floral awakening. Enerjiimass has an interactive atmosphere. Only when there is optimism can there be new growth." Grizelda performed dazzling aerobatics between the hot-air balloons, then landed at the children's feet. "The young buds that grow around Prema are feeding off her positive energy. She has an optimistic aura. Don't you see what this means?"

Nancy and Jimmy exchanged blank expressions. "No," answered Nancy.

"Prema Sarkander is fit and well," proclaimed Grizelda.

"She doesn't look it," replied Jimmy.

"Her inner self is alive," insisted Grizelda. "She is maintaining a positive mindset." Grizelda looped the loop, her joy uncontainable. "It is the same when we pass."

Nancy frowned. "When we what?"

"The spirit outweighs our frame," continued Grizelda. "Energy is constant. It's what Aunt Elma calls the circle of love."

Grizelda hopped onto Prema's chest. "These young rose buds tell us that all is not lost. All we need is the potion to wake Prema. We must continue now that we are refreshed. We are close, children, very close."

Grizelda snatched the map and took flight. Nancy and Jimmy bent down, took hold of the handles, lifted the stretcher, and walked on with renewed energy. Nancy couldn't take her eyes off the floral display caressing Prema's body. With every step, another bud miraculously appeared, surrounded by swathes of lush green foliage. Her body was smothered, a living, breathing work of floral art. They walked with vigour and purpose, hope and excitement driving them forward. Jimmy's legs moved quicker than before, eating up the ground as they descended another gentle slope.

"We are so close," crowed Grizelda from the clouds. "Just a few more steps."

With one final burst of energy, the children climbed out of a shallow valley and reached a flat expanse of land. Nancy realised their journey was at an end. Together, they lowered the stretcher to the ground.

Jimmy fell to his knees. "We made it."

"Yes, you did," chirped Grizelda, triumphantly.

Nancy stood over Jimmy and placed her hands on her hips, her eyes widening at the sight before her. "What on earth is that?"

"Sanitatum," squawked the parrot.

An enormous gate stretched up into the clouds. It was impossible to see the top. It looked as if the sky had swallowed it whole. Two wooden hammers crossed one another, the words 'Hope' and 'Faith' intricately carved beneath them. A sturdy padlock kept out unwelcome visitors. Grizelda vanished momentarily behind the hedge that ran both sides of the gates.

"What are we going to do?" asked Nancy, springing up and down to get a glimpse of Grizelda.

"If we had the bag, we could use the compact mirror," said Jimmy. "It unlocked the cellar doors in Roebuck Woods."

Grizelda reappeared, her wings radiant. "The bag is safe with Ergonwold. Let us think of what we *can* do, not what we *can't*. I believe this to be the outskirts of the village. In the old days these gates opened and closed freely. Unfortunately, times have changed..."

Nancy closed her eyes and placed a hand on the hammers. "I *hope* my friend doesn't sleep forever, and I have *faith* in the spirit of Ergonwold."

As soon as the words left her mouth, the padlock burst open. The great gates creaked, the groans of the rusty hinges revealing how long they had been locked.

"Wow," gasped Jimmy. "How on earth did you do that?"

"Chapter Nine," smiled Nancy. "I have read *The First Book of Cosmo*, you know."

Jimmy was amazed. "Really?"

"Well," said Nancy mischievously, "Prema showed me when we landed Mr Wuu's balloon. The book said that most of the signs in Enerjiimass respond to hearts and minds. So, I surrendered my thoughts to hope and faith. Simple."

"You learn very quickly," replied a strange voice.

Jimmy screwed his hand into a fist. "Who are you?"

A tall, skinny young man stood before them. "I am Inglethwip Limpweed, potion-maker and medicine man."

Grizelda chirped with excitement. "And a gifted alchemist…"

The hot-air balloons sparked into life, radiating heat as if it were high summer. Nancy shielded her eyes as the sky exploded into a riot of colour: a heavenly celebration was unfolding above her. Somehow, she felt connected to the explosive firmament; the tremors of jubilation and excitement were mirrored internally. The penny had finally dropped: Nancy realised that the atmosphere was fuelled by thought.

Inglethwip Limpweed arched his gangly frame and offered Nancy a goofy smile. He was as skinny as a twig, almost malnourished in appearance. Despite his composed smile, the constant twitch of his left nostril revealed his nervous disposition. "Can I be of assistance?" he asked.

"Oh, yes," squawked Grizelda. "Bring the stretcher through, children."

Inglethwip Limpweed inspected Prema's body as she was carried ceremoniously through the gates. "Who is this poor child wrapped in the blossom of Enerjiimass?"

"The Reader of the Cards," proclaimed Grizelda. "Let me introduce the great Prema Sarkander."

"And who might these two be?" questioned Inglethwip, his hands fanning towards Nancy and Jimmy like a court jester. Nancy conducted the introductions. She placed an arm around Jimmy and declared, "This is Jim Jam, and I am Nancy Bo Jones. Nanny Bo to my friends."

"The Chosen One," added Grizelda.

Inglethwip Limpweed raised a hand to his brow, then his legs buckled and he fainted.

24

The Potion

Nancy crouched beside Inglethwip Limpweed, her eyes lingering over his freckly face. She placed her hand on his forehead and brushed away the curtain of red hair that covered his brow. Inglethwip's eyes flickered. "Where am I?" asked the potion-maker. "I haven't touched the elderberry wine. It must have been a dream. Who are you?"

"I'm Nanny Bo, and this is my friend, Jim Jam."

"Oh," said Inglethwip, still dazed.

Nancy turned to the stretcher. Floral garlands smothered Prema's body, weaving their foliage between her limbs, caressing her as if guided by nature itself.

Inglethwip got to his feet and wobbled like a baby calf. "This cannot be true. You are not who you say you are."

"In the name of Ergonwold the Great," squawked Grizelda, "it *is* her. The Chosen One."

Nancy stifled a nervous giggle, then offered her hand to the lanky potion-maker. He grabbed it and gave an appreciative nod as Nancy led him tentatively towards the flower-strewn stretcher.

"What is wrong with this sleeping child?" asked Inglethwip.

"She has inadvertently swallowed Ergonwold's tear," confessed Grizelda. "She needs to be woken from her slumber."

"The prophecy is true," declared Inglethwip, his eyes returning to Nancy. "The Chosen One comes in search of the Bloodstone."

"Yes," replied Nancy. "And Ergonwold is—"

"Alive?" interrupted Inglethwip, his hands clasped like a beggar.

"He sleeps," trilled Grizelda.

"He sleeps forever," sighed Inglethwip. "That is what we creatures of Enerjiimass have been told."

"No!" snapped the parrot. "His nest has been stolen. And Prema Sarkander has made a selfless sacrifice. She has swallowed Ergonwold's tear."

Inglethwip's hand caressed Prema's face, then he picked a small flower from the stretcher and hummed. "She sleeps soundly."

"Can you help us?" asked Nancy, expectantly.

"Maybe," replied Inglethwip, inspecting Prema at close quarters.

"She needs to be woken," pleaded Jimmy. "Please help us."

Nancy tried her best to negotiate. "If you wake her up, you will see Ergonwold before your very eyes."

"I can only dream of such a sight," replied Inglethwip.

"You must have faith in your dreams, dreams can change the world. If Prema wakes, Ergonwold will be re-energised."

Inglethwip fell to his knees and kissed Prema's forehead.

"The Great One's white heart has disappeared," clucked Grizelda. "We don't have much time."

"Oh, dear," groaned Inglethwip. "A time bomb."

"Three days," Grizelda chirruped. "And you, Master Limpweed, potion-maker for Zayock, can help. Let's call it a tonic of forgiveness."

Inglethwip hunched his shoulders and turned away.

Nancy frowned. "What do you mean, *a tonic of forgiveness*?"

"Let the potion-maker answer your question," replied the parrot.

Inglethwip's sunken eyes welled. "I'm so sorry."

"What for?" asked Jimmy.

"I was told Ergonwold had passed," explained the potion-maker. "I was promised a safe haven and an education in witchcraft and wizardry." Inglethwip paused. He ran a finger through Prema's hair and went on: "Zayock forced me to mix Tantibus. He showed me how to make potions. I was tricked, then tortured for refusing to poison the creatures of Enerjiimass." He pulled his sweater up and revealed the letter Z seared into his flesh.

Nancy covered her face and squirmed. "Urgh!"

"I had to run away," said Inglethwip, his voice faltering. "I made a terrible error of judgement."

Nancy closed her eyes and focused: a vision of the sleeping beast was at the forefront of her mind. "Ergonwold will forgive you, I know it. I feel his love for you, Inglethwip."

"Really?"

"Yes."

"The Great One warned me, but I didn't listen," admitted Inglethwip. "I cry myself to sleep every night in shame for what I've done."

"Now, now, Inglethwip," trilled Grizelda. "You have shown yourself to be of good character in the past. Ergonwold knows of your personal sacrifice. You could have stayed with Zayock, but instead you fled, putting your own life at risk."

"Yes, but also the creatures who keep me safe."

Inglethwip ambled towards the laurel hedging either side of the gates and scoured the undergrowth.

Nancy trailed his footsteps. "What are you doing?"

Inglethwip huffed and puffed, his long arms clawing at the roots of the hedgerow. "Got it."

"What?" asked Nancy, twisting her neck to see beneath the laurels.

Inglethwip pulled out a bowl and held it aloft. It was full to the brim with a sticky liquid. Ribbons of green mist spiralled up into the air, the vapour rising slowly above the children's heads. Nancy pinched her nose. "That smells disgusting. What is it?"

"A diffusing potion."

"A what?"

"A diffusing potion," repeated Inglethwip.

"Clever boy," squawked Grizelda.

"Thank you, Grizelda – it's nice to be appreciated," replied the potion-maker.

Nancy scratched her head, oblivious to what was unfolding.

"Let me explain," said Inglethwip in a hushed tone. "I concocted this potion and placed it by the entrance points of Sanitatum. It releases a magical vapour. The green mist that covers our village protects us from the eye of Zayock. But once these bowls are empty, we are in grave danger."

"Why?" asked Nancy. "Can't you make some more? You are a *potion-maker*, after all."

Inglethwip frowned. "Do you know how hard it is to obtain the front teeth of a gremlin, young lady?"

"Er, no, s-sorry," stammered Nancy.

"Well, let me enlighten you. The gremlins of Tu-Nahh are ravenous flesh-eating creatures that take no prisoners."

Nancy winced, her mind briefly visualising a gremlin gnawing away at her flesh. "Sounds awful."

"Ergonwold banished the gremlins to the most northerly part of Enerjiimass," explained Inglethwip. "Until Zayock took control, they were the only dark force within our land. The ingredients for my diffusing potion require a dozen juniper berries, some Youlstride serum, and the front teeth of three gremlins. So, unless you would like to visit the gremlins of Tu-Nahh and ask them nicely for three sets of gnashers, I'm afraid to say we are out of stock."

Nancy stared impassively at the potion-maker. "How did you get them in the first place?"

"Zayock has a jar of them," replied Inglethwip with a sheepish grin. "I stole a handful." He gazed at the balloons flickering above him like a failing torch. "I have been here too long. My mood is affecting the Diwali balloons."

Jimmy observed the balloons and tutted. "And the sky is changing colour. Again!"

"Bad vibes," announced Inglethwip. "And that will only lead to one thing…"

"What?" asked Jimmy, innocently.

"My capture," replied the potion-maker. "The eye of Zayock is finely tuned to fear and negativity. Please, children, bring the stretcher through and follow me."

Within minutes they were in the middle of a bustling village that was protected by a misty green-domed roof. The diffusing potion gave Sanitatum a strange emerald complexion. It was the most bizarre place Nancy had ever seen. Shops, cafés, wine shacks, igloo huts, and market stalls filled the sidewalks as far as the eye could see. A large bandstand formed the centrepiece of the village, a mosaic plaque of Ergonwold adorning its wall. Thousands of creatures walked, ran, and skipped in different directions. Some resembled animals, while others took the form of odd-looking humans. The strangest of all were a combination of the two.

The stretcher wobbled as they were shoulder-barged from the pavements onto the muddy track, where unicorn-drawn carriages sped past them at breakneck speed. Loud horns sounded as the creatures in the oncoming traffic warned them to get out of the way, only narrowly avoiding them.

"My mother tells me the pavements in London are like this," yelled Jimmy. "It's crazy here."

Nancy forced a smile, her arms throbbing under the weight of the stretcher. "*London's not this busy*," she thought. A blue-spotted

Mooyat carrying a trumpet scurried close by. It brushed past her, winked, then trotted off into the distance. To the left of the path, behind the sprawling vegetation, Nancy spied an orchard. There were hundreds of brightly coloured trees, their succulent fruit ripe for picking. She licked her lips and dreamed momentarily of her mother's home-made fruit salads that swam in pools of delicious cream. Loud grunts and munches echoed from the orchard. Nancy bobbed her head up and down, searching the field for any sign of life. Then the munching mutated into a string of loud burps. She couldn't help but laugh when she caught sight of the culprit. Hiding behind a tree was a large orange-feathered creature clawing fruit from its branches. It resembled a fluffy octopus. At the end of each tentacle was a small human-like hand. Nancy flinched when it spun around and stared at her. She stared back in amazement. Then, obviously deciding she was no threat, it returned to what it was doing before. The animal checked each of its hands, unsure of what to eat first. Within a fleeting moment, each fruit was devoured and the orange-feathered octopus slithered off into the crowd, burping and grunting as it went.

The children continued through the avenues and alleyways of Sanitatum, their faces alight with wonderment. A surreal journey through the greatest adventure playground they had ever seen. Some of the creatures followed them, trailing their heavy steps, their curiosity aroused at the sight of Nancy and the stretcher. Then, as the entourage filed through a kissing gate, a terrific *gong* sounded, its metallic clang forcing the children to an abrupt halt. The trailing creatures scurried into the shadows. Nancy twisted her neck to see a small man with antlers blow into a horn, his cheeks blood red, his eyes bursting from their sockets.

Within a heartbeat, Sanitatum was empty. The bustling village was now a ghost town. Inglethwip yelled, "Keep walking," and pointed in an easterly direction. "The horn of Bin-Yew indicates low mist. The eye of Zayock could well be upon us."

The muddy track took a sharp turn and meandered through a sandy stretch of land. Beyond it, a river shimmered, and aquatic creatures jumped through arches of white water like performing seals. On the bank stood a wooden hut, uneven in structure, leaning ominously to one side. Above the door, a rusty sign squeaked as it rocked back and forth in the breeze. Nancy narrowed her eyes – the words were hard to decipher beneath the grime: Flash's Place. The Greatest Elderberry Wine in Sanitatum.

"Quick. In here," instructed Inglethwip. He brushed past the children and pushed against the door. A bell chimed as it swung open. Three steps took Nancy, the stretcher, then Jimmy across the threshold.

Paisley drapes kept out the emerald haze. Inglethwip ruffled the curtains, inviting rods of green light into the room. Nancy's eyes roamed as she inspected every inch of the strange shack. Finally, her curiosity was satisfied. "It's a pub!"

A wooden bar stretched the width of the shack, and behind it was a till and an endless supply of wine. Dried bunches of elderberries and hops hung from the rafters. A crystal ball glistened on the window ledge, and in the corner was a clock, its hands spinning past strange numerical markers in a rapid blur of mechanical tick-tocks. Inglethwip placed his hand on the crystal ball and muttered two strange, unfathomable words: *Lumos Immere.* The glass sphere crackled and fizzed as rays of amber light illuminated the shack. Then he reached for a bottle, gulped a mouthful of elderberry wine, and wiped his mouth. "Put the stretcher on the bar, children, and take a seat. I will be with you in a moment."

Nancy and Jimmy exhaled a chorus of groans as they attempted to lift Prema up onto the bar. Prema's head lolled to the leafy edge of the stretcher as it wobbled dangerously in mid-air. Her hair was knotted in the lush foliage, and her legs slid ominously to one side.

Inglethwip dropped the wine bottle and apologised, "Oh, how silly of me. Let me help."

Slowly and painfully, they lifted the stretcher up onto the bar and rearranged Prema's hair.

Nancy pulled two stools from a table and sat on one of them. Jimmy joined her. Inglethwip fussed over Prema's body, keeping one eye on the flimsy door. "If a bad-tempered man arrives, it'll be Jack Flash."

"Who?" asked Nancy, surprised.

"Jack Flash," repeated the potion-maker. "He's the owner. Don't be alarmed – his bark is worse than his bite. Just send him down to me, okay?"

The name was all too familiar. Nancy's thoughts returned instantly to her father and his bedtime stories of a mad swordsman.

"Are you okay?" asked Inglethwip. "You look like you've seen a ghost."

"Er, yes, I'm fine," lied Nancy.

"I told you Jack Flash existed," cackled Grizelda.

Inglethwip skipped down a flight of stairs and disappeared into the cellar. Nancy couldn't take her eyes from Prema, her body trapped by the blossom of Enerjiimass, her pretty face framed by her trailing black mane. She was a picture of beauty. Nancy wanted her friend awake, reading *The First Book of Cosmo* and passing on all its universal knowledge.

The wooden hut creaked and groaned as if it had a life of its own. The metronomic sound of the clock was a hypnotic, yet comforting distraction as the children waited for Inglethwip to reappear.

"What do you think he's doing?" asked Jimmy.

"I'm not sure," replied Nancy. She stifled a yawn and went on. "Maybe he's making room for Prema in the cellar. After all, she is lying on the bar."

"Yeah, funny little shack this," mused Jimmy. "It's a bit different to the local pub my father visits after church."

"I've never been inside a pub," confessed Nancy. Then she began to laugh. "Better not tell my mother when I get home."

The colour drained from Jimmy's rosy cheeks. "Do you think we'll make it home?"

Nancy's lips tightened. "What do you think Prema would say to that, Jim Jam?"

"I think she would be surprised I even asked."

Nancy reached for Jimmy's hand and stared into his brown eyes. "We all need to be comforted at one time or another. Do you know what my dad says when uncertainty gets the better of me?"

Jimmy shook his head.

"Well, he says that everything will be all right in the end. And if things are not all right right now, then that means it's not the end."

Jimmy slid his fingers from Nancy's and whispered, "It's not the end…"

The sharp *ding* of a bell startled them.

The door sprung wide open and an old man the size of a child walked in. His red beard was longer than his stunted body, its trailing end wrapped around his neck like a scarf. He wore a leather belt that held a sabre as long as his legs. His hair was wild and his face resembled a pumpkin.

"Who is that lying on my bar?"

Nancy didn't know what to say.

"If you make me ask again, I will feed her to the gremlins," shrieked the old man.

Nancy stood up, her indignant face towering above the angry dwarf. "That's my friend," she said. "Prema Sarkander."

The fiery man tilted his head and raised a finger. "Sarema Parksander?"

"No," replied Nancy in a huff. "Prema Sarkander."

"That's what I said," growled the dwarf. "She looks more like a garland of flowers." He prodded the stretcher, then grabbed a bottle of wine. He slugged a mouthful and slid his cuff across his nose. "What are you kids doing in my bar? If you are stealing, I will slice your heads off."

"We are not stealing," countered Jimmy.

Inglethwip's head appeared from the depths of the cellar: "Leave them alone, Flash. They are with me."

"I might have known it had to be something to do with you, my boy."

"Let me introduce Jack Flash," said Inglethwip, stepping into the bar.

Nancy extended a hand towards Jack Flash. "Pleased to meet you. I'm Nancy Bo Jones, Nanny Bo to my friends."

Jack Flash stepped back and covered his mouth. "Never. You are not—"

"It's true," interrupted Inglethwip, with a proud smile. "She has come to us."

Jack Flash shook Nancy's hand with gusto. "Hello, Nanny Bo. It is an honour."

"Hi," replied Nancy. She turned to Jimmy and smiled. "And this is my friend. We call him Jim Jam."

Jack Flash shook hands with Jimmy. "Hello, Jam Jim."

"It's Jim Jam."

"That's what I said, Jam Jim. I'm Jack Flash, the fastest and deadliest swordsman of Enerjiimass. My friends call me Flash."

"Okay," said Jimmy. He mouthed, "Flash," silently to himself and bowed.

Inglethwip pointed to the cellar. "Come with me, Flash."

The two disappeared. A moment later, Nancy heard the gruff sound of Jack Flash's voice. "It's a lie, Master Limpweed."

"It's not," retaliated Inglethwip. "I swear to you – that girl *is* The Chosen One."

"I don't believe it," roared Jack Flash. "It's just a fable."

"It's not," fumed Inglethwip. "Those children need our help; their friend has swallowed the Great One's tear."

"The. G-G-Great. One?" stammered Jack Flash.

"Yes. They need help, and fast. A potion needs concocting to bring her back."

Footsteps followed the angry exchanges. Inglethwip and Flash reappeared. The bearded dwarf was mesmerised by the body on the bar. He drew his sword and bellowed, "For the glory of Enerjiimass. If this is true, I will help wake this child. She has the tear of the Great One within." He jabbed his sabre in the air and shouted, "I fight for the glory of Ergonwold. Let battle commence!"

"We are short of time, Flash," crowed Grizelda. "There is no need for warrior antics. We need to assist Inglethwip with the potion."

Jack Flash continued to swipe his sabre. "This is the move I once used to cut a Jagganath in half, and this is how you chop the head off a gremlin."

"Enough," squawked Grizelda.

Jack Flash froze, his sword aloft.

Nancy, Jimmy, and Inglethwip howled with laughter at the dwarf's theatrical antics.

"How much time do we have?" squeaked Jack Flash from the corner of his mouth; then he winked at the laughing children.

"Not enough," snapped Grizelda. The parrot gave Inglethwip a sideways glance and clucked, "It is time to begin." Then she flew off, disappearing into the depths of the cellar.

Nancy, Jimmy and Inglethwip followed Grizelda, while Jack Flash continued to practise his sword fighting in the empty bar, prancing around like a demented ballet dancer.

It was hard for Nancy to ignore the overwhelming aroma of yeast. She pinched her nose and stared at thousands of miniature glass bottles perched upon a lattice of shelving, each one labelled with a corresponding number. Countless barrels of elderberry wine were stacked perilously on top of one another, wobbling every time Jack Flash thrust his sword and stomped his feet from above. Two wooden benches straddled either side of the room. The left side of the cellar was dedicated to wine-tasting, the right reminded Nancy of a scientist's laboratory. A multitude of test-tubes held all sorts of strange things – coloured liquids, insects, grasses, twigs, bark, smoke, powder, berries, slime, and even eyeballs and teeth.

"Wow," gasped Nancy. "Jangles would love this."

"Who's that?" asked Inglethwip.

"Our science teacher."

"Please do not touch anything," muttered Inglethwip. "Some of these samples are highly toxic." He pulled open a drawer and removed a pamphlet labelled *Home-Made Potions*. "The sacred book is missing. *The First Book of Cosmo* contains the recipe I need to waken your friend."

"We have the book," confessed Jimmy. "And Prema understands it."

Inglethwip's face lit up. "You have the—"

"Not with us," interrupted Nancy. "We left it with Ergonwold for safe-keeping."

"You fools!" shrieked the potion-maker. "My own manual is no match for *The First Book of Cosmo*. It takes time to concoct a potion from scratch. The sacred book has the exact recipe. It is a matter of the right ingredients, temperature, and wizardry."

Nancy nudged Jimmy and tutted.

"Wait a moment," muttered Inglethwip. "There is one of my own potions that might work. But—"

"But what?" clucked Grizelda.

Inglethwip cocked his head and stared at the top shelf. "I think Bottle Three Hundred and Ninety-Nine is empty. I have all the ingredients except the contents of that bottle."

Grizelda fanned her wings and hovered up to the shelf. "What is it you require?"

Inglethwip scratched his chin and whispered, "Three droplets of… er…"

"Come on," said Nancy, urgently. "We need to wake Prema." Inglethwip appeared to have lost the power of speech. His lips moved, but there was no sound. "Speak to us, Inglethwip," insisted Nancy. "What's the problem?"

Inglethwip glanced up the stairs where Jack Flash was acting out his imaginary battle. "I need three droplets of dwarf's blood. It must be drained from the seventh toe."

Nancy rolled her eyes and sighed. "Do dwarves have seven toes?"

"Seven on their right and eight on their left," replied Inglethwip.

"What's the big deal?" asked Jimmy. "Why can't we ask Flash for three drops of blood?"

Inglethwip grimaced. "It's not that simple, Jim Jam. Trust me. Have you any idea how feisty the dwarves of Enerjiimass are?"

"No."

"Well, let me tell you something for nothing," whispered Inglethwip. "Dwarves always keep their feet covered. They never, ever, show them in public. It's a dwarf thing, something to do with honour. I'm not exactly sure why." Inglethwip edged himself over to the stairs, his eyes darting back and forth. "Flash is the proudest dwarf you will ever meet. He thinks he is a gladiator. Ergonwold's warrior."

"Enough of this," squawked Grizelda. "Prema and Ergonwold are comatose. Call that crazy dwarf down here."

Inglethwip froze. His nostrils twitched as he fidgeted nervously on the spot. "I can't do this, Grizelda."

"Call him down," ordered Grizelda.

Through gritted teeth, Inglethwip summoned the dwarf. "Flash, we need you. Can you come down?"

A moment later, they heard the sound of tiny feet trotting down the steps. "I am here, ready for action. When do we fight?"

"Well, the thing is, Flash," babbled Inglethwip, tongue-tied. "You see, the thing is, we need—"

"Spit it out, my boy," bellowed the dwarf.

"We need to make a potion, and we… we require—"

Nancy cut in. "The blood from your toe."

An awkward stand-off followed. The only sound was the creaking of timber.

Jack Flash wriggled his toes, flared his nostrils and growled.

Inglethwip hid behind his hands.

Grizelda ruffled her wings.

Jimmy stared forlornly at his feet.

Then Nancy broke the silence. "Flash, we are running out of time. We need to wake Prema, otherwise she will die on that stretcher."

Jack Flash gripped the hilt of his sabre. "That's not true."

Grizelda attempted to explain their predicament and asked Jack Flash to remove the boot on his right foot. The dwarf shook his head and drew his sword. "There are many potions and many ingredients. Master Limpweed is the best there is. He can find another."

"Please, Flash," begged Nancy. "We need your help."

Jack Flash boiled with anger. "Be off with you, all of you. Go and mix another potion."

Nancy threw out her arms. "You are supposed to be a warrior. Show us what you're made of."

"How dare you!" cried the dwarf. "Do not insult me. I will never reveal my feet. Never."

From the corner of her eye, Nancy spied Jimmy reaching for a test-tube; it was filled to the brim with a fizzy blue liquid. She read the label: *Slumber juice – half a day's rest.*

"Let's have a drink and consider an alternative potion," Jimmy said, hiding a coy smile.

Nancy's face turned to thunder. *This is no time for refreshments*, she thought.

Jack Flash nodded with such gusto, his beard left the floor.

Inglethwip lined up four glasses and nodded at Jimmy. "There you go – is dandelion fizz okay?"

"Yes, that's fine," replied Jimmy, then he slid the bottle of slumber juice into Inglethwip's palm and winked.

Jack Flash sheathed his sword and waited patiently for Inglethwip to pour his drink.

Nancy sulked as the sound of slurps filled the cellar.

"Sometimes in life there is more than one way to skin a Jagganath," said the dwarf. He belched a belly-load of fizz and yawned loudly. "I like you, Jim Jam. You respect the honour of the dwarf." Jack Flash swallowed his last mouthful of dandelion fizz and collapsed on the floor in a small but tidy heap.

"Haw-haw," giggled Grizelda. "You are a cunning little boy, Jim Jam."

Jimmy brushed his fingernails on his chest and raised his chin. "It's what Prema would have done."

"What did you do?" asked Nancy.

"He gave me slumber juice," replied Inglethwip, "so I spiked Flash's dandelion fizz."

"Oh," said Nancy, astounded.

"Magnificent idea, Jim Jam," giggled the lanky potion-maker. "You have the makings of a wizard."

Jimmy blushed. "I'm not sure about that, Inglethwip."

Nancy exchanged a high-five with Jimmy. "Nice one, Jim Jam!" She rolled the dwarf's beard up and placed it next to his oversized head. "Will Flash be okay?"

Inglethwip nodded. "He will sleep for half a day and have no memory of this." He scooped the dwarf into his arms and placed him on the wooden bench. "I will need silence to mix my potion. It has to be an exact concoction."

Nancy sat and stewed as she watched Inglethwip scurrying around, pulling bottles from shelves, inspecting utensils, tasting ingredients, gargling strange fluids, and thumbing his way through the manual of potions and incantations. Time dragged, and the waiting pushed down upon her eyelids. She rested her head on Jimmy's shoulder and drifted in and out of patchy sleep. Grizelda pecked at the elderberries suspended from the ceiling, spitting the pips at the sleeping dwarf. Inglethwip tutted and cursed as he experimented to find the perfect mixture.

Time crept on. And on.

Nancy opened her eyes, yawned and stretched. "How much longer?"

Inglethwip fiddled with a test-tube, then turned to face Nancy. "I'm ready."

Nancy stood to attention.

Jimmy punched the air and mouthed a silent, "*Yes.*"

Inglethwip held a match in his right hand. He struck it and placed it in a large bowl of liquid. Flames danced on the surface, releasing a potent red vapour, its odour reminiscent of burning rubber. "I need help removing Flash's boot and sock."

Nancy yanked at Jack Flash's boot.

"Not that one," said Inglethwip in a panic.

"Oh, sorry."

"The right foot, please."

Nancy pulled with all her might to remove the boot, huffing and puffing as she grappled with the heel. It was a tight fit. "Give me a hand, Jim Jam."

Jimmy grabbed Nancy's waist and doubled the efforts. After much yanking and thrusting, the boot finally came loose and the children tumbled onto the sawdusted floor. "Are you okay?" asked Nancy.

"Yes," replied Jimmy.

Nancy held the dwarf's boot up in a ceremonious fashion. "Good."

Inglethwip wasted no time with his instructions: "Remove the sock and prick Flash's seventh toe with my needle. I will collect the blood, okay?"

"I think so," replied Nancy, half-heartedly.

She pulled Flash's stripy sock. Seven toes curled inwards. They were all exactly the same size and topped with black pointed nails. "Urgh, I've never seen toes like that before."

Inglethwip puckered his face. "Horrible, aren't they?"

"Yes," confirmed Nancy.

"All I need now is the first three drops of blood. We must ensure Prema swallows the entire mixture." Inglethwip pulled a long needle from his pocket and blew the tip. "It must be the first three drops, or the potion will fail. When I count to three, Nanny Bo, jab the needle into his seventh toe."

Nancy's eyes flashed. "I haven't done anything like this before, Ingle—"

"You will be fine," interrupted Grizelda. "Just focus and use the power of positive thought."

Inglethwip wiped the end of his needle, kissed it for luck, then handed it to Nancy. Nancy's hands trembled as she stared at the outstretched body of the dwarf. She focused on the seventh toe, counting them continuously in her head, just in case she pricked the wrong one.

"Are you ready?" asked Inglethwip.

"I think so," replied Nancy with the needle quivering between her fingers.

Inglethwip began to count: "One, two, three…"

Jab went the needle.

The right leg of the dwarf flinched.

Nancy watched as Inglethwip positioned a glass tube beneath the bleeding toe. Three droplets of blood seeped into the vial. He emptied it into the bowl, stirred it with his fingertip, then dabbed it on his tongue. "Perfect."

The elated potion-maker bolted up the stairs towards the bar. Everyone gave chase. Nancy said a silent prayer as she watched Inglethwip push Prema's cheeks together and purse her lips.

"Quick. Pour this in," cried Inglethwip.

Nancy grabbed the bowl and poured the entire contents into Prema's mouth. The flowers began to wilt and die. She panicked, then screamed, "What's happening?"

"The life of the flowers is passing over to Prema, and the fatigue of Ergonwold is passing back into the flowers," said Inglethwip. "It's known as energy transfer. All is well. I am sure of it."

Prema's muscles contracted, her body jarring to the sudden jolt of life. Nancy gawped as her eyes fluttered. A broad smile spread across Prema's face when she saw her friends. She sat bolt upright and stretched her arms. "Where are we?"

"Welcome to Sanitatum," crooned the potion-maker. "I am Inglethwip Limpweed, the greatest mixer of potions in Enerjiimass."

Nancy and Jimmy whooped, jumped, clapped, and cheered.

Inglethwip arched his willowy frame and formally welcomed Prema back to the land of the living. She brushed aside the wilting flowers, climbed down from the bar, and fell into Nancy's arms. "What happened?"

Nancy hugged her so tight, Prema could hardly breathe. "Long story, Pre, a very long story."

"I'm thirsty," said Prema, her throat rasping with dryness.

Nancy laughed. "Ergonwold's tear was your last drink."

"Oh," said Prema, "I forgot all about that."

"I didn't, that tear should've been for me."

Jimmy reached for an empty glass and turned a tap. "There you go, Pre."

Prema gulped the water. "I feel better already."

Distant voices echoed outside the shack. It was a muted chant: *"He's back, he's back..."* Then the boom of a bass drum punched out a pulsating rhythm. It was followed by a fanfare of trumpets and a vocal declaration. *"He's back. He's back..."* Gradually, with every beat of the drum, the chants intensified, reaching a glorious crescendo. *"He's back, he's back, he's back..."*

Something was happening. But no one knew what it was. Inglethwip pulled the door, swirls of green mist spilled into the dusty shack, and the grandfather clock began to chime loudly. Hundreds of creatures whizzed past, chanting, "He's back... He's back."

Nancy pushed Prema out into the emerald haze. "Take a look at Sanitatum."

"Wow," gasped Prema. "It's incredible. Completely and utterly crazy."

"You can say that again," replied Nancy, with her back pressed firmly against the wooden hut. The stampede continued. Thousands surged past her. It was like a tidal wave of euphoria. Every creature carried a flag sporting a white heart bearing a golden letter. The letter *E*.

Nancy scrambled up onto two barrels of wine. Now, she could see the festivities unfolding before her. In the distance the bandstand thrummed with music and dance, Mooyats skipped and leaped amongst confetti and streamers; it was a synchronised mass of celebration.

Inglethwip and Jimmy shuffled out of the hut. "Where's Nanny Bo?" yelled Jimmy.

"Up here," replied Nancy, waving her arms wildly.

Inglethwip jigged merrily on the spot. "I haven't heard this music since, well, since Ergonwold the Great was alive."

"He's not dead," squawked Grizelda.

"We must follow the creatures," bellowed Jimmy over the celebrations. He raced off, calling out to Nancy, before disappearing into the swell of the crowd.

Nancy jumped down from the barrels of wine; as soon as her feet touched the ground, she grabbed Prema and zig-zagged her way through the masses. It wasn't long before the two girls reached a breathless Jimmy. "We need to get closer," said Nancy, emphatically. "There's thousands of creatures here…"

Ecstatic crowds gathered around the centrepiece, where a large grey figure commanded the stage. A leather bag dangled from a tusk, and two glass vials chimed like harmonious angels from a studded collar. The wrinkly beast reared up on his hind legs and roared. "I am Ergonwold. I call upon The Chosen One!"

Jimmy grabbed Nancy and pushed her forward. "He's calling you."

"I can't move," replied Nancy, elbowing herself between two brown bears and a peculiar Elfish creature. "Excuse me…"

"Oh, I do apologise," replied one of the bears, in a haughty voice.

Nancy smiled. "Thank you. Can you ask your friend to move?"

The bear ogled Nancy for a moment, then it slapped the other bear on the back. "Imelda, let her through. It's The Chosen One!"

Nancy squeezed herself closer to the podium until her head was level with the stage.

Jimmy cradled his hands and fell to one knee.

Nancy knew what to do. She placed her foot into Jimmy's hands and sprung up onto the stage.

Ergonwold leaned forward.

Nancy grabbed his snout and kissed him. Then Ergonwold flipped her up into the air. The spectators cheered as she somersaulted twice and landed on the Great One's back.

Fireworks exploded in the sky.

Jimmy stared up at the heavens.

The green haze that shielded the village had begun to evaporate.

Sanitatum was exposed.

25

The Escape

The Duke and Elijah huddled beneath the lobby floor. Two thick candles lit the cramped space, droplets of wax trickled onto a wooden table, where a green stone shimmered in the half-light. Beside the gem was a bowl. The Duke tipped its edge, and a rusty key and glass tube tumbled onto the table.

"What are they?" asked Elijah.

"I don't know." The Duke cupped his ear and concentrated. A distant tapping sound echoed from somewhere beyond, as if a hammer was striking a nail. "Can you hear that?"

Elijah nodded. "Is it Zayock?"

"How do I know?" The Duke was squashed against the wall, the sharp mountain rocks piercing the skin on his back, his shirt absorbing tiny droplets of blood like a paper towel. He pressed a button on the Aero-Strazmicator. "Why doesn't this thing work?" Then he yanked the aerial; but, as hard as he tried, it wouldn't extend.

Elijah crawled back to where they had landed and pleaded with his friend, "It's a dead end. Maybe we should go back."

The Duke refused. He reached across the table and grabbed the glass bottle. Sparks of light singed his fingertips, his nails burnt to the quick. "Ouch!"

Elijah cowered back, shivering on his haunches. "Are you okay?"

"Yes," said The Duke, emphatically. He blew the ends of his smoky fingertips and sighed. "These things are cursed. Arnus told me so."

"Don't touch them, then," squealed Elijah, in a panic. "Leave them alone."

"No. We need them. Arnus told me to break the curse. But I can't remember how. What was it he said?"

Elijah shrugged. "Don't look at *me*. I was strapped in the chair and I'm no magician."

"Neither am I, but—"

"But what?" interjected Elijah. "You have a magic wand tucked up your sleeve?"

The Duke relived the giant's dying words with a sad, faraway look in his eyes. "What was it Arnus said? *Intenta...* No... *Incanta, Maloto. Incanta Malouchia.* That's it!" he exclaimed. "*Incanta Malouchia!*"

The legs of the table began to move, clattering against the ceramic floor. They shuddered back and forth as wisps of smoke circled the room.

"Wow, that's cool," said Elijah. "Who taught you that?"

The Duke opened his eyes and held his hand over the bottle. He stared at it, drew breath, and repeated the strange words to himself... "*Incanta Malouchia...*" Then he grabbed the bottle.

There were no sparks.

He had broken the curse of Zayock. He puffed his chest out and placed the glass vial in his pocket. Then he eyeballed the green jewel. He pinched it with his thumb and forefinger and rolled it into the palm of his hand. An immense wave of euphoria caressed him. Suddenly, The Duke was energised.

"What are you going to do with them?" asked Elijah, nervously.

The Duke's eyes sparkled. "I don't know. Arnus only told me to find them. Maybe they will help us."

Elijah stared at his friend. "Are you all right?"

"Yeah, I've never felt better." In truth, The Duke felt as if the entire world loved him. His mind was clear, his body strong, and his heart filled with unbridled hope.

"I wonder what that's for," Elijah said, staring at a mechanical lever protruding from the wall.

"Only one way to find out," replied The Duke. He reached out and pulled the lever. A deep grinding noise was followed by the sound of a steam valve opening somewhere in the distance. Slowly, one of the rocky walls slid open, revealing a path that wove its way into the depths of the mountain. Thousands of candles flickered in glass jars either side of a track – a dusty path, glowing as far as the eye could see.

"Look at that," proclaimed The Duke. "It's the way out. A path of candles."

"What about that t-t-tapping noise?" stuttered Elijah. "It sounds like Zayock is hammering something. And it's getting louder. He might be here – somebody must've lit those candles."

"We have two choices," said The Duke, flatly. "Go back to the castle and *that chair*, or take this path that could lead us to the Tree of Hearts."

Elijah raised his hand to his brow and studied the multitude of wicks glimmering either side of the pathway. The Duke stepped out of the cramped recess into the open expanse of the pathway. It was a welcome relief to be able to stand. He stretched his arms, bounced up and down, then sprinted off. "Come on, Eli. Let's get out of here."

Elijah grumbled his misgivings and followed. "I'm as far from home as I'll ever be."

The Duke turned to face his friend. Elijah's lowering gait and timid face was all too evident. The Duke reached into his pocket and removed the glass bottle, whose label was barely legible: 'One mouthful repairs one's mind'. He removed the lid and sniffed. The sharp scent of lemons darted up his nostrils. *What harm could it do?* Then he curled his arm and gestured at Elijah. "Hurry up."

"I'm tired," moaned Elijah, his long legs trailing behind his friend's.

The Duke held an imaginary cup to his mouth. "Are you thirsty?"

"Yes, I am."

"Here," said The Duke, holding the glass vial above his head, "come and take a swig of this."

"What is it?"

"Do you want some or not?"

Elijah trotted up to his friend and sipped a mouthful. He went to take another, but The Duke stopped him. "Easy, Eli. One mouthful at a time. It's all we have."

Elijah's eyes widened. "Oh, wow! I feel better. In fact, I feel amazing," he proclaimed. "Give me some more of that stuff."

"No, only *one* mouthful."

Elijah's face was now radiant. "What's in that bottle?"

"I don't know," replied The Duke. "Arnus told me it was for troubled minds."

Elijah bounded off like a gazelle. "Come on, let's get out of here…"

"Hold on," yelled The Duke. "Wait for me!"

Clouds of dust trailed behind them as they raced along the pathway, the constant tapping of metal growing louder and louder as they followed the long line of candles. Elijah skidded to a halt. "Look," he cried. "A light. It must be the way out."

The Duke strained to see the small opening in the distance. Once he realised it wasn't a figment of his imagination, he fist-pumped Elijah and boomed, "Magnificent!"

"That's strange," said Elijah, narrowing his eyes. He prodded the mountain wall. "There's another handle poking out of this rock."

The Duke dragged Elijah towards the light. "Come on, ignore it, we need to get going."

Elijah wouldn't budge. "Stop it, there's someone in there. Maybe they could help us."

"Or maybe it's Zayock hammering the nails into our coffins," sniped The Duke.

"Don't be silly," replied Elijah. "We need to investigate…"

The Duke couldn't believe Elijah's transformation. His courage was astounding, his outlook positive, and his strength seemed to be growing with every passing second. He felt for the glass bottle in his pocket and considered taking a mouthful.

Elijah twisted the door handle.

"What are you doing?" asked The Duke.

As soon as the handle turned, minute cracks split the mountain wall. Elijah tried the handle again. The splinters in the rocks morphed into the shape of a doorframe. He pushed against the handle, but the door wouldn't open. "Give me the key, Duke."

The Duke furrowed his brow. "What key?"

"The key you took off the table."

The Duke fumbled within his pocket and presented Elijah with a rusty key. "There you go."

Elijah placed the key into a small hole beneath the handle, then twisted it to the left, then back to the right. A latch unhinged itself and the rocky door creaked open. The Duke stood on tiptoe and prepared to run from whatever was lurking behind.

Elijah crept inside.

The Duke picked up a candle from the path and followed. He crossed the threshold and sniffed. The room reeked of solvent. He held his candle aloft and marvelled at their shadowy figures dancing across the flinted walls. At one end stood a huge desk, and at the other an electronic panel spewing out ribbons of paper. A robotic arm ferociously stamped the tickertape at regular intervals.

The Duke breathed an almighty sigh of relief. "So that's what the tapping sound was." He skipped towards the machine and inspected the labyrinth of cogs and pistons. "It looks like some sort of coding machine."

Every time the robotic arm retracted, a jet of steam hissed beneath the electronic panel. Valves opened and closed at irregular intervals, and hundreds of names flashed upon a screen as the arm swiped down and stamped the next name onto a ribbon of tape. The Duke's eyes followed the coils of ribbons. "Maybe it's a list of people Zayock is targeting."

"Really?" said Elijah, untangling the coils of paper.

"Look at the names on the screen," insisted The Duke. "They get printed onto the tickertape and then the metal arm stamps them."

"That's weird," replied Elijah.

The Duke grasped a strip of paper and unravelled it. His stomach knotted as he read the extensive list of names. "These are real people, Eli. In fact, these are people *we know*."

"Are you joking?"

"No," answered The Duke, seriously. "Look at this..." He held his finger beneath a name. "It's Anthony Musgrove, the taxi driver. My mum says he is the most miserable person she knows: always banging on about how unfair life is." The Duke scrolled further down. "Here's another one – Monty Henderson."

"That's Billy Henderson's father," said Elijah. "He's in our class."

"Yeah, and Billy says his father is a real grumpy so-and-so. He calls him a mood-hoover."

Elijah pulled a face. "A what?"

"A mood-hoover," repeated The Duke. "Billy says his father's doom-and-gloom can suck the life out of a room in seconds." The

Duke's eyes were drawn to the name beneath Monty Henderson. "Bessy Jones. Isn't that Nanny Bo's mum?"

"Not sure," replied Elijah.

"Bessy Jones," said The Duke, as if he was trying to remember an old friend. "I'm sure that's Nancy's mother."

Elijah shrugged. "What if it is?"

"It means there is a connection between Enerjiimass and home." The Duke dropped the roll of tickertape and held out his arms. "What on earth is going on?"

"I don't know," whispered Elijah. "But I do know one thing."

"What?"

"Whatever it is, it's sinister."

The Duke scurried across the room towards the desk. An inkpot and quill sat beside a leather-bound manual. He blew the dust from its cover: *The Identification of Negative Thinkers via The Ether.* "Oh my—"

"What?" interrupted Elijah.

"Zayock is using the internet to find susceptible people. People who are troubled."

"Are you sure?"

The Duke thrust the book in Elijah's face. "Take a look at this."

Elijah stared at the manual. "That's scary."

"Yes. And I know it sounds crazy, but somehow Zayock is using the internet to access people's minds and identify the so-called *mood-hoovers*."

"How on earth can he do that?" asked Elijah.

The Duke placed a finger on his temple and grinned. "Think about it. He wired you up in that chair and extracted all of your fears, then processed them into smoke and released it into the atmosphere."

Elijah grimaced at his friend's recollection.

The Duke continued, piecing together his thoughts, his finger prodding at the air. "Zayock is a clever man and he needs dark thoughts to create the Elixir of Life. If he can identify all the negative folk back home – and there are plenty of them – he has an endless supply of negativity to draw from."

Elijah shook his head, unable to comprehend the sinister plot. "That's mental."

"Yes," confirmed The Duke. "He's an internet hacker of mood. Not only does he want to turn Enerjiimass into a pessimistic hell-hole, but he obviously has plans for our own world, too."

Elijah took a moment to digest The Duke's words. "Maybe you're right. Sounds like he wants everyone to experience the same miserable outlook on life he has."

"Shared depression," mumbled The Duke. "People like him are happiest when everyone else is suffering. They can never be content if someone else is happier than they are."

Elijah threw out his arms. "Let's get out of here. Shall we take the book?"

"No. Leave it. Let's go."

The boys left the room and ran the short distance towards the opening at the end of the cave. The Duke trailed, straining under the weight of the Aero-Strazmicator. They left the candlelit path behind them and clawed their way out of the subterranean chamber into a field of rye grass. The Duke raced after Elijah, slipped his hand into his pocket and touched the Bloodstone. Adrenaline shot through his veins as if he had just swallowed a wonder drug. He turned back to face the mountain. Castle Zayock – no longer their prison – peered down at him from above. He followed Elijah through the field and hid behind a screen of trees.

"What's that noise?" asked Elijah, pointing at the Aero-Strazmicator.

"Shh," hushed The Duke. He unstrapped the contraption and placed it on the ground. The speaker emitted a low humming sound; then, miraculously, the aerial extended. He pressed a button and waited patiently. The humming grew louder, and louder. Then, without any warning, a laser fired out of the aerial, up into the night sky, lancing the darkness. A large red arrow appeared, followed by four neon letters:

H-O-M-E.

"Look at that," observed The Duke, "it's pointing the way home."

Elijah nodded. "It's like a firework..." He picked up the Aero-Strazmicator and kissed it. "You beauty. I always knew something good would come of this machine."

The Duke slapped Elijah on the back. "You are unbelievable."

"What?"

"You said this box was a piece of junk." The Duke held the Aero-Strazmicator aloft. "And now you're praising it."

Elijah pointed to where the arrow had flashed moments earlier. "We need to go in that direction. I bet the others will be waiting for us. At last, my friend, we are *going home*."

The Duke strapped the Aero-Strazmicator over his shoulder and trudged through the undergrowth, fiddling with the array of knobs and buttons, hoping that the strange contraption would respond. Time and again he pressed the power button, but it didn't respond. Then he tried the auto-tune. Something clicked. A loud *beep* was followed by a crackle of distortion. The Duke's heart fluttered when the LCD display flashed. A green line traced the outline of Enerjiimass. At last, he had a map, a point of reference, something to give him his bearings. A trail of white dots sparkled on the screen, the final dot stopping at the Tree of Hearts. "This is going to be a piece of cake, Eli. It's guiding us back to the portal."

Elijah studied the buttons on the Aero-Strazmicator. "I thought you said this machine had a voice?"

As soon as The Duke released the mute button, a soft female voice emanated from the speaker. Elijah crouched beside it, cupping his ear. "Turn it up."

The Duke twisted the volume knob. The Gaelic tones of Aunt Elma echoed from the speaker. "Continue straight ahead. Don't stray from the path of white petals; avoid the swamp to your left. Bear right at the windmill, follow signs to the village of Gobaith, and continue along the trail of petals... They will lead you home."

Elijah whooped and cheered. "We're going to be home before you know it, Duke."

"Maybe."

Elijah bobbed his head from side to side. "I can see lights. Red lights."

The Duke spun on his heels. "Where?"

"Look," said Elijah, excitedly. "Over there, to our right."

The Duke squinted. "Oh, yeah. According to this machine, there should be a trail of white petals to guide us home."

"Everything is going to plan," declared Elijah.

"Maybe a little too much to plan."

"What do you mean?"

"Well, where on earth are the Jagganath?" asked The Duke; "and look at the sky."

Elijah stared at the heavens. "What's wrong with it?"

"It's bleak, and I can hear the dawn chorus."

"So?"

"That's when Zayock said he was going to return. At dawn."

"Stop fretting," said Elijah, angrily.

"Can you smell anything?" asked The Duke, with his nose in the air.

Elijah pinched his nose and laughed. "Only your fear."

"I'm being serious, Eli. I can smell them. You know what I mean."

Elijah tipped his chin and sniffed. "Mmm, maybe you're right. I can smell *something*."

The Duke continued to inhale and exhale, exaggerating every lungful. Then a terrible feeling of despair spread outwards from his heart. He pointed west-bound and whispered, "*Over there.*"

"Where?"

"There," replied The Duke. "In the bushes." He silenced the Aero-Strazmicator and ducked beneath a hedge.

Elijah focused on the distant lights. "Those red lights are moving."

"They're not red lights. They're eyes."

"Eyes?"

"Yes, eyes," confirmed The Duke. He swallowed hard. "What's seven-foot-tall with red eyes?"

"Jagganath!" croaked Elijah.

A fierce howl echoed throughout the woodland. Birds fled their nests as the Centurion of the pack strode towards the two boys. The Duke closed his eyes in anticipation of the approaching monster, its heavy hooves slapping against the sodden earth. Then, feeling extremely vulnerable and expecting the worst, he opened one eye and glimpsed the monster. The rotten stench of the Jagganath was unbearable. It stood within a metre of the bush that shielded the two boys.

Elijah gritted his teeth, his lips barely moving. "It hasn't seen us."

The Duke signalled for silence.

The Jagganath's tongue flicked at the air, tasting the atmosphere, then it reached over, pulled a handful of berries from a low-hanging branch, and swallowed them whole. The monster picked a leaf from one of his shark-like teeth and trudged back to his pack. The Duke was convinced he could hear something: the rumbling of machinery – cogs turning, pistons moving, and the hissing of steam. It was unmistakable: the Engine Room had re-started.

It was then that the Jagganath became restless. The Centurion snatched a fruit from one of his foot soldiers and threw it to the floor. One by one, they began to howl like a pack of hungry wolves. The serene dawn chorus was drowned by the menacing cries of Zayock's soldiers. The Duke's eyes scoured the woods for the elusive white petals. All he could think of was finding the route home, but all he could see was a carpet of decaying leaves. And all he could hear was the demonic rallying call of the Jagganath.

Elijah pressed his mouth to The Duke's ear and whispered, "They're over there."

"What are?" asked The Duke, pulling at a small branch that impaired his view.

"The white petals," replied Elijah, softly. "Next to that fallen tree."

The Duke twisted his neck ninety degrees and hugged Elijah. "Well spotted. They're beautiful, like confetti."

A trail of petals snaked off towards Berringer Hill, but the boys' pathway to freedom was blocked by the Jagganath. Elijah clenched his fists and groaned, "If we can't get past those monsters, we're going to die."

The Duke glared at his bedraggled friend. "I'm not going to die. I have too much to live for." He knew the effects of the tonic were waning. He reached for the Bloodstone and presented it to Elijah. "Here, hold on to this."

"What is it?"

"I don't know, but it'll help you."

"Give me a swig of that tonic," demanded Elijah, "it perked me up. I don't want to hold a silly stone."

"One mouthful is enough, Eli. No more."

Elijah snatched the green stone. Instantaneously, his face lit up.

At that same moment, The Duke winced as if he had just been stung. Pain seized his body and his mind became clouded, hope draining from his tired limbs.

The howls of the Jagganath intensified, their hooves drumming a muted rhythm on the leaf mould. The Duke braced himself as the slimy creatures marched towards the hedgerow. Within three strides, the Centurion had reached the bush where they hid. The beast snorted, bent its big, gooey head towards them and dragged the boys from the ground with his teeth. Two pairs of legs dangled helplessly as beastly roars of approval rang out.

The Duke fought back tears as he was carried back to the foot of the mountain and thrown to the ground. He cocked his head, stared up at the summit and locked eyes with Zayock. The sorcerer sprinkled a grey powdery substance onto the tip of his wand and released a bolt of lightning. The boys disappeared from the base of the mountain and reappeared, miraculously, at the feet of the magician, their garments scorched, their skin singed. The Duke coughed and groaned, his body riddled with pain and anxiety. "I'm burning... I feel sick."

"Fools!" hissed Zayock. "How dare you think you could outwit me!"

The Duke crawled to the mountain's edge and vomited. Zayock followed, his boots teetering on the precipice. He ruffled his cape and screamed at the top of his voice, "For thine is the glory, the power, and the kingdom, forever and ever, Amen!" He dragged the boys back into the castle and led them down three flights of stairs.

The Duke's throat constricted as the rising vapour from the engine room filled his lungs. The mountain walls trembled from the thunderous momentum of the machinery.

"Not the chair!" groaned The Duke.

"Not just yet," replied Zayock, taking a sideways step into a small triangular room. He bolted the door and reached for a grainy black-and-white photo.

The Duke wrapped his arm around Elijah. "I'm gasping."

"Me, too," echoed Elijah.

"There's a jug of water by the window," growled Zayock. He perched himself on the edge of a desk and faced the boys. "Drink as much as you want. You will need to be hydrated before I strap you into the chair."

The Duke offered Elijah the jug. Elijah took a mouthful, then passed it back to his friend. The Duke quenched his thirst, crooked his neck, and studied the photo in Zayock's hand. A tall man with snow-white hair and piercing blue eyes stared back at him.

"I wasn't yet a man when you left me, father," mumbled Zayock. "Why did you not listen? Oh, why?" The sorcerer brushed a tear from his cheek and slammed the photo onto the desk.

The Duke glugged another mouthful of water, breathless at the spectacle unfolding before him. The man's madness seemed to be getting worse. Zayock brushed the frame towards the edge of the desk. "I had so much I wanted to share with you, father, so much, but you didn't listen. It could have been so different. We could have left the old world behind us and shared in the fruits of Enerjiimass."

The Duke prodded Elijah, his bottom lip quivering as Zayock unfolded the ornate painting he had snatched from Arnus Pilkus. The sorcerer held it at arm's length and sighed. Two halves had been hastily taped together. For one brief moment, The Duke thought Zayock was admiring the image of Nancy Bo and the mystical elephant. Then he realised that the blonde girl's eyes matched the eyes of Zayock's father in the photo.

"I knew you would come," whispered Zayock.

The Duke remained statuesque as Zayock paced the angular room. He dared not blink, scared that he might miss something, or might himself be noticed.

"I tried to warn her parents," confessed Zayock. "It was written in the stars. I sent the bottle. Why did they not heed my warnings? I am sorry, father. I know it is family, but it *has* to be done… *again*!"

284

The Duke stepped forward. "There's something moving behind us."

Zayock pushed The Duke to one side. "Who goes there?" barked the sorcerer, his wand aimed precariously at a cloth curtain. He pulled a cord and the curtain parted. There was nothing but an empty chamber. "I will not ask again," yelled Zayock. "Reveal yourself or the power of my wand will be unleashed."

The Duke tilted his head to one side and stared in disbelief as a small, furry hand appeared, its talons arched and razor sharp. Zayock placed his wand in his cape and grabbed the creature by the membrane of its wings.

"Master, you inflict pain so easily," squealed the creature. "Please release me. I come with news of the girl."

The Duke nudged Elijah and winked.

Zayock dropped the animal to the floor. The creature manoeuvred its wings back into position and stared curiously at the two boys. The furry animal swished its tail and released a high-pitched wail, constantly twitching its pointed ears like mini antennae. "I have news, master."

Zayock spread his cape with both hands. "You know I find it hard to trust gremlins. If you have come for your teeth, Drinyak, you have wasted your journey."

Drinyak rolled his tambourine eyes. "No, master, I have *news*."

"What news?"

"Ah, master, I heard you crying. Is everything going to plan?"

Zayock shuddered with anger. "How dare you eavesdrop, you dirty little gremlin. I could kill you right now!"

"If you kill me now, master, you kill the only gremlin that is on your side. My family in Tu-Nahh knows of our arrangement."

Zayock faked a smile. "What news do you have for me?"

Drinyak remained tight-lipped for a full thirty seconds. Then he opened his mouth: two sets of pink gums were punctuated by small holes, saliva dribbling from his toothless mouth.

"Speak, damn you. Speak," said Zayock, his patience thinning.

"Remember, master, we have a deal," replied the gremlin. "When you capture the girl, you will remove the curse upon me and return my fangs." Drinyak clawed at the holes in his gums. "I miss my teeth."

Zayock opened a cupboard and removed a jar of metal teeth. "I have these for you, but all in good time, my friend. As I said, I cannot trust the gremlins of Tu-Nahh. I had to remove your teeth for my own safety. Now, tell me what you know."

Drinyak bowed with reverence to his master. "I flew over Sanitatum. The emerald charm shrouding the village is fading and the mist is clearing. Soon, we can attack."

Zayock stroked the gremlin's chest, his voice cajoling. "Please continue, my furry companion."

"The girl has been seen with your apprentice."

Zayock cleared his throat and spat on the floor. "Inglethwip Limpweed? The boy is a traitor. He was the only one I trusted. I taught him all he knows – potions, incantations, and transformation. He betrayed me and now he shelters that girl."

Drinyak flew up onto the desk and clawed the photo. "I see my master has a heart. Is this your father?"

"Yes," confirmed Zayock. "He possessed more skill with a wand than any other sorcerer in history. He was a powerful man – a politician, a magician, an alchemist, a spiritual medium. He could connect with the other side. He was a man of genuine influence. But—"

"But what, master?" asked the gremlin, quietly.

The Duke's head flitted back and forth between the sorcerer and the gremlin. He wondered at Zayock's sudden talkativeness. He'd never imagined that evil man sharing anything so private or heartfelt.

Zayock fell silent. A tiny chink in his armour had been revealed.

Drinyak probed again. "You were saying, master. Your father…?"

"My father followed that holy beast," confessed Zayock.

"Ergonwold?" said Drinyak, nonchalantly.

Zayock's pale complexion became almost translucent. "That name is not mentioned in my castle."

"What name?" asked the gremlin, innocently. "Do you mean *Ergonwold*?"

Zayock swallowed hard, then flicked Drinyak's nose.

"Ouch! I apologise, master."

"My father came from a bloodline of humans blessed with the skill of crossing over. He was a dual-star."

Drinyak twisted his head three hundred and sixty degrees. "Crossing over, master?"

"Yes, he had the gift of being able to live in both worlds – the world of Enerjiimass and the Earth realm."

"Ah, yes, I understand."

"He spent little time in Enerjiimass, and when he did, he devoted himself to the teachings of *You Know Who.*"

Drinyak nodded, then grinned a toothless grin. "Er-gon-wold?"

"*DO NOT SAY THAT NAME!*"

Drinyak chuckled, then placed a paw over his mouth and apologised.

Zayock composed himself and continued. "My father married beneath himself; a poor woman from the city."

"There are many cities in the Earth realm," purred Drinyak. "Which one, master?"

"London. She came from the east side. That's where the poor congregate and breed." Zayock pondered the thought of his Earth Mother, "…uneducated vermin." He rubbed his hands as if he were washing them. "When I was born, my mother died – an exchange of life. My father grieved throughout my childhood. His only concern was to pass on the knowledge of potion-making. He told me, 'The greatest potion ever to be made was never to be made.' I never understood him. It sounded like a riddle to which only *he* knew the answer." Zayock paused, licked his lips, then continued: "On my eighteenth birthday, he revealed the portal between the Earth realm and Enerjiimass. From that day on, I was mesmerised. A world of interactive thought and magic."

"And here you stayed, master?" said Drinyak, wistfully.

"No, I flitted between the two worlds as only a dual-star can, just like my father. After I graduated from medical school, I cured a few ill-gotten diseases, then I was made a lord, a knight of the realm. But I craved more. A world on a higher plane." Zayock gazed at the monochrome photo and sighed. "One day I visited my father's mansion. The cellar had been flooded in the autumn storm. He had business to attend to, so I decided to help."

Drinyak bowed reverently. "So *kind* of you, master."

"I spent all day clearing the debris and rummaging around my father's cellar. I found a wooden box embossed with the crest of the Magic Circle. Inside was the answer to my father's life-long riddle." Zayock drew breath, savouring the memory. "The ingredients for the greatest potion never to be made." He stroked the gremlin's ears and sighed. "That was the moment I finally understood him."

Drinyak nestled his face into Zayock's palm. "What was the greatest potion never to be made?"

Zayock pondered Drinyak's question as he fanned his cape.

No one uttered a word. It was a moment of tranquillity; the only sound was the distant hiss of steam from the engine room, a painful reminder that the dreaded chair waited for The Duke. He swigged another mouthful of water, passed the jug to Elijah, and waited with bated breath for the sorcerer to answer the gremlin. Zayock revelled in the silence. He pulled the strings on his cape and exhaled a pleasurable sigh. "The Elixir of Life."

"I do not understand, master," replied Drinyak. "Why was this potion *never* to be made?"

"To concoct a potion or tonic that grants everlasting life is a remarkable feat. It would be the greatest potion ever made. No one thought it possible, except me." Zayock's lips tightened over his crooked teeth. "My only problem was *You Know Who*."

"Ergonwold?" asked Drinyak.

Zayock placed his hands around the gremlin's neck and shook him ferociously.

"I'm sorry, master," squeaked the furry creature. "Please, I beg you, release me."

Zayock loosened his grip and went on: "The reason the followers of *You Know Who* believe that the everlasting potion should never be made is something to do with eroding the magic of life." He slammed his palm on the desk. "When my father returned from business, I told him that I had found the ingredients to the greatest potion never to be made. I told him that it was my destiny to make it, and we could live together in Enerjiimass forever. Death would never find us."

"Never?" quizzed the gremlin.

"Never!" confirmed Zayock. "My father lost control of his senses. He tried to banish me from Enerjiimass. He even turned *You Know Who* against me, and eventually he disowned me. It was the start of our family feud, a feud that lasted until his untimely death. I have always kept the ingredients close to hand. They belong to me!"

"What are they?" asked Drinyak, peering at the jar of metal teeth on the desk.

"A vial of healing liquid, seven hundred and seventy-seven bottles of Tantibus, and a shard of the precious Bloodstone. I spent years locating them. For the love of my father, I swore to myself that I would find every ingredient and concoct it for him."

Zayock grabbed the photo and pressed his thumb against his father's face. The glass shattered into tiny fragments, tearing his skin. Blood trickled behind the glass and seeped into the frame.

"When I was close to acquiring the final piece of the jigsaw, I…" Zayock stopped himself. He kissed the photo and stuttered, "I… killed… him." Then he licked the blood from his thumb and, inexplicably, grabbed the gremlin by the wings.

Drinyak sunk his toothless gums into Zayock's hand.

"Your gums are no threat to me, Drinyak. I have said too much. Now, return to the skies of Enerjiimass and bring the girl to me."

Zayock held the jar of teeth in one hand and threw Drinyak against the wall with the other. The gremlin yelped as he landed at The Duke's feet. Zayock released the bolt from the door, pointed his wand towards the stairwell, and continued his descent towards the engine room.

The Duke hesitated. The thought of being strapped into the chair curdled his stomach.

"Come on," yelled Zayock, from two flights below. "The chair is waiting for you."

Reluctantly, The Duke followed, keeping a constant check over his shoulder, the damp mountain walls scratching his skin. It was the pathway to hell, every step a cold realisation that the onset of pain and torture were only moments away. Elijah was the last to reach the confines of the engine room. The Duke pulled him to his side and awaited his fate.

"You silly little boys," sniggered Zayock. "You have no idea what type of magic you are dealing with, do you?"

"No," answered The Duke. From the corner of his eye he noticed Elijah slip his hand into his pocket and grab the Bloodstone.

"We haven't got a clue what's going on," confessed Elijah, his face glowing with confidence. "We followed our friend and now we are lost. Let us go. We mean you no harm."

The tip of Zayock's wand glowed blood red. He strode forward and laughed in Elijah's face.

"Release us," pleaded The Duke over the sorcerer's haughty laughter.

Zayock's wiry frame bent double as he released another fit of spluttering giggles, beads of spittle flecking onto Elijah's cheeks.

Elijah stood firm, hands on hips, accentuating his broad shoulders, the effects of the Bloodstone masking any sign of weakness.

"Don't touch the stone, Eli," whispered The Duke. "You're making it worse."

Elijah took a confident step closer to the sorcerer until their noses touched.

The Duke watched in horror as it happened.

Elijah reached for Zayock's wand.

Zayock roared with laughter as an electrical current consumed Elijah, his entire body attacked by a surge of purple sparks, his hair on end, and his body now quivering in a heap by Zayock's boots.

"How dare you even touch my wand!" growled Zayock. "It will always protect me. It is fashioned from the dark forests of Enerjiimass and charmed with an everlasting pulse. Only one of a specific bloodline – mine – can handle this wand."

The Duke huddled over the electrified body of Elijah. The sorcerer was unflinching. His icy stare locked on the cowering boys. Then, for a brief moment, he looked down at them with pity and sighed. "You are in the wrong place at the wrong time. Why were you so stupid as to follow that girl?" He twiddled his wand between his fingers and continued. "She was warned off, but still she came. Like the rest of that family, she is too courageous. It is her weakness, her undoing."

"We made a mistake," replied The Duke. "Please, release us."

Zayock ingored The Duke and continued. "You are caught up in something so great you could not comprehend it if you tried. You are Earth-bound whippersnappers. The girl, on the other hand, has power and strength of which she is unaware. I must protect what is mine."

"I'm alive," groaned Elijah. His arm was charred black, and ribbons of smoke curled up from where his fingernails once were. The power of Zayock's wand had left its mark.

"Please don't kill us," begged The Duke. "We'll do anything you want. Just spare us our lives."

Zayock stared at him pensively. "Life, huh. What is a life if it is unfulfilled?"

"What will you do with us?" asked The Duke.

"You are too weak for my chair. I need you fully conscious to extract the best of your woe. It is your sadness that creates my Tantibus. I will tie you up and review the situation." Zayock turned from the boys and stomped around the room, his cape trailing behind him like a black sail. "I can sense her. She is getting close. I feel a change in the atmosphere. She is coming for the Bloodstone."

The Duke mustered enough courage to address his captor. "Who is coming?"

"You know who – that curly-white-haired brat."

The Duke returned a blank expression. "What brat?"

Zayock grimaced as the words left his mouth. "Nancy Bo Jones." It was as if he had tasted something so foul it made him gag. He rolled out his tongue and slurped saliva from his chin. "I promised myself never to mention her name, but the time has come and I am ready."

The Duke drew a nanosecond of comfort from the sound of his friend's name. Nancy Bo Jones seemed like a distant, happy memory for him – a memory of a time before imprisonment. The reality was that he could feel the life draining from him, as if his soul had taken enough and was asking for rest. He was filled with remorse. He cradled Elijah in his arms and wept.

Elijah began to cough, purple phlegm spewing from his mouth, the wand's power contaminating his lungs. He raised his head. "Take it," he croaked. "Take the stone."

The Duke shook his head.

"Take it," insisted Elijah.

The Duke's thoughts were clouded with uncertainty. He never put himself before others, but he knew this time he had to. He slipped his hand into Elijah's pocket, removed the green stone, and hid it in his jacket. The colour returned to his face as quickly as it left Elijah's. His eyes sparkled as he watched Zayock tinker with the dials on the machine. He was energised by the mystical Bloodstone. It was a gift. From whom, he did not care.

Zayock pressed a button on the centre console; he waited for the cogs to turn, then dipped his wand into a powdery substance and ran it through The Duke's hair. A silver rope appeared above his head, twitching and turning like an albino snake. Zayock stepped back, drew his wand and sent a ray of light onto The Duke's chest. The white snake followed the light from his master's wand and wrapped itself around the two boys. Zayock grinned. "Let's see you get out of that."

The Duke's face reddened. "It's too tight."

Zayock placed a finger between the rope and his prisoners. "Maybe a little tighter." He flicked his wand and the rope-snake slinked another of its coils around them. The tension increased, constricting their lungs, robbing them of breath. The Duke's chest expanded as he gasped for air. With each desperate intake of breath, the rope squeezed against his pocket, pushing against the Bloodstone. Then, as the tension became unbearable, it popped out, rolled across the floor and landed at Zayock's feet.

"Well, well, well. What do we have here, then?"

26
Attento

The iron gates of Sanitatum creaked open.

The emerald haze protecting the village had all but vanished. The sky was filled with Diwali balloons, fizzing like effervescent light bulbs. Nancy edged past the gates and stepped out into the bright sunshine. The impressive hedges either side of the entrance dwarfed her. Her slender frame was microscopic against the wide valleys of Enerjiimass. She peered out at the magical land, waves of joy crashing against the lining of her stomach, every muscle and sinew tingling with excitement. She turned to face Ergonwold and the gathering crowd. They bowed before her. It was her moment, a moment she had to act upon. "I'm ready, O' Great One. I follow you. My heart is yours," she said, reciting the words from *The First Book of Cosmo.*

Ergonwold raised his snout and trumpeted a long continuous note. The creatures brave enough to leave the inner sanctum of the village jostled for position next to Ergonwold the Great.

Nancy's eyes were drawn to the dark mountain range, the smoke bellowing from Castle Zayock's chimney was a constant reminder of the sorcerer's reign of terror.

Ergonwold stood proudly on his hindquarters, his strength temporarily restored after the energy transfer, his tusks now sharper, ready for battle. The strange motley crew of creatures fell to their knees and waited patiently for their spiritual leader to address them.

"We are about to undertake a perilous journey," bellowed the Great One. "The Reader of the Cards has swallowed my tear... I have energy!"

The crowd got to their feet and applauded. Ergonwold waited for the elation to fade before he continued. "Unfortunately, it will not last. We must find the maternal nest and regain the Bloodstone. The future of Enerjiimass and the wider world depends upon it. The greatest weapon we have at our disposal is belief in one another. Solidarity!" Ergonwold dipped his head towards the leather holdall that contained their precious cargo. "I carry the sacred book, the music box, the compact mirror, a vial of healing liquid and the spyglass. These artefacts have proven their worth and will continue to do so. But, most important of all, we have The Chosen One with us."

The crowd whooped and cheered. Ergonwold chuckled as the blood rushed to Nancy's cheeks. "Nancy Bo Jones is a child, and a brave one. We must thank her with all our hearts." More applause rang out. Ergonwold paused, then continued: "If we had waited until she was of age, there would be no Enerjiimass and the Earth realm would fall into perpetual darkness." He turned to face the crowd, his green eyes sparkling. "Our journey cannot be completed without rest and recuperation. We will need to gather our strength prior to reaching Castle Zayock. Between where we stand and our final destination lies Berringer Hill. The trusted Night Fairies will offer us sanctuary." Ergonwold ruffled his snout and prepared himself for departure. "It is time for us to leave."

There was a frenzy of goodbyes as hands were slapped and cheeks kissed. Nancy stood alone, away from the well-wishers, gazing out at the phenomenal landscape. A tiny spark flickered in the distance: it was the flame of Berringer Hill and it burned brightly. Her head swam in a giddy bout of emotion. She couldn't wait a moment longer. She had to leave. Time was ticking and lives were at risk.

The swaying crowd waved an assortment of flags and handkerchiefs as Nancy and her entourage joined a narrow path that eased its way downhill towards the outer reaches of a forest. Grizelda flew high above them, her crest unfurled, darting in and out of the balloons, clucking and squawking. Nancy vaulted onto Ergonwold's back and gripped his collar. Her friends followed. Jimmy squeezed her waist, Prema clung onto Jimmy, and Inglethwip rode side-saddle at the rear.

Their journey had begun. The leather holdall dangled from the underside of Ergonwold's collar. Beside it, the two vials clanged against one another, the Wisdom Stone safely concealed within one, the other empty – awaiting the return of the Bloodstone. Nancy tugged on Ergonwold's collar as they entered the forest. "Giddy-up," she joked. Her friends laughed as Ergonwold cantered on. The clear air of the open fields was soon replaced by the odour of decaying leaves and wet bark. Ergonwold slowed, his large frame squeezing through the myriad of trees and vines. Low branches clipped the children's heads. It wasn't long before the temperature dropped and the light faded to a murky gloom.

"Something's wrong," said Nancy, her senses now finely-tuned.

"The balloons have lost their power," replied Ergonwold.

"It's a strange darkness," said Nancy, "like a black fog."

"Do not worry," replied Ergonwold, "to see a light in a room of darkness is a test of one's character – maybe the first of many, Nanny Bo."

"Now is the time for The Chosen One to be told," squawked Grizelda.

Nancy tapped Ergonwold's head. "Told what?"

"She needs to know," clucked Grizelda.

Ergonwold cast the parrot a sideways glance. It was enough to silence her. "You are a brave girl, Nanny Bo. Your frustration with

Aunt Elma was partly my fault. We had to withhold information from you.”

“Why?” asked Nancy.

“I informed Captain Carbunk—”

“Branch!” interjected Nancy at the top of her voice.

Everyone ducked.

Ergonwold slowed to walking pace. “I informed Captain Carbunkle to withhold certain information. In our wisdom, we decided the less you knew, the better our chances were of you raising the portal.”

Nancy hunched her shoulders. “I understand.”

Inglethwip chimed in. “Good girl!” He hopped off Ergonwold’s back and followed on foot. “You are in tune with The Great One.”

“There are two things I must burden you with,” announced Ergonwold.

Nancy prepared herself for the worst. It was all she knew. Her mother’s mantra had been passed on like an unwanted baton. The usual feeling of dread now percolated within.

Ergonwold flapped his ears and declared, “You come from a bloodline of gifted magicians.”

“Me?” responded Nancy, with a look of astonishment. “I’m related to… magicians?”

“Yes,” replied Ergonwold. “Unfortunately, one of the greatest magicians in your distant family made a wrong turn.”

Nancy prepared herself. She knew what was coming. Somehow she had known all along.

“I’m afraid Zayock is that magician,” confessed the Great One.

“I don’t believe it!” Jimmy exclaimed.

“It is true,” countered Ergonwold. “Nanny Bo is related to Zayock. His father had a sister. That sister was known as Beatrice.”

“That was my gran’s name,” admitted Nancy, “she died when I was a baby.”

Ergonwold snorted, then completed the ancestry: "Beatrice gave birth to Edward Jones at Saint Andrew's Hospital; Edward Jones married Bessy Hart, and the rest is history. That is why we are here."

Nancy's world was now spinning off its axis; it was too much to digest. Ergonwold continued to unravel the past. "It is an ancient bloodline. Only one of the same family can reverse Zayock's dark magic and claim his wand. Many have tried. All have failed."

"Who has failed?" asked Nancy, tugging on Ergonwold's collar, desperate for an answer. But he walked on, trudging over decaying trunks and sprawling roots.

"If the wand finds a good soul, it will replicate the feelings of its keeper," explained Ergonwold. "The wand will not leave Zayock unless it is in the hands of a blood relative."

Nancy's mind was a whirlpool of unanswered questions. Her face flushed with uncertainty as she contemplated the concealed truth of her family tree. She lifted Ergonwold's ear. "You said there were *two* things you needed to tell me."

"Yes," Ergonwold replied.

"Well, what's the second?"

"Your birth sent out a dual-star that illuminated the cosmos. It shone high in our skies."

Prema reached past Jimmy and tapped Nancy on the shoulder. "I told you. You are a dual-star, Nanny Bo."

"A what?"

"My gran says a dual-star is a special individual," explained Prema. "The star shines brightly in two different worlds. They get two shots at life."

"Correct," said Ergonwold. "Unfortunately, Zayock spotted the dual-star in the sky of Enerjiimass. I believe that day in your Earth realm to be 20th April."

"My birthday," whimpered Nancy.

"Yes," confirmed Ergonwold. "A special day for all of us. And since that day, Zayock has kept a close watch on you. He knows everything about you, Nanny Bo – what makes you laugh, what makes you cry, every little thing." Ergonwold stopped, his passengers unwittingly falling forward from the momentum of the sudden halt. "He has placed a spell upon you. And only *you* can break that spell."

"Are you saying," Nancy shuddered, "that I'm cursed?"

"Yes, and it is a dark spell. In our world, it is known as *Attento*. It bewitches the individual and strengthens their worst characteristics."

"Oh, no," groaned Nancy. "Can you get rid of it for me?" She waited for a brief moment, then whispered, "With your *magic*?"

"Only you can conquer this curse," declared Ergonwold. "It is a personal challenge, a test. You must overcome your own failings."

Nancy hid her disquiet behind a fake smile.

"Zayock is a clever man," added Ergonwold. "In addition to this curse, he has cast a reversed spell of *Attento* upon his castle."

Nancy thought long and hard. "Cursed himself?"

"Sort of," replied Ergonwold. "You will find it impossible to enter the castle grounds unless you break the spell. And without you, your imprisoned friends will perish."

Inglethwip brushed his mop of hair to one side and explained. "You and Zayock are like the same pole on two magnets: you will repel one another when in contact. Without breaking the curse of *Attento*, you cannot enter the castle – if you do, you will die."

Nancy watched helplessly as the colour drained from her friends' faces. The collective mood was plummeting, and a cold, damp, murky gloom encapsulated the woodland. She acknowledged Inglethwip with a stiff, yet regrettable nod.

"I need to address something close to your heart," said Ergonwold. "It may upset you, but I need you to control your emotions."

"Sure," replied Nancy.

"I know how much you love your mother—"

"What has my mother got to do with this?"

Ergonwold swiped his snout and reprimanded Nancy. "Control your feelings!"

"I'm sorry. But why mention my mother?"

"Zayock is aware of her pessimistic nature, he has ways of getting into people's psyche. He is a master of trickery and deception."

Nancy felt the clunk of a dead weight within. The heavy load of anxiety had returned in an instant. She felt as if she was digesting all of her mother's frailties in one fateful gulp.

Ergonwold walked on. "Somehow, Zayock has found a way to feed your mother's negative view on life."

"How?" asked Nancy.

"That we do not know," replied Ergonwold. "But, what I do know is that being around a woeful person can be testing at the best of times, even if you love them with all your heart."

Nancy hid her face at the revelation of a dark family trait. It was too much to bear amongst friends.

"There's nothing to be ashamed of, Nanny Bo," whispered Prema.

Nancy jumped from Ergonwold's back and shook the mud from her pumps.

"Look into my eyes, young lady," instructed Ergonwold.

Nancy stared at her feet, unwilling to co-operate.

"Nancy-Bo-Jones," bellowed Ergonwold, "I asked you to look into my eyes."

"Do as the Great One asks," squawked Grizelda.

Slowly, Nancy raised her head.

Ergonwold lowered his neck and fluttered his feathered lashes.

Nancy stared into his huge oval eyes. They were immense, deep wells of emerald green. Her mind cleared and her surroundings faded into the periphery of her vision. She pulled Grizelda's white feather from her pocket and lowered her eyelids. When she opened them, a ghostly figure appeared at the rear of Ergonwold's misty eyes. It waved at Nancy, then blew her a kiss.

The shadowy figure walked closer.

It was her mother. Nancy waved the feather and mouthed the words, "I love you." Then the sob that had been building in her chest escaped. "I'm here, Mum... I'm alive."

Ergonwold blinked and the apparition vanished. He wobbled, then steadied himself, his magical powers draining his strength. "Beneath your mother's pessimistic exterior is a glimmering light of hope." He rubbed his snout against Nancy's forehead, blowing jets of warm air onto her locks.

"My mother has happiness tucked away somewhere," admitted Nancy. "I know it exists. She needs help."

"And only you can do that, Nanny Bo – for her, and for us," replied Ergonwold. "A child raised in woe will only seek woe. Zayock is unsure how much of your mother's nature has rubbed off on you. His plan was to infiltrate your mother's mind and hope that her cynical view was passed on to her only child."

"Why?"

Inglethwip reached for Nancy's hand and answered. "If Zayock manipulated your mother's mind, you could have been raised as a carbon copy."

"I guess so," said Nancy, quietly.

"You would never have been able to help the creatures of Enerjiimass, because your mindset would have been so predisposed to negativity." Inglethwip tried his best to rouse Nancy. "We need the best of you. The real Nanny Bo, the one we adore."

"And that is why you are with us at such a tender age," said Ergonwold. "If you were any older, there would have been more time for you to take on your mother's personality. I know this is a great shock to you, but we have little time. The challenge of *Attento* is upon us."

"What challenge?" asked Nancy, her brow wrinkling with uncertainty.

"*Attento*," replied Ergonwold. "The light has left us. I cannot lead you to Berringer Hill. It must be you and you alone. You must have faith that all will be well." The Great One paused, his entourage dumbstruck, waiting silently for him to continue. He yawned and went on: "Your biggest weakness, Nanny Bo, is your pessimistic nature."

Nancy felt as if she was drowning in a sea of truth. Ergonwold stared at the girl before him and offered a final warning, "If all appears lost, your optimism and belief must remain. That is the only way of breaking Zayock's curse. I give you my word."

Nancy smiled. "I trust you."

"This is *your* failing and this is *your* challenge," instructed Ergonwold. "Do you understand?"

"I think so."

"There will always be a little piece of me that lives within you, you know that, don't you?"

Nancy placed a hand on her stomach.

"In there, Nanny Bo," said Ergonwold, moving her hand towards her heart with his snout.

Nancy's friends clambered down from the Great One's back and hugged her.

"You can do this," said Jimmy, passionately. "You can do anything you put your mind to, Nanny Bo."

"Thanks, Jim Jam."

Prema squeezed Nancy's hand and kissed her on the cheek. "Remember, you're a dual-star."

Nancy chuckled. "Oh, yeah, I forgot about that."

Prema raised a fist. "One for all, and…"

"All for one," added Nancy.

"That's more like it," crowed Grizelda.

Nancy, Jimmy and Prema linked arms and formed a circle of hugs. Inglethwip reached for the leather holdall and grabbed the spyglass. "I think you might need this."

Nancy took it and twisted the lens. A beam of light cut its way through the darkness. She raised it to the sky, then back to the ground. Ergonwold swished his tail and nudged Nancy forward. "You must lead us out of the forest. Berringer Hill lies on the other side of the silver lake."

"I'm not that good at navigating," confessed Nancy.

"Have faith," squawked Grizelda.

"The curse of *Attento* will not let us help you," instructed Ergonwold. "It is said we must remain silent or the curse will remove the dual-star from both skies."

It was time for Nancy to face her demons. "To Berringer Hill," she said in a half-hearted whimper. The spyglass lit her footsteps as she brushed aside the dense vines and creepers of the forest. Ergonwold, Grizelda, Jimmy, Prema, and Inglethwip followed. It seemed like a never-ending march through a dark abyss of foliage, the only sound being the heavy stomp of Ergonwold's paws. From time to time, Nancy glimpsed a balloon through the canopy of trees. They looked so dull without their brightly lit canvases. Her instincts were to take the path of least resistance. She strode through the overgrown maze of the forest. Privet walls merged with the trees, and rambling ivy grew thicker with each and every step, engulfing her in a sea of yellow and green. The privet walls grew higher and higher, new leaves sprouting before Nancy's eyes. She marvelled at the high-speed growth, the earth parting as new roots gave birth to another row of hedging. She walked on, undeterred by the horticultural magic unfolding before her. She knew she was close to the mysterious Berringer Hill, as she could hear the roar of its beacon in the distance. Her stride lengthened as she approached a three-way intersection.

She stopped to consider her next move. The forest had all but vanished, replaced by a cultivated maze. Nancy clambered up the green walls in an attempt to gain a vantage point. It was impossible: the higher she climbed, the taller the privets grew. She slid back down to the ground, dejected and defeated.

There were three options – left, right, or straight ahead.

She needed help. A decision needed to be made. She turned to face Ergonwold and her friends. The narrow alleyway of shrubs had become deserted of life. *Where are they?* Nancy's hands trembled as she peered into the spyglass – all she could see was an endless corridor of privet walls. She made a left turn into the maze. The flickering spyglass flashed like a strobe against the leafy walls. She scurried forwards, then halted, unsure of herself. Then she sprinted back to the intersection and pointed the faltering torch in every direction. There was nothing other than a vacuous, leafy tunnel of darkness. Then the light of the spyglass died and a fine sheet of rain began to fall. The night was her only companion. She took two blind steps. Her toes pushed against something. Something soft. She took another step forward and tripped over the object. The leather holdall cushioned her fall.

Nancy curled up into a ball and cried. She had failed. Her thoughts returned to the dark void of negativity she had grown so accustomed to. Then, in her curled-up state of sorrow, she heard a voice.

Ergonwold's words echoed: *"This is your failing, and this is your challenge."*

The wind howled as cold droplets of rain poured down upon her tired body. She promised Ergonwold she would remain optimistic. Guilt now piled itself upon her despair. "Stop this!" she screamed, in a fit of defiance. "Pessimism has taken my mother, but it will never take me."

In that brief moment of refusal, something changed. A neurological pathway became unblocked, so her thoughts and emotions dictating the immediate living space ran free through her mind.

The curse of *Attento* was broken.

Nancy unzipped the bag, her fingertips probing for the music box. She found it and turned the key.

The lid sprung open. Light spewed out, clouds of glitter surrounding the diminutive fairy as she hovered in the air. Nancy clapped enthusiastically as the Night Fairy sang her heart out. "I am glad you appreciate my song," said Shaanue, her voice trailing off into the dead of night.

Nancy smoothed away tears of joy and kneeled before the fairy. "Oh, Shaanue, you have no idea how happy I am to see you."

"But you appear so sad?"

"I was… but now, I'm—"

"You allowed yourself to slip down the path of despair," interrupted Shaanue, her wand pressed firmly against Nancy's chest.

"I'm sorry," replied Nancy, allowing her curls to hide her embarrassment.

"There is no shame in fear or despair," said Shaanue, "we all encounter that. Every youngster carries the burden of self-doubt and anxiety."

"Really?" asked Nancy. "I'm not the only one?"

"No," replied Shaanue, resolutely. "You are certainly not. The curse of *Attento* has exaggerated those feelings. If you look hard enough, there will always be a way out of the darkness."

Nancy got to her feet, held out her arms and conceded, "I'm sick of fearing the worst." Then her voice became stronger. "I refuse to allow this fear to control my life. I've had enough of it!"

Shaanue whizzed through the air and looked straight into her emboldened eyes. "What a thing it is for one so young to have stood against the darkness and banished the spell of *Attento*." The fairy leaped onto her shoulder. "You are a brave, wonderful little girl."

Nancy emptied her lungs and slumped to her knees, the soft earth squelching as she landed. "At last," she gasped. "It's gone..."

The Night Fairy returned a blank expression, and with a swish of her wand she said, "Gone? What has?"

"That feeling – the fear and dread," exclaimed Nancy. "I feel different. Lighter."

Shaanue sang a joyous, uplifting melody, an offering to the higher echelons of light and energy. She threw handfuls of fairy dust into the air, the glittering confetti raining down on Nancy, every fleck fizzing against her skin, puncturing any cloud of worry or doubt.

Nancy opened her mouth and swallowed the sparkling dust. "More!" she said, as laughter erupted uncontrollably from her stomach.

"What's so funny?" asked Shaanue.

Nancy shrugged. "I don't know. I'm lost, wet through, cold, tired, and hungry. But I feel great."

"You should feel great, Nancy Bo Jones. You are free from Zayock's curse. You have overcome the exaggerated weakness imposed upon you."

Nancy held out her hand. Shaanue landed in the middle of her palm. She lifted the fairy up to her face. "I feel brand new."

Shaanue smiled. "It's a rebirth."

"How will I find my way out of this maze?" asked Nancy, as she inspected every avenue of foliage.

The Night Fairy lit the walls of the maze with her wand. "You stand at a three-way intersection. Make your choice. Only you can decide the direction in which you travel."

Nancy grabbed the leather holdall. To her left was a dark alleyway of privets; to her right, a mirror. Somehow it was nestled amongst the shrubberies, glistening to the eye. She turned to the right and spoke quietly to her reflection. "Everything's going to be all right. Be positive – one step at a time, no need to worry..."

She clambered through the shrubs and placed a hand on the glass. It rippled like water: what appeared solid was now fluid. A large, reflective, aquatic-looking glass. Nancy held her breath, pinched her nose, and plunged into the water. Sparks flew from the edges of the glass as her skin was doused by a luscious silvery liquid. Static energy fizzed and crackled all around her. She reappeared moments later, breathless, standing behind the looking glass, looking back at her entry point.

The sweet sound of birdsong echoed throughout the forest: nature calling her, pulling her forward. Nancy shook the remaining silver droplets from her garments and walked on. "That was incredible."

"The mirror of change," said Shaanue. "We all need a time of personal reflection." The Night Fairy continued, swooshing her wand, encouraging her: "Life's path is easier if we walk with certainty."

Nancy pushed her way through the branches, repeating the fairy's words over and over, her inner radar now guiding her towards Berringer Hill. Then the horizon appeared – a white line intersected by two green eyes.

Trails of fairy dust followed Shaanue as she flew off into the distance, scouting the way, checking that no Jagganath hid nearby.

The peak of Berringer Hill was now in full view and could be seen over the walls of the maze. The privets were no longer a hindrance, their roots shrivelling and walls reducing.

Navigation was restored. Nancy could see her goal. She knew where she was going. She imagined her friends waiting for her. She knew they would be. She *believed* they would be. They *had* to be there. Her doubts had vanished as quickly as the effects of the curse of *Attento*. As the forest thinned and the trees parted, Nancy felt the radiant heat of the beacon, its orange flames caressing the sky. She carried on, relentless, her belief intact, and her doubts crushed.

Finally, as she crawled through a barrage of weeds and vine, she saw them.

Her friends appeared at the foot of Berringer Hill. Jimmy and Prema ran with open arms to greet her. They embraced as Nancy's tired legs finally gave way. "I knew you would be here. I just knew it."

Inglethwip scooped Nancy up in his arms. "We were here all along, Nanny Bo. You just had to believe it. And with a little help, you did. Well done."

Nancy pushed back her curls and blew Inglethwip a kiss.

He hid behind his fringe and blushed.

"Any chance you could carry me up Berringer Hill?" Nancy asked.

"Certainly, madam," replied the potion-maker.

Ergonwold approached and nuzzled his snout into Nancy's face. She giggled as the snout looped her left ear. "I never thought I could lose a friend as big as you."

"As long as you believe, you will never be alone," insisted the Great One. "Remember that when I'm gone."

Nancy reached out with the tenderness of a loved one and stroked his snout.

"As soon as you took the challenge of *Attento*, we left you," confessed Ergonwold. "Well, physically speaking. We were nothing more than ghosts following you through that maze."

"You mean you were never actually with me in the maze?"

"No. As you ran off, we were transported."

"How?" asked Nancy.

"Dark magic, I'm afraid to say," confessed Ergonwold. "Once the challenge of *Attento* began, Zayock's spell took control. You had to be alone. I tried my best to help. I conjured our images for as long as possible. Unfortunately, my powers are failing me. Magic saps my strength. Our minds are more powerful than our bodies. I'm sorry I—"

"Don't apologise," interrupted Nancy. "Sometimes you just have to make it on your own."

Ergonwold raised his snout and trumpeted, his mighty legs pulling him up towards the furnace. "We can rest here. The colony of Night Fairies will be a welcome relief. You may recognise some old faces."

Nancy's eyes followed the tip of Ergonwold's snout. A polka-dot balloon floated down towards her and landed on the crest of Berringer Hill. The wicker basket contained three passengers. Clouds of smoke swirled around them as they climbed out and kneeled before Ergonwold the Great. Nancy recognised the soft Irish lilt. She jumped from Inglethwip's arms and raced towards the balloon, her legs wobbling and her lungs smarting at the smoke. She fell to the ground in a fit of coughs and grunts.

An old lady walked through the haze and appeared like an angel, the beacon colouring her face as she opened her arms and pulled Nancy to her feet. "How the devil are you?" asked a weary Aunt Elma.

"I'm all the better for seeing you," replied Nancy.

Aunt Elma took a sideways step and revealed the High Priest of Enerjiimass. Captain Carbunkle giggled, his gold tooth gleaming in the firelight. Then, with a click of his fingers, his impish body levitated six feet above the ground.

Mr Wuu straightened his bow-tie and offered his hand to Nancy. Nancy slapped his palm, planted a wet kiss on his cheek, and introduced Jimmy to her acquaintances from The Home For The Incurably Curious. Thousands of glimmering Night Fairies buzzed and hummed around them, their trailing tail lights reminiscent of rockets fizzing across the night sky. Mr Wuu opened a hamper and pulled out a slab of cheese, numerous bunches of grapes, crackers, and a tray of jam tarts.

The feast had begun. There was a frenzy of wild conversation as the sky returned to an array of ever-changing neon colours.

Diwali balloons glowed brighter than ever and the silver lake shimmered, reflecting light onto the cluster of igloo huts. Shaanue continued to express her joy through song, her fellow fairies harmonising perfectly, like a Cathedral choir. Captain Carbunkle entertained all with his acrobatic dancing and vanishing tricks.

Nancy squeezed herself next to Prema. "Budge up! Let me in."

There you go," smiled Prema. "Room for all."

Nancy watched her friend flicking through the elaborate optical cards, twisting them one way, then the other. She finished by arching the pack between her palms, then placed a solitary card on the grass.

"That's so cool," said Nancy. "Who taught you that?"

"My gran."

Nancy pointed at Jimmy. "Go on, turn it over."

Prema laughed out loud. "Yes, do as The Chosen One desires, Jim Jam; it will inform us of the present."

"Okay," grunted Jimmy, between slurps of fizzy drink. He turned the card and gulped another mouthful. "Five gold rings."

"Correct," replied Prema. "That's us."

"Us?" grunted Jimmy.

"Yes," replied Prema. "Otherwise known as the circle of friends – you, me, Nancy, Elijah, and The Duke."

At the mention of their missing friends, Nancy's smile disappeared. "I hope they're all right."

Prema dealt another card. "And now, for the future."

Jimmy wiped his mouth and turned the card. "It's a shield protecting two stars. And there's a wand." He sipped another mouthful and narrowed his eyes. "Why is the wand firing at the shield?"

"There's going to be a battle," replied Prema.

Jimmy prodded the card. "What are the two stars?"

Prema hesitated, then looked at Nancy and lowered her voice. "The two stars are—"

"Me," interrupted Nancy. "Otherwise known as dual-stars."

"Yes," whispered Prema.

Nancy chewed her nails as Prema dealt a third card. Jimmy pinched the corner of the optical card and spun it over. "It's the same as the first card – gold rings."

Prema's hand covered her mouth. "Oh, no!"

"What?" asked Jimmy.

Prema looped her arms around her friends. "It's the ring of friendship. Again."

"What's wrong with that?" asked a bewildered Jimmy.

"Count them," said Nancy, her eyes glued on the card.

Jimmy placed his index finger on each ring. "One, two, three, four." He counted again. "One, two, three, four."

Nancy turned away, her head falling into her hands. "A death."

Jimmy grabbed Prema and drew her close, their foreheads bumping. "Does this mean there will only be four of us when the battle is over?"

Prema nodded and placed her finger over his mouth. "We cannot speak of this."

"But—"

"Enough, Jim Jam," said Nancy, abruptly. "We carry on as normal. Okay?"

Jimmy pronounced, "She's going to die," from the corner of his mouth.

"Never interfere with or mention the future," said Prema. "It is the golden rule of the optical cards. My gran says a dark cloud will never leave the person who breaks the code."

"But Nanny Bo will—"

Nancy cut Jimmy short. "We must continue as planned, Jim Jam. Think of the consequences if we don't."

"And think of the consequences if we do!" screamed Jimmy, in defiance of his friend.

An uncomfortable silence followed.

The jubilation around them stopped, as if someone had hit the pause button. All eyes fell upon Jimmy. He cleared his throat and apologised, gradually, the background noise returned. Prema rested her hand on his shoulder and tried her best to raise his spirits. "Sometimes the cards can rework their imagery."

Nancy pulled Prema to one side. "Over there."

"Where?"

"There," pointed Nancy. "To the right of the beacon, I think the High Priest wants us."

Captain Carbunkle waited for the right moment to address the crowd. He made sure that everyone had been fed and watered and was in possession of sufficient air berries. He climbed onto Ergonwold's back and waved his hand back and forth. Nancy marvelled at the sound of invisible bells chiming, giggling at her friends, whose eyes scanned the hillside for the elusive bells.

"The curse of *Attento* has been broken," proclaimed Captain Carbunkle. Cheers rang out on the summit of Berringer Hill. "Aunt Elma, Mr Wuu, and I can return to the land where we belong. Our status as dual-stars returned." He gave a grateful wink at Nancy. "We have waited eleven years for The Chosen One to raise the portal and come to our rescue. We have spent every waking hour planning for this day. We have sorely missed Ergonwold and the love he spreads throughout this magical land. But, during the Great One's absence, Zayock's power has multiplied. It is our priority to find the maternal nest and return the Bloodstone to its rightful place."

Nancy held up her hand.

"Speak, my child," insisted Captain Carbunkle.

"Forget the Bloodstone – surely our priority must be to find Ergonwold's Nest?" The bigger picture was now forming in Nancy's mind's-eye. "If he cannot recharge himself on the maternal nest, he will—"

"I am well aware of the Great One's predicament," interrupted Captain Carbunkle, "but if we do not locate the Bloodstone, Zayock will continue to concoct Tantibus and fill our land with his smoke." The High Priest held out his palms and concluded, "It is impossible for us to radiate optimism through the veil of smoke. Eventually, it will kill all of us."

Nancy remained tight-lipped. Her eyes found Ergonwold, who turned his head to face the fiery beacon. The deep plunging sensation in the pit of her stomach returned. She knew the Great One was troubled.

Captain Carbunkle continued to address the crowd. "After we have rested, we will cross the glades of Enerjiimass and land our balloons within the mountain range. There, you will be instructed of our plans to breach the castle, find the Bloodstone, and, hopefully, Ergonwold's Nest."

Aunt Elma pulled Nancy to her feet. "Sometimes, we have to sacrifice for the greater good."

"At last," crowed Grizelda, "the children get to ride in the balloons of Diwali."

"We can ride in the balloons?" asked Prema, her face a picture of childish excitement.

"Yes," replied Captain Carbunkle. "Our gathering creates much positivity. It has been quite some time since a force of positive energy has filled the air of Enerjiimass. It is like the old days," joked the High Priest of Enerjiimass. "Years ago, the Diwali balloons had enough light and power to guide passengers from one side of this land to the other. It was our mode of transport until Zayock began poisoning the skies."

Inglethwip wedged two fingers in his mouth and wolf-whistled. A small cluster of Diwali balloons began their descent, floating towards Berringer Hill, their empty baskets swaying in the breeze.

"Let us join Grizelda and take to the sky," yelled Captain Carbunkle.

The children were led to their balloon. Nancy kept one eye on Ergonwold, who walked down the hill, his enormous paws crushing the floral carpet, his snout pointing in the direction of Castle Zayock.

Captain Carbunkle barked his instructions: "On the count of three, release the sand bags and place your feet onto the circular board." He clapped and giggled like a naughty child. "This is your steering wheel, children. Whichever way you spin the wheel is the direction you will travel."

"Be careful," cried Mr Wuu from his basket. "The wheel is very sensitive."

Captain Carbunkle lit his pipe and screamed, "One, two, three... Follow me!"

The sand bags were thrown overboard and the balloons left Berringer Hill. Nancy's yellow canvas rose effortlessly into the bright sky, up, up and away, aimlessly drifting over the spectacular landscape. The three children jumped onto the steering board and began to rotate it with their feet, puffing and panting as the Diwali balloon's furnace roared. Nancy chuckled as she watched Jimmy pull himself up onto the ledge of the basket, his feet swinging back and forth as he admired the Night Fairies whizzing around them like fire-flies, their soprano voices filling the air with choral bliss.

"Sorry for interrupting, Jim Jam," said Nancy, grinning. "Are you going to give us a hand or spend the rest of our journey star-gazing?"

"Oh, I'm sorry," replied Jimmy, "it's such a fantastic view." Then he pushed himself off the ledge and attempted to land on the spinning wheel.

Nancy roared with laughter as Jimmy crash-landed onto the pedal board, which spun to the right, then the left. The balloon was now zigzagging like a wayward rollercoaster.

And with that, Nancy, Jimmy, and Prema began the ride of their lives.

27
The Piano and the Bulb

Zayock arched his elongated frame and clenched the Bloodstone. He held the precious jewel to the light and kissed it. "My search for the Elixir of Life is coming to an end. Soon, with this stone and the last of the remaining ingredients, I will live forever."

The Duke's petrified eyes followed the magician across the engine room to an electric piano. Wires spewed from beneath it, meandering their way to a computerised panel, where digital sound waves and musical notes flashed on a miniature screen. Zayock pulled the fabric of his trousers high over his knees as he sat. "If only you had listened, father, we could have ruled together." He danced his bony fingers across the black-and-white keys, his head rocking as the notes filled the air. He was lost in the depths of his music. A melancholic sonata seducing body and mind.

It was then that The Duke spied a light bulb. Somehow it was powered by the keyboard, its filament glowing blood red as the music reverberated throughout the cluttered room. The pistons shuddered as valves released jets of steam, the machine pounding in time with Zayock's music. The cable that linked the bulb to the piano looped its way through a nest of tangled wires to the glass orb in the corner of the room.

"Every note of music has a purpose," cried Zayock. He finished his virtuoso performance and proclaimed, "I can refine any energy. And music is energy." He lifted his fingers from the keys and sniggered, his madness showing in all its glory. "This tune creates a pillow of sadness for the creatures of Enerjiimass. My beautiful smoke increases with every minor note."

The Duke's heart sank: it was in that moment he understood Zayock's plan. He knew from his own experience how music could alter mood, but not at the bidding of such a twisted purpose.

"The light of my life," said Zayock, softly. "Can you see it?" asked the sorcerer, poking his wand at the bulb.

The Duke shifted his eyes towards the light and nodded.

"That *is* the light of my life," confessed Zayock, "all of my feelings illuminated." The Duke stared at the bulb, the glow of the lamp blurring his vision. "Ordinary folk have no idea," added Zayock. "Music has a power – it's an invisible source of energy. And light is what fuels our soul."

The rumble of machinery and the wizardry of Zayock were too much to contend with. The Duke had nothing to lose. He had all but capitulated. He fixed his sights on the piano and summoned the music from within. His fingertips tingled as a strange, distant, harmonic chime filled the space between his ears. Something guided him. A flutter of creative energy pulled him to his feet. He ambled towards the keyboard, the last morsel of determination etched upon his weary face.

Zayock looked on, puzzled, his tongue lolling to the side of his mouth. "What do you think you're doing?"

"Musical balance," whispered The Duke. He stepped over Elijah's body and perched himself on the piano stool. He stretched his fingers and thought of his mother's favourite piece. "This is my last offering. I dedicate this to every good soul…"

The hairs on his neck stood firm as he began to play *Rhapsody on a Theme of Paganini*. The music lifted him out of the engine room, high above the gloom of the mountains, catapulting him into a clear sky of hope. The churning of machinery was disabled. The bulb faded from a fiery red to an angelic white.

A look of astonishment spread across Zayock's face as the young boy caressed the piano keys.

Then the final note rang out.

The Duke looked up and smiled.

For the first time since his father's death, Zayock offered a kind gesture. He returned a smile of respect for the music within the boy, his angular features softening for a split second as if a pilot light shone from a pitch-black soul. The Duke's heart boomed in his chest as the silence seemed to immobilise them both. *Could music be his salvation?*

His hopes were dashed in an instant.

"Get off my piano," ordered Zayock. "Your talent has saved you. You were next in the chair. Now, your friend can take your place."

"No!" cried The Duke. "Elijah's had enough."

Zayock snorted, then he picked Elijah off the floor, strapped him into the chair and pulled the lever. A slow, resounding, mechanical groan followed. The machine started to chug and churn, lights flickered on the control panel, then the cogs jerked into action. The walls vibrated, the floor shook, and the pistons hissed like a nest of angry vipers. "One more bottle of Tantibus and I can formulate the Elixir of Life."

The Duke slammed his fist on the keyboard. "Leave him alone."

Zayock connected the skullcap to the machine and pushed a button. Elijah's body stiffened, arrested by the surge of electrical power. "At long last, the final extraction of Tantibus. I have succeeded, dearest father." He applauded his own malicious masterplan and glared at The Duke. "The ingredients are complete: seven hundred and seventy-seven bottles of Tantibus, a vial of healing liquid, and a shard of glass from the precious Bloodstone. I have it all. Eternity awaits."

"Take me," pleaded The Duke. "Elijah is weak."

Zayock dismissed The Duke's pleas, emphasising every word with his wand: he was a conductor with an orchestra of one. "You are too hopeful, a firm spirit, but your friend's dark mood will generate my final bottle. Soon, I will be immortal."

"You're sick," said The Duke. "You need help."

"Come here!" ordered the sorcerer. "I need to keep an eye on you…"

The Duke reluctantly obeyed.

Zayock grabbed his collar, turned on his heels and dragged him up the flinted staircase.

The noise of the engine room was but a distant rumble as they stepped into the castle lobby. The cold night air crept through the windows onto The Duke's face, rousing his senses. His eyes were now fixated on the huge drape fluttering like a purple flag in the medieval room. Zayock stood beneath it, reciting the words with melodic glee: "*Forever is not long enough.*" He pranced across the flagstones, fell to one knee and pushed the serpent's eye. "At last," he sighed. "*Forever* is within reach."

The stone slab slid open.

The Duke felt the panic rising, an icy cold liquid filling his lungs to bursting point. Zayock salivated as the secret void appeared. "You may have stolen the Bloodstone, but I cursed the bottle of healing liquid. My incantations and charms are undeniable."

The Duke held out his scorched fingertips and mouthed, "*Incanta Malouchia,*" silently to himself. A loud clunk reverberated throughout the lobby. The slab stopped and fell into its resting place. Zayock jumped into the dark chamber. He drew his wand and released an orb of light, then he fell to his knees, scampering around like a rat for any sign of the healing liquid. Bewilderment quickly turned to rage. "Where is it? Only *I* can handle the healing liquid!"

The Duke peered down at the sorcerer and shrugged.

Zayock sprung from below like a wild animal and lunged at him. His hands clamped around his neck, his nails tearing his skin. "Where is it? Tell me!"

"Elijah," rasped The Duke.

Zayock panicked. "I must release him!" He ruffled his cape and scarpered towards the staircase. "The mechanical vibrations will shatter the vial. I need that tonic. My future depends upon it."

The Duke gulped desperately for air. He stumbled towards the stairwell, teetering on the edge, fear and trepidation crippling him as he stared into the dark void. The distant groan of his friend sparked his tired limbs into life.

Breathless, he entered the engine room and was immobilised at the sight before him.

Elijah had been unbuckled and Zayock had him pinned to the floor, rifling through his garments like a man possessed.

"Leave him," said The Duke, his hands aloft in a pose of surrender.

The plea fell upon deaf ears. "There is only one place for you," scowled the demented sorcerer. "The chair!"

Within seconds, The Duke was strapped in and the skullcap was attached. His body jolted as the machine was set into motion.

"Now we can talk without being disturbed," growled Zayock. "Where is my healing liquid, Elijah Lincoln?"

Elijah's lips were sealed.

Zayock's eyes drilled into Elijah's. He drew his wand and pulled a drawstring-bag from the lining of his cape. He released the cord and dipped his wand into a powdery substance.

The Duke wriggled beneath the chair's restraining straps, the sharp metal buckles breaking his skin, his wrists bleeding, his scalp burning.

Zayock thrust his wand onto Elijah's temple, his voice a rasping, hate-fuelled whisper. "Where... is... my... healing... liquid?"

28
By the Light of Shaanue

Three Diwali balloons landed within the castle grounds. Nancy stared up at the torn canvases tangled in the treetops. They reminded her of gigantic streamers. *What a shame.*

"Worry not," replied Ergonwold, interrupting Nancy's thoughts. "The balloons are happy to serve us."

Captain Carbunkle and Aunt Elma tugged on their shredded canvas and released it from the sprawling branches. Mr Wuu and Inglethwip were nowhere to be seen. A deflated pink balloon drooped over their basket, shielding them from prying eyes. Nancy clicked her fingers and connected her thoughts with Grizelda's. The parrot grabbed the remains of the canvas and flew up into the clouds, the bright pink material trailing behind her like a torn sail. Mr Wuu and Inglethwip sat cross-legged in the basket, their cheeks bursting with scones, and jam smeared all around their lips.

A brief moment of laughter was brought to an abrupt halt. The distant howls of the Jagganath echoed beyond the woodland. Nancy held up a finger for silence, her stomach knotted as a strange, yet familiar voice echoed within. As it grew in volume, she plugged her ears.

"You can hear him, can't you?" said Aunt Elma, sharply.

"Yes," confirmed Nancy. "It's jumbled, incoherent. He's looking for something, and he's angry…"

Aunt Elma took Nancy by the hand and led her to Ergonwold. "The girl has attained mind skills."

"Your observation is accurate," confessed Ergonwold. "Nanny Bo has evolved."

Aunt Elma witnessed the fading light behind Ergonwold's eyes. "You are struggling."

Ergonwold returned a slow, painful nod. He yawned loudly, then raised one of his paws. Nancy tickled it, then blew the wrinkly beast a kiss. "Be strong, you are our hero."

"Thank you, NannyBo," groaned Ergonwold. "Unfortunately, my energy levels are depleted."

Aunt Elma addressed the tired beast. "We need the last drop of your magic to overturn Zayock." She placed her hand over her heart and said, "You, and your precious energy, are our only hope."

Ergonwold swished his snout. "I know."

Nancy stroked him affectionately. "The maternal nest will restore your powers, O' Great One."

"I hope so," replied Ergonwold.

"You are our spiritual leader," said Aunt Elma. "Lead us into battle; we are here to serve you."

"Yes," said Nancy, confidently, "we are your army." She took a step back as Ergonwold extended his tusks and peered through the screen of trees.

Captain Carbunkle bowed before Ergonwold and mumbled a string of reverential words. One by one, they linked fingers and formed a circle. "We have three objectives," Captain Carbunkle confided. "One – find the Bloodstone and the healing liquid. Two – release the prisoners; and three – find Ergonwold's Nest. Without the nest, a regeneration will be needed."

"What's a regeneration?" asked Nancy, pulling herself free from the circle.

"It's the *real* everlasting," replied Captain Carbunkle. "If you clip an old flower, a new one will follow."

Nancy pulled a disgusted face, unwilling to digest such prophetic words. "We *must* find the nest and my friends."

"No!" retaliated Captain Carbunkle. "First we need to deal with the Jagganath; their weakness is light. The next difficulty will be to enter the castle. Climbing the mountain-steps would be foolish. Zayock would pick us off one by one with his wand."

Jimmy squealed his disapproval at death by wand. Swirls of dark mist appeared above him, floating up through the trees, forming a small yet visible cloud.

Nancy was the first to notice it.

Captain Carbunkle was the second. "What is this cloud of worry, Jim Jam?"

Jimmy shrugged, looked up at the cloud, and then down at his slippers.

"Speak up, lad," squawked Grizelda. "The dark clouds are gathering."

"Surprise will aid us in our battle," added Captain Carbunkle. "Your cloud of negativity will alert Zayock."

Jimmy apologised, avoiding eye contact with Nancy. "What's wrong?" she asked, tugging at Jimmy's sleeve. "You are the most optimistic person I have ever met."

Jimmy turned his cheek. "I'm okay. Leave me alone."

"Once we are inside the castle, I will take responsibility for finding the Bloodstone," instructed Captain Carbunkle. "Ergonwold will locate his nest, and the rest of you must help the humans."

"The Duke and Eli!" said Nancy. "They have names, you know."

"Forgive me," said Captain Carbunkle. "We must release The Duke and Eli."

Nancy bowed before the High Priest. "And then what?"

"Then your fate awaits," muttered Captain Carbunkle. "You must face your long-lost relative – Lord Bymerstone." Nancy felt the blood surge through her veins. She gave Captain Carbunkle a pointed look and clenched her fists. "If you succeed, you must find the Tree of Hearts before the timeline elapses," concluded the magical dwarf.

Nancy arched her brow. "Timeline?"

"Not enough *time* to explain," replied Captain Carbunkle.

"You make it sound so simple."

"It is," replied Captain Carbunkle, his gold teeth glimmering through his impish smile.

"We've never had to enter a castle or had to defeat a magician before," said Nancy.

Captain Carbunkle tapped the heels of his clogs together and said, "Use your instincts, Nanny Bo."

Ergonwold pulled his head from the trees. "They are close."

"Urgh, I can smell them," said Nancy, pinching her nose.

"We need to fill them with our light," whispered Captain Carbunkle. "Children, I need you to surrender yourselves."

Jimmy scowled, folded his arms and addressed the High Priest. "No way!"

"Surrender to the Jagganath," replied Captain Carbunkle, quietly. "That's what you need to do."

"But why?" asked Jimmy. He waited patiently for the High Priest to answer.

"To give the Night Fairies a chance."

"A chance of what?"

Captain Carbunkle's playful tone changed, agitation accentuating his words. "Success, Jim Jam. They will use their magic to overcome the Jagganath."

Jimmy swiped his arm. "That's madness."

"But there is a method to it," said Captain Carbunkle, casually. "You must leave the woods and walk out into the open fields. The Jagganath will be overwhelmed at the sight of The Chosen One."

Jimmy pointed at Nancy. "They'll kill her... the optical cards foretold it."

Nancy fixed Jimmy with her blue eyes, her words escaping through gritted teeth: "Enough of that. We must do what's needed."

Captain Carbunkle raised his arms above his head, his tiny fingers pointing at the cluster of Night Fairies above him. "Come to me, Fairies of the Night..."

Shaanue fluttered down between the branches, reciting an ancient song from *The First Book of Cosmo*. She was followed by her entourage and a tapestry of merging glitter trails.

"Shaanue," hooted Captain Carbunkle. "I need you. The Great One is weak."

"Yes, Your Highness," answered the fairy. "I am here to serve."

Captain Carbunkle's voice was laden with remorse. "Shaanue, I need you to put light into the souls of the Jagganath. Their eyes *must* be penetrated. Do you understand?"

Shaanue didn't answer. She hovered momentarily, a fine haze of dust lingering behind her. She wiped a tear, bowed before the high priest, then whizzed up to the larger congregation of fairies in the treetops.

A cold, darting arrow of pain ran the length of Nancy's spine. Death was calling, but she wasn't sure whom it was seeking.

Captain Carbunkle lifted his hat and raised a toast. "In the name of Ergonwold the Great and the wider world, we hereby offer our energy to the stars and our hearts to our loved ones." He sighed heavily, followed by what sounded to Nancy like a hushed prayer. "Children," he cried, "you must leave these woods and walk towards the Jagganath. Have faith. It will reward you."

Nancy acknowledged Captain Carbunkle with a firm nod. Then, as she started forward, and without warning, a series of high-pitched screams attacked her inner ear. The pain was unbearable. A sonic attack tore her emotions to shreds. Nancy spun in every direction, searching frantically for the owner of the screams. Then she found Ergonwold's eyes, their senses aligned. Ergonwold raised his snout and gestured to the Night Fairies. Nancy crooked her neck. The pain came from up there. Hovering in the treetops were the wailing Night Fairies, bidding farewell, embracing one another, their shrill cries way above the frequency of human ears. Only three felt their pain: Ergonwold – the Great One, Nancy – The Chosen One, and Grizelda – Reader of Hearts and Minds.

The pain passed through The Chosen One and rose up into the skies of Enerjiimass. "I can feel everything," groaned Nancy, the declaration bursting free. "Not just the pain, but the love, the fear. It's scary."

"An omniscient observer," replied Captain Carbunkle. "That means you are ready. You are a true conduit of energy. You are our seer!" He clapped his hands and boomed, "Walk without fear, children."

Aunt Elma blew Nancy a kiss and waved her off. Nancy left the woods and, after a few short steps, turned to face Ergonwold. Their eyes met again. Their minds still entwined. She scurried back and embraced him. "*Go*," said Ergonwold. He nudged her gently from the woods back into the field. "Your destiny awaits. Do not be late."

Nancy trudged forward, glancing over her shoulder, unconvinced she would lay eyes on the magnificent beast again. She stared up at the castle. It was enormous, perched on the highest mountain, its chimney reaching to the sky like a giant smoke-filled finger. Her friends' steps laboured behind her. They were scheming and bickering, their thoughts and voices interfering with her own – a crackle of unwanted interference.

"What if this is when Nanny Bo—?"

"Be quiet, Jim Jam," snapped Prema.

"But the optical cards predicted—"

"Jim Jam!"

"What?"

"We must not talk of the future!"

Nancy turned, her face grave. "What are you arguing about?"

Then came the sound of the marching Jagganath. Jimmy's fear outweighed his guilt. "Sorry, Nanny Bo."

"That's all right," replied Nancy, her voice calm and controlled. "Let's hope Shaanue knows what she's doing."

With Nancy in the middle, the three linked arms and continued to walk in the direction of the largest mountain, the wooded area behind them growing smaller with every step. "I can hear the Jagganath," declared Nancy, "and I can smell them, but I can't see them."

Suddenly, a golden ray of light shone through the clouds, splitting the sky in two. Nancy marvelled at the divided heavens. It was a strange sight, as if one half was pitted against the other. Then something on the ground caught her attention. Her skin prickled as the outline of a dozen Jagganath appeared. They marched in perfect time, swinging their limbs back and forth, their capes flowing in the wind, their red eyes shining like lasers, howling at the sight of The Chosen One. The Centurion panted in exhilaration, slime seeping from the slits in his nostrils, his razor-sharp teeth chattering wildly. Then he halted, forced his staff into the ground, pushed out his webbed claw, and continued to walk alone. As the leader, he wanted the glory of apprehending The Chosen One.

Nancy strode on, dragging her two reluctant friends in the crooks of her arms. They were less than ten metres from the monster. She stopped in her tracks and faced her companions. "When you believe in your heart of hearts that everything is going to be all right, it doesn't matter what life throws at you."

Jimmy and Prema nodded, then closed their eyes. Another two steps brought them within a hair's-breadth of the monster. The

Centurion's sticky mucus trickled from his head onto Nancy's ringlets, slithering down her cheek like a translucent slug. He howled with delight, then opened his arms to seize his prize.

Nancy ducked.

Then she swung a fist at the lunging monster. Wild Jagganath howls filled the air as a distant speck of light hurtled towards the children. Nancy fought with all her might, arms flapping, legs kicking. The Centurion lifted Nancy by the throat with one claw and slapped Jimmy and Prema to the ground with the other. At that precise moment, the speck of light released a high-pitched wail. "I am Shaanue, here to sacrifice myself and lighten your soul. Be gone with you, Jagganath!"

Shaanue turned to face Nancy.

In the nanosecond before she disappeared, Nancy witnessed her goodbye. With a final wave of her wand, the Night Fairy sped through the air and penetrated the red pupils of the Centurion, disappearing deep into his skull. The giant monster glowed bright white, then crumbled into a pile of dust. Eleven more sparks of light flew past the children, aiming for the remainder of the Jagganath. Nancy gagged, the terrible sound reminiscent of flies splatting against a car windscreen. One after another, the fairies crash-landed into the pupils of the Jagganath.

Shaanue and her entourage had made the greatest sacrifice.

Ergonwold trotted towards the children. "The Night Fairies are carriers of light. It is painful for them to see the light of day."

Nancy struggled to get the words out. "She's dead, Shaanue's dead!"

"Their sole purpose is to pass light on to others," rasped Ergonwold. "And there was never a creature in greater need of light than the Jagganath. Surely you must understand the sacrifice, Nanny Bo?"

"But why Shaanue?" asked Nancy, choking back her grief. "She was my friend. You knew that. You could have chosen another fairy."

"If you are a leader, you must lead," replied Ergonwold, "and never hide from what needs to be done."

"She lost her life to save me," croaked Nancy.

"Death is part of life," mused Ergonwold. "We will never forget Shaanue. If you make it home, she will live in your music box forever – I promise you that – she will always be able to sing for you."

Nancy wiped a tear from her cheek. "She had the voice of an angel."

The remaining Night Fairies mourned the passing of Shaanue and the others with a sombre choral interlude, their trails of light creating a tapestry of colour against the twelve piles of dust that were the Jagganath.

Inglethwip waited patiently for the choir to finish, then pointed to an opening at the base of the mountain. "It's over there. That's the secret entrance. It leads up into the castle lobby."

"Well done, Master Limpweed," said Ergonwold. "You know this castle better than most. Lead the way, young man."

Inglethwip grabbed Nancy's hand and entered the tunnel. After a dozen strides, she asked, "What's that tapping?"

"Another one of Zayock's machines," replied Inglethwip, grimly. "Before I planned my escape, Zayock told me he had devised a way of identifying pessimistic humans. He needs their negativity to power his machinery."

Nancy stared at Inglethwip, mystified. "How does he do it?"

"He did tell me," replied Inglethwip, scratching his head for an answer. "I can't remember."

They filed past the encoding room and observed the trail of candles either side of the path. The noise of the engine room gained in volume as they made their way up the dusty track.

"Ah, that's it," cried Inglethwip. "I do remember..."

Nancy slapped Inglethwip on the back. "Go on!"

"Something like *in-turn-and-nets...*"

Nancy's face puckered. "The internet?" she suggested, half-heartedly.

"Yes, that's it," said Inglethwip. "The in-ter-net." His nostrils twitched and his lips curled. "Do you know what it is?"

"Of course we do," said Jimmy, squeezing himself between them.

"But how does he do it?" asked Nancy.

"He mentioned something about a survey. That's how he identifies the maudlin. Then he accesses negativity through the *ether*."

"My mum was completing a happiness survey before I left," said Nancy.

"We need to focus on the task at hand," countered Aunt Elma. She placed a hand on Nancy's shoulder and reassured her. "All in good time, my child. The story of Zayock and the internet can wait. Right now, we need to find the Bloodstone."

"And Ergonwold's Nest, and our friends," Nancy retorted.

"Of course, dear. Of course."

They continued the long walk through the dotted line of candles. Prema searched her pocket for an air berry, steadied herself from what felt like a mini earthquake, opened her mouth, and swallowed. Jimmy threw a berry up into the air, stuck out his tongue, and waited for it to land. They prepared themselves for an onslaught of stomach cramps and vomit, but nothing happened. Nancy shrugged, not convinced the berries had worked. "Try another one, Pre."

"No need," squawked Grizelda. "Your bodies are acclimatising to Enerjiimass."

"That means you are dual-stars," said Nancy, cheerfully. "Just like me."

"Not quite," replied the parrot. "The longer you are here, the harder it will be to cross the threshold and return home. And if you don't make it home in time, you will be trapped here. Forever."

Nancy watched helplessly as fear arrested her friends' faces.

"Unfortunately, you are not dual-stars," added Grizelda. "You should not even be here. Although, without you, we would not have come this far."

"Don't worry," said Nancy, with a comforting smile, "we will soon be home. I promise."

Ergonwold huffed and puffed as he attempted to squeeze his enormous body through the narrowing tunnel, his back scratching against the sharp rocky passageway, the two vials chiming together with every one of his uncomfortable jolts. Nancy knew he was weak. She walked by his side, their hearts entwined. Finally, the trail of candles finished at a slate wall.

A dead end.

Inglethwip ran his palm across the craggy wall, searching, feeling, and probing. He tapped his fist on a rock and waited.

The wall slid back and Nancy's face lit up. "Wow, that's awesome."

The room beneath the castle lobby revealed itself.

"I am too big to enter," declared Ergonwold.

"All in good time, O' Great One," said Captain Carbunkle. "Zayock is unaware of our presence. The longer we remain undetected, the better our chances."

Nancy tiptoed onto the mosaic tiles and inspected every inch of the chamber. Captain Carbunkle placed his finger on his lips and levitated through the opening, his impish body disappearing up into the castle lobby. Nancy's heart sent a hot thump of blood to her stomach. The thought of meeting a distant relative troubled her. She knew that family was the eternal thread, like different strands to the same rope. She crossed her fingers and hoped that this particular rope would be a lifeline, not a cord of restriction.

Captain Carbunkle returned, his pipe dangling from his mouth. "The lobby is clear, but I heard voices below the staircase."

"That's Zayock," said Inglethwip, anxiously.

"We need to find Ergonwold's Nest," instructed Captain Carbunkle. "We need you alive, O' Great One."

Ergonwold yawned, flopped onto his stomach, and coiled his snout. "I am weak. I need to recharge."

Nancy stroked his brow, reassuring the tired beast. "It won't be long. The maternal nest is here somewhere." She breathed deeply and focused on a flickering candle. "Like you, I can sense it. We are close."

"I was frozen for eleven years, Nanny Bo. I can wait a little longer."

One by one, they pulled themselves up into the castle lobby. Captain Carbunkle scoured the grand hall for the precious Bloodstone. He was followed by the remaining fairies and the hobbling Aunt Elma. Grizelda swooped up into the rafters and perched herself. Nancy stood resolute by the serpent's head, her feet close to the emerald eyeball, her hands clasping her hips, her eyes devouring the gothic splendour of the castle and its keep. Inglethwip shivered by her side, his face ashen as he recalled his previous life. Nancy whispered, "It's gonna be all right," from the side of her mouth, then linked fingers with him.

"I can't do this," admitted Inglethwip.

Nancy stared at the potion-maker, his entire body twitching with nerves. "Inglethwip Limpweed..."

"Y-yes, N-Nanny Bo?"

"If you seek forgiveness—"

"I do, I really do," interjected Inglethwip.

Nancy embraced him. "Then be strong for Ergonwold."

"Okay."

"If it wasn't for you, potion-maker extraordinaire, I wouldn't even be here. You are a wonderful person. A very talented man."

Inglethwip swallowed the lump in his throat. "Thank you."

"Defeat Zayock and banish your past, your memories will never haunt you again."

"But you don't know him," whimpered Inglethwip. "He is so powerful."

"And so are we," replied Nancy, her tone masking any trace of self-doubt.

Inglethwip fist-pumped Nancy. "Perhaps, with you by our side, we have a chance after all." He turned to face the velvet drape. "That's what he's searching for."

Nancy read it: *Forever is not long enough.*

Somehow it was familiar. A distant voice came to her – a voice spoken over Nancy when she had been a babe in arms. "If you live forever, my darling, it will not be long enough."

Inglethwip prodded Nancy in the midriff. "Come on, we need to find Ergonwold's Nest and the Bloodstone." But Nancy was mesmerised by the tapestry. A subliminal message penetrated the mind of the dual-star, her senses momentarily scrambled. Just like Zayock, the expansion of time was the object of her desire.

Captain Carbunkle clicked his fingers and bellowed, "*Refreshuumaatra.*"

Nancy's limbs jerked as if she had been resuscitated. She inhaled deeply and addressed the High Priest. "What happened?"

"Let's just call it a family trait," replied Captain Carbunkle. "Always wanting more. It's your family's spiral of torment."

Nancy shook her head, refusing to allow the idea of *forever* to take hold and seduce her. "I won't do it."

"Do what?" asked Captain Carbunkle.

"Meddle with time," answered Nancy. "It's wrong – all we have is the here and now."

"Good girl," replied the High Priest. "Your journey is near its end. To practise the art of mindfulness is the realisation of Ergonwold the Great."

Inglethwip swiped his arms towards the overhanging balcony. "Up there, that's where he keeps things."

"Live in the moment," cried Captain Carbunkle, "and the moment will deliver."

Grizelda swooped down from the rafters and landed on the balcony. Nancy was spurred into action. She raced up two flights of steps and entered the concave room. Inglethwip and the Night Fairies followed. Two rugs were crumpled next to a smouldering fire, and an upturned bowl of berries lay scattered across the floor. "They were here. I can sense it," said Nancy, in a fit of excitement.

"Who was?" asked Inglethwip.

"The Duke, Eli, and... him!"

"Trust your senses," replied Inglethwip. "You are our seer."

The Night Fairies hovered above Nancy, radiating light as they followed her steps. Where Nancy went, they followed – a protective and colourful ball of energy.

"We need to search this place from top to bottom," instructed Nancy. "The nest is here somewhere."

"And so is the Bloodstone," added Captain Carbunkle.

Suddenly, the mechanical noise from the depths of the engine room stopped. The tremors that had shaken the castle ceased. An eerie silence was followed by the shrill cries of the magician.

29
Nothing Lasts Forever

"You thieving scoundrels," screamed Zayock. "Where is my healing liquid? I need that glass vial... now!"

The Duke mustered a faint groan. The electric chair had taken its toll. Saliva dribbled from his jowls as he watched Zayock torment Elijah with the nib of his wand. Elijah edged backwards until the mountain wall pressed against his spine.

"Where is my tonic?" growled Zayock.

"I don't know..."

"Leave him alone," cried The Duke from afar.

Zayock ignored the heartfelt plea, obsessed with obtaining the last of the vital ingredients. "Don't play childish games with me, Elijah Lincoln. You stole the Bloodstone, the healing liquid, and my magic key."

"No, I—"

"Quiet!" ordered the sorcerer. "I have the Bloodstone. Now, return the vial of healing liquid."

"Don't do it, Eli," whimpered The Duke. He had accepted defeat and was now focused on preventing Zayock getting his hands on the ingredients that would make him live forever. The very thought of Zayock ruling for eternity filled him with despair. A solitary tear trickled down his bedraggled face. His head lolled to one side, droplets of blood seeped from his wrists – the restraining straps had a life of their own, tightening like magical constrictors.

Zayock continued to interrogate Elijah. "Where is it?"

"I'm not sure," replied Elijah.

"Give me the tonic," demanded Zayock. "I want it now!"

"I think The Duke has it."

Zayock dragged Elijah to his feet and pushed him towards the electric chair. "You're playing games with me." He shifted his glare from one boy, then back to the other, unsure who spoke the truth. "Go and retrieve my tonic, Elijah Lincoln."

Elijah froze. Stuck between his friend and his captor, unsure of his next move.

Zayock flicked his wand and reminded Elijah of his magical powers. "Let's see who conceals the glass vial. Go and get it... NOW!"

Elijah took one step towards The Duke, then stopped.

Zayock stabbed the wand into Elijah's back. "Go. And. Get. It."

Silently, with his weeping eyes, The Duke pleaded with Elijah not to do it, but Elijah tiptoed across the engine room towards his weak friend. He pulled the glass vial from The Duke's pocket and dabbed his brow.

Zayock lowered his wand and softened his tone. "Well done, young man. You spoke the truth."

"Don't give it to him," groaned The Duke, the last glimmer of hope within him fading fast.

Zayock tutted. "Bring it to me, and be very careful. Don't drop it."

Elijah didn't move. Indecision gluing him to the spot.

The Duke stared helplessly at him. "*Eli... don't... do... it...*"

Elijah raised the glass tube above his head, like a trophy. To his left was The Duke. To his right was Zayock, the embodiment of evil, a mind consumed with greed for more – more time, more power, and more control.

Zayock slapped his thighs, as if calling a pet. "Come on, Elijah, bring the liquid to me. Soon, I will be the 'Father of Time'."

Elijah stood perfectly still.

Zayock's lips quivered as he waited for the boy.

For one fleeting moment, The Duke thought he heard voices from above, and his eyes flickered as he croaked, "*Help.*"

"No one is going to help you," replied Zayock, nonchalantly. "Now bring me the healing liquid, Elijah. And I will reward you handsomely."

Elijah took half a step towards the deranged sorcerer and, very slowly, very deliberately, unscrewed the lid.

Zayock pushed out his palms. "Be very careful! That liquid has been extracted from beneath the maternal nest."

"Don't do it," begged The Duke, his voice a hoarse whisper.

Elijah spun on his heels and scurried back to the electric chair. He lifted The Duke's head and tilted the glass vial over his mouth. "One drop of this and my friend will be re-energised."

A look of terror swept across Zayock's scrawny face, aghast at the boy's impudence. Elijah's hand trembled as he pushed the bottle closer to The Duke's lips. "He deserves to live."

Zayock fell to his knees. "Don't be silly… I'm sure we can work something out."

Sparkles of light crept into The Duke's peripheral vision. He tried to focus, but a brief moment of blindness was followed by the outline of Zayock's willowy frame. He heard something, something so desperate it grabbed his attention. It was Zayock. He was pleading desperately with Elijah, offering him anything he desired, goading him to name his price in return for the precious liquid. The Duke's cries filled the room. "Don't listen to him, Eli, he can't be trusted."

"Shut up!" roared Zayock. "Come to me, Elijah; bring me that vial of healing liquid." Elijah tilted the glass vial precariously over The Duke's mouth, the precious liquid just millimetres from his tongue. Zayock's desperation was palpable as he pointed his wand towards the spherical orb that contained the black vapour. "My machinery has extracted all of your friend's worst nightmares. Soon they will be refined into the last bottle of Tantibus. It's all in there – fear and loathing, processed and ready for the potion of eternal life."

"You're sick," said The Duke. "Don't give him the liquid, Eli..."

"Your friend is a lost cause," said Zayock. "The liquid will not help him. It's too late – time has beaten you. Return the bottle; it belongs to me."

Elijah inhaled and gave a defiant shake of his head.

"It's the *everlasting*, young man," explained Zayock, desperation now saturating his words. "Think about it – the gift of life. I can offer you all the time in the world." He opened his arms wide, as if he wanted to embrace the boy. "Once that liquid is infused with Tantibus and the Bloodstone, we can walk the path of eternal life – you and me, together, hand in hand, forever and ever. You will want for nothing."

The Duke's fingertips tugged at Elijah's cuff. "Nothing lasts forever."

"It does," remonstrated Zayock. "And I can prove it."

Elijah ignored Zayock and pressed his face against his friend's. "Open your mouth."

The Duke's jaw widened.

Slowly, and purposefully, Elijah drizzled the last drops of the healing liquid into The Duke's mouth.

Zayock's hysterical scream filled the engine room: "NO!" He raised his wand, circled it above his head, then thrust it towards

Elijah. A purple bolt of lightning flew through the air and punctured his heart.

Elijah Lincoln fell to the floor. Dead.

30
Omnia Vincit Amor

Nancy felt a sudden tug upon her heartstrings. Something was wrong. Captain Carbunkle raced to the stairwell. Nancy needed no invitation. She bolted down the stairs as fast as her legs would carry her. The Night Fairies flew after her, their multi-coloured tail-lights illuminating the dark recesses of the mountain walls.

Everyone but Aunt Elma followed.

Grizelda's wings flapped and fluttered, leaving plumes of feathers trailing in her wake. Captain Carbunkle clung to Mr Wuu. Inglethwip held Prema's hand and Jimmy lagged behind, puffing, panting, and coughing out the industrial fumes that clung to his lungs.

Nancy stalled as she reached the final turn of steps. She was about to come face to face with a maniac, someone who could turn out the lights to the entire world. She muttered a silent prayer, then burst head-first into the engine room and screamed, "LEAVE HIM ALONE!"

"Nanny Bo!" yelped The Duke, his eyes bulging at the sight of his friend.

Zayock froze. He stared at Nancy, captivated by her, astounded by her presence. Finally, he had lured The Chosen One to his castle.

He turned and quickly tapped the bands around The Duke's wrists: one, two. He was released. An unwanted prisoner in the shadow of The Chosen One. Zayock stood perfectly still, fixated on Nancy Bo Jones. His lips moved. Nancy read them: "*The prophecy.*"

The Duke pushed Zayock to one side and ran to his friends.

Zayock rubbed his skeletal hands and repeated more loudly, but still in a hushed tone, "The prophecy."

"That's right," replied Nancy. "The prophecy."

Nancy glared at the scrawny man clutching his wand, his eyes a chilling reminder of the family thread. Then she saw Elijah's body. She took three tentative steps forward, panic clawing at her throat. There was no sign of life as she approached the body. A tear trickled down her cheek, her thoughts quickly returning to the circle of friendship. She whispered, "Some things are written in the stars," and held her palms aloft as Zayock raised his wand.

Captain Carbunkle stepped forward. "Lord Bymerstone, your rule of terror is over. You need to regenerate."

"Never," hissed Zayock. "How dare you refer to me by that Earth name!"

"We trusted you," replied Captain Carbunkle. "Your search for the everlasting has turned Enerjiimass into a living hell. Our lives are ruined by your constant spreading of negativity."

Nancy's eyes flitted one way, then the other, as angry words were exchanged.

"I have seven hundred and seventy-seven bottles of Tantibus and the Bloodstone," confessed Zayock. He jabbed his wand at The Duke. "That vile excuse for a boy has drunk the last of my healing liquid."

"That wasn't your healing liquid to begin with," screamed Inglethwip. "It belonged to Ergonwold the Great."

"Look who speaks," snarled Zayock. "The boy who ran away."

"You tricked me," replied Inglethwip. "You even fooled the gentle giant, Arnus, into stealing the healing liquid for you. You conniving swine."

Zayock flicked his wrist, shooting a spark from his wand towards Inglethwip. Inglethwip ducked, then held his hands up in a moment of surrender. "And where is your spiritual leader when you need him?" asked Zayock. He spun around and called for '*Ergonwold*' in a childish voice. Then he flung his arms up into the air. "He's nowhere to be seen, is he? His time is over."

"He will return," said Nancy, with a curt smile.

"He's frozen. Dead, you fool – an overgrown wrinkly elephant who relinquished his power to me, the greatest magician of all time." Zayock twirled his cape, as if performing an illusion to a paying audience. "And now, ladies and gentlemen, I will defy the hands of time."

"Your dream is over, Lord Bymerstone," interjected Captain Carbunkle.

"If you call me that once more, I will—"

"What?" interrupted Nancy. She cocked her head and struck a defiant pose.

"Kill you," replied the sorcerer. Zayock shuffled closer to her. "You are Nancy Bo Jones, the girl who should have stayed away."

Nancy stood firm. "And what if I am?"

"If you are, you are the most foolish girl for siding with these weaklings, and you will lose. I am stronger than you. It is inevitable…"

"No, it's not," retaliated Nancy. "You stand alone. I stand with my friends and with the love of the Great One."

"Oh, spare me the pathetic sentiment," cackled Zayock. "Your heart is entwined with Ergonwold, and your blood is mixed with my own." He looked down his nose at Nancy and tutted. "What a strange concoction you are."

"I'm not strange," retaliated Nancy, her heart thumping an anxious beat.

"Come closer," mused Zayock. "Let me inspect you." He wielded his wand again, as if to lasso her. Then he pulled her forward. She took one step towards the magician. Then another. She had no choice.

"You fight my magic," muttered Zayock. "You are strong in spirit, Nancy Bo Jones." He gave Grizelda a sideways glance, then brushed a bead of sweat from his brow. "That stupid parrot has meddled with your mind and bolstered your resilience."

Grizelda squawked loudly, then flew towards Nancy, her crest emitting a radiant arc of white light.

Zayock aimed his wand at the parrot.

Captain Carbunkle levitated, positioning himself between Zayock and Grizelda.

Zayock sprinkled particles of dust onto the tip of his wand and shoved his hand forward. A purple beam flew through Captain Carbunkle's hat and hit Grizelda. The white parrot landed at Nancy's feet, lifeless. Nancy fell to her knees and lifted Grizelda's body, brushing her crest in a vain attempt to connect with the Reader of Hearts and Minds. It was too late: Zayock's wand had severed the connection. Nancy stared through her tears as Zayock swayed his wand from left to right. Behind him, the machine rested, the array of levers, switches, knobs and buttons flashing intermittently. Standing in front of him were Nancy and her entourage, immobilised by their fear of the wand.

Inglethwip wept at the sight of Grizelda's head drooping over Nancy's forearm. "She was the last spiritual parrot in our land."

"Elijah's dead," whispered The Duke.

"I know," replied Prema.

"The five rings of friendship are now four," added Jimmy.

Prema stifled a sob and nodded. "Poor Eli…"

Zayock grabbed Nancy's arm and pulled her close.

"Leave her," shouted Jimmy. "Take me!"

"I don't need you, you pathetic mound of lard. All I want is the tonic." Zayock wiped the spittle from his lips and prodded Nancy. "I know *she* has some."

Nancy kissed Grizelda's crest. "I don't have a clue what—"

"There is a spare bottle of healing liquid," interrupted Zayock. "I know it exists."

Nancy lowered the dead bird and bit her lip. "I don't have any."

"I can sense it," remonstrated Zayock, flaring his nostrils, "and I can smell it."

"Leave her alone," pleaded Jimmy. "She has told you—"

"I am a dual-star with a sixth sense," interrupted Zayock. "Now, get out of my way, before my wand takes another life."

"Do as he says," insisted Captain Carbunkle.

Nancy glared at Captain Carbunkle and pleaded for help. "Someone do something!"

Mr Wuu took one step forward, then stopped. He bowed his head and gave a defeated shrug of his shoulders. "I'm sorry, Nanny Bo…"

Zayock shuffled towards the door. "Move!"

Captain Carbunkle, Mr Wuu, Inglethwip, Jimmy, Prema, and The Duke edged out of the sorcerer's way. They huddled against the machine in a semi-circle of remorse.

Zayock pressed his wand into Nancy's spine, forcing her out of the engine room towards the staircase. The spiralled climb filled Nancy with dread, her mind at a loss, her heart empty as pain replaced hope. Halfway up, Drinyak waited, his mouth twitching like a vampire bat.

"You have the girl, master. I would like my teeth back. A deal is a deal."

Zayock kicked a door and pushed Nancy into a small room. She slumped onto a desk and brushed the shattered remains of a photograph to one side. Zayock reached for a jar of metal teeth and unscrewed the lid. He tapped it three times. Drinyak purred with delight. He opened his mouth to receive his metallic fangs. Zayock pressed his finger into Drinyak's furry chest. "You can have your teeth on one condition."

"Anything, master, anything," replied the gremlin, eagerly.

"I want your first meal to be those fools in the engine room. Do you understand?"

"No!" shrieked Nancy.

"Yes, master," replied Drinyak. "I promise to feed from the flesh of your prisoners. Now, please return my fangs."

Zayock waved his wand in a figure of eight and pronounced three words: "*Seellana, Dutrait, Escombo.*"

Nancy winced as Drinyak ran his tongue over two rows of metallic pincers. He flapped his wings and flew from the concealed chamber, up and into the sky, screeching with excitement. She knew Zayock cared for only one thing: the final ingredient for the Elixir of Life. She had something he craved and it was up to her to lay her life down for the future of Enerjiimass. There was nobody else who could do it. But Ergonwold was close. She sensed his energy, his prophetic words resonating within: "*To be loved by someone is the greatest protection anyone can hope for.*"

Zayock dragged Nancy out of the room. He skipped up the final flight of stairs and shoved her into the castle lobby. "Get the healing liquid. I know it is close. I can sense it."

"I haven't got any," lied Nancy.

"Don't play dumb," snapped Zayock, his head twitching for any sign of the magic tonic. From the corner of her eye, Nancy spotted the leather holdall, its zip pulled tight, the healing liquid concealed from the eye of Zayock. Her stomach knotted as she tried to mask her thoughts from a fellow dual-star.

"I want the healing liquid," roared Zayock. "I know it's here somewhere."

"And if I find it," chirped Nancy, "what will happen to me?"

"I will leave *you* in the Earth realm, unscathed, and *I* will return to Enerjiimass as the everlasting king," replied Zayock. "The portal will be frozen once and for all. You can consider yourself lucky to be alive. Now, get me the healing liquid."

Nancy stood firm.

"Move," ordered Zayock.

"Only if you let me have a keepsake."

"No bargaining."

"Kill me then," said Nancy, nonplussed. "You will never find eternity without the healing liquid."

Zayock considered the compromise. "What do you want?"

"Ergonwold's Nest."

"What?"

"Let me have the maternal nest you stole."

Zayock narrowed his eyes, a tiny smile tugging at his lips. "You are like me. A collector of magical artefacts."

"You could say that," replied Nancy, her eyes fixed on the chiselled snake beneath her feet.

"A family trait," said Zayock. "Let me share something with you, Nancy Bo Jones."

Nancy's eyes sparkled with expectation. "Please do..."

Zayock curled a finger. "Follow me." His cape swished as he walked from one side of the castle to the other, his sights fixed upon the tasselled drape hanging at the rear of the lobby, constantly repeating the words embroidered upon it.

Nancy followed, checking over her shoulder for any sign of Ergonwold.

Zayock lifted the velvet mural and chirped sarcastically, "Ta-Dah."

"What is it?" asked Nancy. "It looks like a safe?"

"You could say that," replied Zayock. He twisted a dial to the left, then to the right, and back again. The door slid open. He

346

reached within and placed a wooden box into Nancy's hands. "Hold this."

Nancy stared at it. "What is it?"

"The remains of what you asked for." Zayock tapped the lid with his wand and grinned. "Take a look."

Nancy opened the box and stared at its contents. "It's just a mound of ash." She pinched a small amount of the grey powder between her thumb and forefinger. "I don't understand."

"That ash is my secret," replied Zayock. "What do I care if you know? Soon you will be on the other side, never to return."

Nancy blew the ash from her fingertip and raised her voice. "Where's Ergonwold's Nest?"

Zayock pointed at the wooden box cradled in Nancy's hands. "That's it, you fool…"

Nancy said nothing. Her lips tight-pressed together.

Zayock's sardonic laughter filled the lobby. "I burnt the maternal nest and kept the remains. A sprinkle of that ash on the tip of my wand makes me the most powerful man in the universe."

Nancy covered her mouth, forcing her desperate yelps back down her throat. Zayock dipped the tip of his wand into the wooden box and licked his lips. The cold realisation hit Nancy like a sledgehammer. Her face reddened with rage. She hurled the box up into the air and watched as Zayock frantically tried to collect as much of the precious ash as possible, scurrying around on all fours like a rodent.

Nancy seized the moment and lunged at him.

Zayock wrestled her to the ground, his hands clawing at her face as they grappled, the powder raining down on them like cigarette ash. Nancy kicked and screamed, but her efforts were overpowered. Zayock pinned her by the throat, his sharp fingernails drawing blood from her neck.

Their eyes locked. The family connection had reached breaking point.

Nancy felt something move beneath her: a deep, thunderous tremor. It felt as if the ground was giving way. She stared up at Zayock's eyes, inflamed with hate. She couldn't move. The last oxygen left her lungs, like squashed bellows waiting to be filled again. But there was no air coming.

Large cracks appeared in the floor between Zayock's legs, followed by an immense shattering. Then, with a deafening crash, Ergonwold burst through the floor of the lobby. Debris rained down and rocks flew through the air. Walls split as dust shrouded the air like a grey veil. Zayock coughed and spluttered, hyperventilating at the large shadow hurtling towards him. His castle was no longer his keep.

Ergonwold roared.

The magician looked up. "This is not happening. It's a mirage. You're dead. You are not—"

"I am Ergonwold. You are Lord Bymerstone. Like you, I have been waiting for the girl. Without her, I would be as if I were dead, where you put me."

Zayock cowered back. He dropped the wand and covered his face. "How did she conjure such magic?"

Nancy writhed on the floor, inhaling deep, purposeful breaths. She reached for the wand. It flew through the air of its own volition and landed in her palm. White light fizzed around her fingertips.

The wand had a new master. She raised it and pointed it at the magician.

"No," pleaded Zayock. "We are family. I need a brave young potion-maker. I could teach you everything you need to know."

Nancy locked eyes with Zayock. All she could think of was Elijah and Grizelda. Her heart pounded as the two dual-stars' minds were infused.

"I have a potion for the dead," said Zayock, softly.

"I don't believe you," countered Nancy.

Zayock pressed his hands together. "Trust me, I'm blood. Let me show you the fountain of youth. It has a miraculous rejuvenating serum within it."

"You're lying."

Zayock stepped towards her. "Let me show you. The boy who loves you could return. And the parrot."

Nancy was set rigid, her mind whirring with endless scenarios. All she wanted was Elijah and Grizelda alive. Her body contained a combustible box of emotions. She jabbed the wand at Zayock. "I can't trust you."

"Yes, you can," replied Zayock. "Come to me, let me create eternity. The Elixir of Life. Think of the endless passage of time. You desire it as much as me. Imagine everything you loved lasting forever."

"Be strong, Nanny Bo," warned Ergonwold. "Do not succumb. The nest has gone, but I will always be with you."

Tears welled in Nancy's eyes.

Ergonwold's strength was waning, his eyes flickering, and breath failing. "Live… in… the… moment… Nanny… Bo…"

"Live in the future, Nancy Bo Jones," said Zayock, with a menacing grin. "You would have nothing to fear. Nothing at all." The sorcerer's words were alluring. A family trait tickled Nancy's alter ego. Just as she relented and lowered the wand, Zayock sprung forward, drawing a dagger from his cape, screaming, "For the love of eternity."

Ergonwold summoned the last of his strength and roared.

Nancy came to her senses and swiped the wand.

Shards of penetrating light cut Zayock's body in two.

Nancy gagged, fighting off the nausea as blood spewed from the severed body, splattering against her garments.

Ergonwold collapsed to the floor, his eyes fading to a ghostly grey. "You are a brave girl, Nanny Bo. We have asked so much of you."

"That we have," said Aunt Elma, her friendly face appearing from behind Ergonwold. "I think it's best if I take this," she said, removing Ergonwold's dog collar, paying particular attention to the two glass vials.

Ergonwold yawned loudly. "Be my guest."

Nancy wiped away a trickle of blood from her nose and held out her arms. "I love you, Ergonwold."

"*Omnia Vincit Amor*," groaned Ergonwold.

"Love Conquers All," whispered Aunt Elma.

"I love you, Ergonwold," repeated Nancy, her eyes glazed with tears.

"I will always love you, Nancy Bo Jones," replied Ergonwold. "I have two final requests."

"Anything. I'll do anything," said Nancy, her fingers caressing the Great One's face.

Ergonwold's voice was nothing more than a tremulous whisper. "Retrieve the Bloodstone from Lord Bymerstone."

Nancy squirmed. The thought of touching a dead body unnerved her. She clambered over piles of rock, broken flagstones, and the embers of burning tallows. The force of Ergonwold's entrance had reduced the supporting wall to nothing more than a pile of rubble. Swirls of dust circled Nancy as she searched through the haze for the body of her tormentor.

Then she saw it. The frayed hem of Zayock's cape protruded from a pile of rock. She clawed away fragments of rubble and stone, then spun the severed torso over. She yanked the sorcerer's cape and watched as his tongue drooped to the side of his mouth. The cloak was secured with a double knot, so she loosened the bow, and tried again. This time it came free. Nancy slipped her thumb and forefinger into the lining of the material and retrieved the emerald stone.

"Wow. That feels good," she cried, racing back to Ergonwold.

"I will take that," Aunt Elma said, holding up the dog collar. Two glass vials dangled like charms on a bracelet, one empty, the other encasing the Wisdom Stone. "Now, let us return it to where it belongs."

Nancy placed the green stone into the empty vial and watched as the Wisdom Stone shone brighter than ever. She unzipped the leather holdall and retrieved the healing liquid. Aunt Elma clipped the magic tonic onto Ergonwold's collar and proclaimed, "The three vials are back where they belong."

The dog collar glowed, its magical powers restored.

"My life is over," gasped Ergonwold.

Nancy shook her head.

"Remember this, Nanny Bo," spluttered Ergonwold. "When you clip an old flower, a new one grows. I need to regenerate."

"No. I won't let this happen," countered Nancy. "We can keep you alive. We can use the healing liquid."

"It's over, Nanny Bo," replied Ergonwold, his ivory tusks shattering as his head slumped to the floor. "The healing liquid is for the mind, not the body. The Wisdom Stone and the Bloodstone need to be passed on. My collar is blessed with hope. I will live on in your heart. Whenever you need me, I will be here." Ergonwold brushed his snout against Nancy's forehead. "I have one last request."

Nancy stared into his eyes, her tears raining down on his coiled snout. "What is it?"

"Put me out of my misery," whispered Ergonwold. "Only you can do it. I do not want to struggle for a moment longer. Since you released me from the ice I have been in pain. The search for my nest is over. It was my last and only hope. I want to go now. Use your wand. It belongs to you. Please, release me."

"No!"

"Let the new guardian of Enerjiimass be born," pleaded Ergonwold. "My collar will serve the new one well."

Aunt Elma pushed the palms of her hands together and prayed, "A sacrifice of souls, two hearts beat as one, a regeneration has begun."

Nancy bit her lip and fought back her sobs. "I can't do this."

"Forever is too long," Ergonwold gasped. "Don't let me suffer."

Nancy closed her eyes and pointed the wand, her arm quivering, tears streaming. "This isn't right… I'm so scared…"

Aunt Elma stepped in front of the dying beast. "Nancy Bo Jones."

"Y-yes."

"Don't be scared. Make sure the wand knows of your intentions. Just say the three magic words, otherwise you will follow in the footsteps of Lord Bymerstone."

Nancy knew what to say. "*Omnia Vincit Amor.*" With that, she pointed the wand to release Ergonwold from his agony. Sparks shot across the lobby. Every muscle in Nancy's arm contracted. Then her knees buckled. Aunt Elma pulled her away from the Great One and led her to the mountain's edge. "Look!"

Hundreds of gremlins flew towards the dilapidated castle, its huge chimney now leaning ominously to one side. Nancy let out a ghastly wail. "They're going to eat my friends."

"Use the wand," replied Aunt Elma.

Nancy raced down the stairwell while the gremlins of Tu-Nahh circled above the turrets, waiting their turn to enter the lop-sided chimney. One by one, the furry creatures disappeared within. Nancy lunged into the engine room, wand in hand, exhausted, but ready to fight.

Jimmy's head appeared from behind the centre console. "Nanny Bo."

"Jim Jam," replied Nancy. "Are you all right?"

"Yes," replied Jimmy. "How about you?"

Nancy nodded and made the okay sign with her left hand. She circled the machine, her eyes darting from side to side, searching for something. Then she found what she was looking for. Grizelda. She placed a small cloth over her body and blubbered, "Where's… Eli?"

Prema pointed at the glass bowl that housed the sticky black substance. "We moved him over there."

"A wonderful boy," added Captain Carbunkle.

Nancy side-stepped the machine and kneeled beside Elijah. She kissed his forehead and whispered, "Good night, my friend."

The Duke removed his jacket and placed it over Elijah's face. Nancy hugged The Duke as he choked back his grief. Then she heard something. A scratching noise. The fireplace shuddered, dislodging clouds of soot from the chimney stack.

"Gremlins," whispered Nancy.

"Flesh-eaters," added Mr Wuu.

"The gremlins are above the castle," said Nancy, pointing the wand at the fireplace. "They are going to use the chimney to get to us."

The Duke raised his fists. "Let's fight them. Eli gave his life for me. I must honour that."

"Ergonwold banished the gremlins centuries ago," said Inglethwip. He brooded for the briefest of moments. "They cannot overrule him. It is impossible – they have no leader."

Nancy swallowed the lump in her throat. "I'm so sorry, Inglethwip, Ergonwold is dead."

"Dead?"

"Yes."

"But, how?" asked the potion-maker.

"By the wand of Zayock," replied Nancy.

Captain Carbunkle raised his hat and declared, "Sacrifice always precedes success."

Nancy gestured at the fireplace. "And Drinyak has returned."

"Who's Drinyak?" asked Jimmy.

"The ringleader of the tormenters," answered Inglethwip.

"Behind the machine, children," instructed Mr Wuu. "Now!"

Everyone obeyed. The sound of scratching claws grew louder and louder. Captain Carbunkle was lost in a sombre deliverance of prayer.

Mr Wuu rested his head between two stationary pistons and stared at the fireplace.

Tension filled the silence.

Then Nancy broke it. "They're in the chimney. It won't be long before they reach us."

Mr Wuu left the makeshift barricade and tiptoed towards the glass orb. He tapped it with his knuckles and laughed.

Nancy's eyes widened. "What?"

"I have an idea." Mr Wuu eyeballed the mass of tangled pipework above them. "We need to act fast." He jumped up and touched one of the metal tubes. "This is the main pipeline that feeds the orb."

Nancy's eyes followed a metal pipe that wove its way from the machine, along the wall, across the ceiling, over the electric chair, past the piano, and finally to the glass orb. Two rusty bolts joined the pipe to the orb.

"We need to unscrew this pipe," instructed Mr Wuu.

Nancy shrugged. "Why?"

"It's our only hope," whispered Mr Wuu. "Let's release the fumes of Zayock!"

"Yes," cried Nancy, "let them eat smoke!"

While they worked, Mr Wuu formulated his plan. His face creased with exertion as he grasped the bolt between his fingers and twisted with all his might. Nancy steadied the pipe as he puffed and pulled. Finally, the connection gave way. Mr Wuu raised the glass globe from the floor. "How long can you hold your breath?"

Nancy and her friends stared at one another.

Mr Wuu tapped his wrist impatiently. "Quickly! The gremlins are seconds away."

"Maybe half a minute," said Nancy. She stared forlornly at Mr Wuu, drew breath, and waited for his answer. It came quickly, and sharply.

"Longer!"

Jimmy held a single finger aloft. "One minute."

"Okay," said Mr Wuu, balancing the glass orb and the length of pipe precariously by the fireplace. "Inside this orb is raw negativity, life's most deadly drug. When the gremlins arrive, I will smash it. Once the smoke fills their lungs, it will kill them. Whatever you do, do not breathe. Hold your breath until the smoke has cleared. It should take about a minute or so."

"A minute or so?" questioned Nancy.

"Yes," replied Mr Wuu, rocking from side to side, his cheeks ballooning like an Olympic weightlifter. "Your life will depend on how long you can hold your breath."

The flapping of wings was incessant. The gremlins were inches from the open fireplace, their claws scratching against the stone flue.

Nancy grabbed Captain Carbunkle and her friends, pulled them all behind the machine and issued her command. "On the count of three, close your eyes and pinch your nose. Do not breathe until I say so." She stared into Jimmy's eyes, squeezed his hand and winked. He tried his best to raise a smile, but failed.

"Ready?" asked Nancy, preparing her lungs for one final intake of air. Jimmy, Prema, The Duke, Inglethwip, Captain Carbunkle, and the Night Fairies followed her lead, inhaling and exhaling continuously, all breathing in rhythm.

Then the scratching inside the chimney stopped. A furry body slipped from the chimney into the fireplace and surveyed the engine room.

"A feast awaits us," squealed Drinyak.

The engine room filled with tiny predators, their mouths salivating and their teeth chattering like metallic castanets. Mr Wuu inhaled. Then he dropped the orb and covered his face as the glass dome shattered into tiny fragments.

"One, two, three!" cried Nancy.

The children took deep breaths, pinched their noses, and covered their faces.

Dense black, acrid smoke filled the room.

Nancy opened one eye. There was nothing but a sea of black fog. She couldn't see a thing, not a single chink of light. Seconds passed like minutes as they waited with swollen lungs. She counted silently to herself, "Twenty-seven, twenty-eight, twenty-nine, thirty…" It was the longest minute of her life.

The gremlins flapped wildly in the poisonous atmosphere. The seconds ticked by. Nancy's head swirled in a sea of giddiness. Then there was a thud, followed by another, then another. Soon the gremlins were falling in their droves, and the smoke began to clear.

Jimmy grunted, then rolled onto Nancy's lap. He was the first to empty his lungs, his wild gasps for air loud and uncontrolled. A solitary gremlin flew towards him. It was Drinyak. Half-intoxicated by the smoke, half-alive, he flew in a drunken zigzag fashion, then raised his top lip and revealed two rows of serrated teeth. He aimed directly at Jimmy's neck.

Nancy grabbed the wand and directed it at the gremlin. A ray of light struck the gremlin's head. Drinyak crashed to the floor. The last of the gremlins of Tu-Nahh was dead.

31
Five Goms and a Purple Balloon

The residue of smoke smelled like a concoction of ammonia and glue. The battle was over, the floor strewn with furry corpses and smeared with a sticky black liquid. Nancy and her friends sat silently amongst the squalor, the ever-present Night Fairies hovering above them like neon specks of light. "We have to leave," she said, her eyes drawn to the shattered remains of the orb. "It's time to go home."

"You… are… h-h-home," stuttered Inglethwip, his words smeared with hope.

Nancy got to her feet and surveyed the carnage. "We need to say goodbye to Aunt Elma before we leave." She kicked Drinyak's body to one side, traipsed past the electric chair, and left the engine room for the very last time.

"She will be waiting upstairs," said Mr Wuu, with a lop-sided grin.

Everyone trailed Nancy. They climbed the rocky steps in silence, their tired limbs straining all the way. Nancy crawled agonisingly up the final flight of steps and into the ruin of the lobby. Aunt Elma stood by the castle doors, their ornate hinges now bent and buckled. Ergonwold's body was slumped between a huge pile of rocks and the bloody remains of Zayock's garments. The leather holdall balanced precariously on a broken flagstone, the sparkle of the serpent's eye now gone, shrouded by dust.

Aunt Elma acknowledged Nancy with a tight smile.

Nancy avoided eye contact. Her bottom lip trembled as she croaked, "Eli and Grizelda are—"

"I know," interrupted Aunt Elma.

Inglethwip pressed the palms of his hands together and prayed for forgiveness beside Ergonwold the Great.

A brief silence passed. Heads were bowed, and eyes were shut.

Then, a gentle breeze whistled through the castle lobby and ruffled the velvet drape, its golden tassels swaying like mini pompoms. Nancy clambered between the debris and stood beneath it. "Why do people always want more time?" She wiped her face, then shook particles of mortar from her hair and continued, "Ergonwold said that forever is too long."

"Forever is a curse against life," concluded Aunt Elma.

Nancy yanked the drape. She watched as it fell to the floor in a crumpled heap. "Yesterday is gone, tomorrow is coming. That means we only have today."

"Who said that, Nanny Bo?" asked Prema. "It's *so* true."

"Lillie Lincoln."

Prema stared at Nancy, bewildered. "Who's that?"

"Eli's mother," replied Nancy, waving a sheet of paper. "I found this in my pocket. Eli must have put it there before he scarpered."

She cleared the dust from her lungs and read it to her friends.

Dear Nanny Bo,

I wanted to write this down just in case I didn't make it home. If I do, please destroy this note!

You are a special person, someone I admire. It is important that you know that. Please tell my parents that I love them and I'm sorry for the pain I have caused. Tell The Duke it was all my fault. I shouldn't have led him into Roebuck Woods. He is not to blame. Whenever I'm bored and wishing the days away, my parents get frustrated with me. My mother always says, 'Yesterday has gone, tomorrow is coming, so we only have today.'

Tell her I get it!

Maybe it's too late, but now I know what she means.

My heart is yours, Nanny Bo.

I love you.

Elijah.

Nancy folded the sheet of paper and placed it in her pocket. She hung her head and felt her heart sink. Elijah's words had painted an unfamiliar picture of someone she thought she knew. Now, when it was too late, she wanted him by her side.

Aunt Elma pushed against the castle doors. They swung out, then crashed to the floor. Sunlight streamed into the dusty room, like an iridescent tidal wave. It flooded the decrepit castle and lit every nook and cranny.

Outside, the sky changed colour with every passing second. Diwali balloons bobbed up and down, their baskets full of strange folk letting off fireworks. Thousands of creatures gathered beneath the castle, clapping and waving at Aunt Elma, desperate for her attention. She gestured for Nancy to join her on the mountain's ledge. Nancy toddled towards her, squinting as the sunshine struck her face. She gazed out at the sea of people, their voices reaching a crescendo as she acknowledged them with a nervous wave. Aunt Elma attempted to speak above the celebrations, but it was no use: the crowd were lost in their elation.

Nancy reached for Aunt Elma's hand. The frail old lady grasped it and gazed at the towering young girl. Her voice was tarnished with remorse: "I feel your pain, Nanny Bo. I have lost my light, my everlasting love, my Ergonwold."

Nancy kneeled before her. "So have I."

"Sometimes in life we have to think of the greater good," said Aunt Elma. She kissed the top of Nancy's head and went on: "You have saved our world, and, indirectly, yours. Enerjiimass stores all the positive energy and feeds it back to planet Earth."

"Yes, I know," mouthed Nancy, in a silent confirmation.

"Zayock was close to reversing that. We may have lost loved ones along the way, but we have saved the next generation. Fill your heart with joy, not sorrow. You are our saviour, Nancy Bo Jones."

Nancy forced a smile.

"Your childhood was interrupted," Aunt Elma added. "Only *you* could defeat Zayock. Be proud, go home, and live your life positively."

Jimmy, Prema, The Duke, and Inglethwip embraced, their friendships now cemented. Aunt Elma gave a regal wave to the swaying crowds, then pulled Nancy to her feet. "Arise. Your audience awaits."

Nancy sprung up and blew a string of kisses to the jubilant crowd. The creatures of Enerjiimass erupted with joy, sparking the Diwali Balloons into a riot of colour. They fizzed and crackled above the crumbling castle, thousands of them, a multi-coloured sky of canvas. "They're beautiful," declared Nancy. "They fill the entire sky."

"What's your favourite colour?" asked Aunt Elma.

"Purple," replied Nancy, without thinking.

Aunt Elma clicked her fingers and summoned a purple Diwali balloon from beneath the swell of clouds. The balloon floated closer to the mountaintop. Nancy gawped at the strange-looking passengers leaning out of the basket. Peering out beneath their pork-pie hats were five odd looking creatures, their noses bright red, their hair a mishmash of frizzy green and yellow. They reminded her of the clowns at Cirque Du Soleil. Aunt Elma waited for the balloon to land, then welcomed the strange-looking characters with a curtsy and introduced them to Nancy. "Say hello to the five Goms."

Nancy waved as the five Goms kneeled before her. "Why are they kneeling?"

Aunt Elma looked straight through Nancy, raised her walking stick and pointed it at the lop-sided chimney. "These creatures have been in hiding for eleven years, Nanny Bo. They have been trying to avoid Zayock's smoke-induced depression."

"It must've been awful," said Nancy, in a low voice.

"Yes, it has been…" Aunt Elma paused, inhaled the clean air several times, smiled, then went on, "You have restored their freedom and they are eternally grateful. You will always be welcome here."

Nancy acknowledged the open invitation with a stiff nod, then Aunt Elma lifted her arm and the five Goms stood. The crowd began to chant Nancy's name, in three excruciatingly loud syllables, "*Na-Ny-Bo, Na-Ny-Bo, Na-Ny-Bo.*"

She was adored, and her inner thoughts and feelings were so different from the place that she had left behind: 145 Oxon Road. She closed her eyes and drifted. *I belong here. I fit in.*

An anxious call from Inglethwip brought Nancy swiftly back to her senses. "Timeline!" cried the potion-maker. "That's if you *want* to leave us?" he added, staring at a non-existent wristwatch.

"The heart will soon be sealed," added Mr Wuu, as he ushered Nancy towards the balloon and whispered his goodbyes.

Aunt Elma climbed aboard the wicker basket. "Come on, children, we need to leave."

One by one, they joined Aunt Elma and squeezed into the basket. Inglethwip walked towards them, clutching the leather holdall. "Don't forget this."

Nancy wrapped her arms around him. "Thanks, Inglethwip. I didn't want to leave that here."

"You could have returned to collect it," replied the potion-maker with a cheeky grin. "I'm going to miss you, Nanny Bo."

A broad smile lit Nancy's face. "Thanks for waking Prema up. It was a life-saving potion."

"Oh, don't thank me. That was one of Lord Bymerstone's."

Nancy kissed Inglethwip on the cheek and ruffled his hair. He blushed, grabbed her hand, and pleaded with her: "Stay."

Nancy looked him in the eye and contemplated an alternative life.

The wicker basket left the ground.

Inglethwip squeezed Nancy's hand. "You belong here." His arm strained against the rising balloon. "Enerjiimass is a world of colour. Your world. Don't go. *Please stay...*"

Nancy's hand slid from Inglethwip's. "I'm going to miss you, too, Inglethwip Limpweed, but we *really* need to go."

Inglethwip bit his lip and mouthed, '*Goodbye.*'

Nancy waved her final farewells and blew three kisses towards the sparkling light of the Night Fairies. The purple Diwali balloon left the mountaintop and floated up and beyond the clouds into the kaleidoscopic sky. Below them, the floral-carpeted land of Enerjiimass sparkled in all its glory. Lakes and rivers shimmered in a blaze of mercury silver. Lush forests punctuated the rolling hills and tumultuous valleys. The tiny igloo huts were like grains of sugar spilt upon a lush green canvas.

The wind rushed through Aunt Elma's thinning hair, the purple glow of the canvas highlighting every wrinkle on her face. She grasped Ergonwold's collar in one hand and tugged Nancy's sleeve with the other. "There is a timeline connected to the portal. When you entered Enerjiimass through the Tree of Hearts, you inadvertently started the dual-time continuum."

"Oh," said Nancy, flabbergasted. "I'm sorry, I didn't realise."

"Don't apologise," replied Aunt Elma. "It is possible to raise the portal and enter Enerjiimass without the clock ticking in your own world."

"Great," said Nancy, clapping her hands in anticipation of home. "That means we should arrive back in Roebuck Woods at midnight."

"Correct," confirmed the old lady. "But…"

"But what?"

"If you breach the duration of the dual-time continuum, the time you spend here will be exaggerated back within the Earth realm."

"Meaning?"

"It won't be midnight," interrupted Prema. "The final chapter in *The First Book of Cosmo* explains the dual-time continuum. We are in the fourth cycle of time. The last lunar cycle."

Aunt Elma nodded her appreciation and congratulated Prema. "Outstanding. Good girl."

"How much time will pass if we breach the dual-time continuum?" asked The Duke.

"A decade," replied Aunt Elma, over the roaring flames.

"A decade!" Jimmy exclaimed.

"Or two," yelled Aunt Elma.

"How much time do we have left?" asked Nancy.

"Not much," admitted Aunt Elma. "There is a membrane that grows over the heart-shaped hole. After the fourth new moon, it seals itself completely until the next cycle begins."

Nancy frowned. "And how long have we been here?"

"The fourth moon has just passed," replied Aunt Elma. She winced. "And the membrane is close to sealing itself."

"Oh, no," groaned The Duke. "I'm going to be thirty-two when I get home. And I still won't have a girlfriend. Thirty-two and single. I'll be a laughing stock."

"No, you won't," said Prema, fluttering her lashes.

"How come?" asked The Duke, innocently.

Prema slid her fingers into his palm. "I'd love to be with someone like you."

Nancy stifled her laughter as the blood rushed to The Duke's cheeks, his face now a furnace of embarrassment. "Well, Master Duke," said Nancy in a fancy voice, "do you, the musical man of Enerjiimass, accept the hand of the Great Sarkander, the Reader of the Cards, and the mystical queen of Bhopal?"

The Duke nodded, then yanked Prema to his side.

Nancy and Jimmy clapped as The Duke embraced Prema.

"Time is our enemy," mumbled Aunt Elma.

"Can't you fly this balloon any faster?" asked Nancy, impatiently.

Aunt Elma tutted. "We are close, young lady, very close."

They began a gradual descent, bobbing and weaving through the canopy of the forest. Aunt Elma carefully pedalled the steering board, navigating their landing with meticulous precision. Nancy peered down at a small clearing beside a pond. "Down there – that will do." The Diwali balloon shunted itself left, then right, then left again. It was a wet landing.

"Ah, I'm soaked," cried Nancy, as she wriggled out of the basket.

"Sorry about that," said Aunt Elma, graciously. "Landing isn't my forte."

Nancy stood waist deep in the middle of the pond, covered in algae. The children crawled out of the pond and shook the excess water from their garments.

"Which way?" asked The Duke, already on his toes for the race against time.

Aunt Elma buckled Ergonwold's collar over her shoulder, hobbled past an igloo-hut, and prodded her cane at a Silver Birch. "Go past that tree, turn left at the wishing well, and you will see the Fountain of Youth. Beyond it is the Tree of Hearts." She paused, took a breath, then continued, "That is your portal back to the Earth realm. Unfortunately, there is no time for goodbyes. Go. Be off with you. Your journey is at an end."

The Duke was the first to run. Jimmy followed, shouting, "Goodbye, Aunt Elma," over his shoulder. Prema hesitated, kissed Aunt Elma on the cheek, and turned on her heels.

Nancy stood motionless, looking one way, then the other, her emotions torn between two worlds.

"You need to go home, Nanny Bo," said Aunt Elma.

Nancy flung her arms around the old lady. "I will visit you at The Home For The Incurably Curious."

"I'm afraid you will not find me there."

"Why not?"

"I must find the new spirit of Ergonwold. Somewhere, here in the vast lands of Enerjiimass, a baby will be born. It is the way of life. When you clip an old flower…"

"A new one grows," said Nancy, quietly.

Aunt Elma smiled, then placed her hand on Nancy's shoulder. "I will not rest until I find that creature. You must go now."

"What about *The First Book of Cosmo?*"

"I will take that for safekeeping," replied Aunt Elma. "All good books belong in libraries."

"It's in here," said Nancy, unzipping the bag. She reached inside and passed the book to Aunt Elma.

"Thank you, Nanny Bo."

Nancy smiled. "That's okay, I didn't get time to read it all." Then she pulled the wand from her pocket. "Here, take this."

"Keep it," replied Aunt Elma.

"But—"

"You may need it one day. Nobody else can use that wand."

"But—"

"You need to go," insisted Aunt Elma. "Time is running out."

Nancy strapped the leather bag over her shoulder and bolted. She darted left at the wishing well and caught sight of the Fountain of Youth. It was beautiful – jets of water spewed up from the ground, sparkling as they caught the rods of sunlight that penetrated the woodland. She ran straight through it, her skin prickling as the water rained down upon her. There it was, in all its rustic glory: the Tree of Hearts, its copper bark glistening like an orange monolith.

"We were going to wait another ten seconds," shrieked Jimmy.

The heart-shaped hole was smothered in a sticky, translucent, elasticated membrane. At the arch of the heart was a tiny opening. "We need to squeeze through," instructed Nancy. She pushed Prema forward. "Go on, Pre, hurry up."

Prema resisted. "No. You can go first."

"I don't need air berries," replied Nancy. She tapped her wrist. "Tick-tock-tick-tock."

Prema squeezed herself through the narrowing gap at the top of the heart. Jimmy was next. He held his breath, pulled his stomach in, and attempted to clamber through. He was stuck, halfway between two worlds, his legs kicking wildly as if he was swimming. The Duke pushed against his backside, while Nancy pulled against the membrane.

Jimmy yelped, then finally fell through.

"Your turn, Duke," said Nancy, casually.

"You are coming, aren't you?" asked The Duke, unsure of Nancy's intentions.

Nancy winked at him. An instant later, he was gone. She took one last look at the place she had grown to love, the place where she felt she truly belonged – a parallel world where emotions coloured the sky, and mood altered the atmosphere. Somehow, she fitted in here. She *had to stay*. But she knew she couldn't. Two emotional tides collided against one another. She watched agonisingly as the membrane began to seal the last of the heart. Then, with a rush of blood to the head, she squeezed herself through and landed face down in the damp earth of Roebuck Woods.

32
A Sort of Homecoming

"We're home!" yelled The Duke at the top of his voice. He punched the air repeatedly like a prize-fighter. "We're home; we made it home..."

"Not a word of this to anyone," said Nancy, sternly.

The Duke clapped the mud from his hands. "And who would believe us?"

Nancy brooded on The Duke's question. As hard as she tried, she couldn't answer him. She passed the leather bag to Prema, slid the wand into her pocket, and ogled the gaping hole she had just crawled through. Buckled hinges hung from a wooden frame, the cellar doors lying splintered at her feet. She stepped back as a pile of leaves rustled over the void. Within a fleeting moment, the gateway to Enerjiimass had vanished. Then she pulled Elijah's note from her pocket and felt her entire body contract, as if she had jumped feet first into an ice-bath.

"What about Eli's parents?" asked Prema.

Nancy raised her eyes from the letter. Roebuck Woods stared back at her, dark, calm, and sedate, its monochrome surroundings jogging her memory as to why she had run away.

Prema raised her voice and tried again. "What will we say to Lillie Lincoln?"

"I don't know," croaked Nancy, unable to reconcile her thoughts. "It's going to be crazy around here. How are we going to explain ourselves?"

The children stood in a stony silence, each looking at the other for an answer. The grim realisation of a missing child and no feasible explanation forced Nancy into a deep chamber of thought. In the race to beat the dual-time continuum, she had forgotten something, something very important, something the inhabitants of Enerjiimass had overlooked. A body! She grabbed the wand and pointed it at the pile of leaves shrouding the cellar.

Jimmy leapt in front of the wand. "What are you doing, Nanny Bo?"

"This is all my fault, get out of my way."

"No."

"Move, Jim Jam. We owe it to Eli's parents."

"What do we owe?"

"We owe them Eli's body," replied Nancy, emphatically. "Only then can their lives move on from this nightmare."

"She's right," admitted Prema.

"Maybe," said Jimmy, "but—"

"But what?" asked Nancy, flicking the wand to accentuate her words.

Jimmy ripped the end from his cape and dabbed his face. "Look at us. We look like refugees. We've just escaped from the clutches of Zayock, and we were nearly eaten by an army of gremlins." He took three short steps and straddled the cellar frame. "Before this crazy journey, I was packing a suitcase for Bournemouth. We need to go home. And we need to *think* before we act."

Nancy withdrew the wand. "Okay. But maybe, just maybe, I could finish the recipe Zayock started and—"

"And what?" interrupted The Duke. "Bring Eli back to life?" He reached out to Nancy. "This is *not* your fault. You have the letter as proof that he loved you. Don't start searching for the everlasting."

"I'm not!" protested Nancy. "I just want to see if it could work."

"You're starting to sound as desperate as Zayock," sniped The Duke.

Nancy glared at The Duke. "What if that potion could bring—?"

"Nothing can bring back the dead," interrupted Prema.

"But Zayock told me there was a magic serum."

Prema shook her head. "There's nothing wrong with retrieving Eli's body. As long as—"

"That's your sole intention," said The Duke.

"*All right*," conceded Nancy. She screwed her hand into a fist and raised it above her head. "For Eli and his parents, I vow to bring his body back."

One by one, The Duke, Jimmy and Prema edged closer to Nancy and raised their fists to the heavens. As their knuckles touched Nancy's, they heard the echo of their voices resounding throughout the grounds of Bymerstone Hall.

"*We will bring him back!*"

Nancy closed her eyes as the voices trailed off into the night. Behind her eyelids, visions of Elijah began to form. Flashing images cascaded through her mind, one after the other, a rapid, non-stop storyboard of what she knew of his short life. His body was radiating an angelic glow, his muscular arms beckoning her towards him, his words a distant echo from a far away land, "*Come back, Nanny Bo. Please, come back. I'm here, in the Fountain of Youth.*"

Nancy squatted on her haunches, tormented by the celestial visions. Her fingers were embedded in the sodden earth, mud squelching within her palms as she wrestled with her emotions. Then she felt something, something protruding from the ground. She rustled through the leaf mould and grabbed a torch, its long metallic shaft smothered in dirt. She brushed away the debris and stared at the initials carved upon its shaft – *E.L.*

She flicked the switch. A beam of light darted across the forest floor. "Follow me!"

Slowly, she led the way out of Roebuck Woods, at one with her thoughts, each and every step illuminated by the light of Elijah Lincoln. As they approached the perimeter fence, Nancy turned to her friends and swung the torch up into the inky sky.

"We will return…"

'*A stumbling block for the pessimist
is a stepping-stone for the optimist.*'
- Ergonwold

Nancy Bo Jones is a member of The Young Greens
www.younggreens.org.uk and can be found on Facebook or
emailed at nancybojones123@gmail.com

Acknowledgments

At the bottom of my garden is a shed. I sit in it whilst writing, listening to weird, ambient music as I tap, tap, tap the keys. Sometimes, it can be very lonely, and when the isolation gets the better of me I remind myself that I'm part of a team. A beloved team. A kind, understanding, tolerant group of individuals without whom this novel would never have found its way to you - The Wonderful Reader.

First and foremost, I'd like to thank Gillian James (Mother Goose,) for her patience, knowledge and countless re-reads of my early drafts. Graham Gladin and Gareth Worgan are two men I greatly admire, I feel privileged that they accepted the daunting task of embryonic edits, the feedback you offered as we traipsed along the Thames was invaluable: The only impossible journey is the one you never begin.

I am indebted to GP Taylor for kindly pointing me in the direction of Dr Mark Stibbe, (who opened a window into the world of publishing and editing.) Annelisa Christensen has held my hand the entire way. My writing rock. A 'literary' force of nature, an outstanding writer, editor, thinker, and most importantly, a do'er. Your friendship, encouragement, and the full bloodied, microscopic edit you conducted will never be forgotten, (even though it scared the life out of me.) Jan Marshall, you do exactly what it says on the tin... You are the Super-Proofer! And a fantastic formatter, thank you for taking my mid-afternoon calls and listening to my tea-slurped waffle. Dave and Pat Paine trusted me with the keys to the greatest sea-side writing retreat in England. The Southbourne Beach and cliff-top views are embedded in my families' memory (forever.) Dave's oil paintings of Ergonwold hang with pride in my hallway. Thank you!

Everything changed after a pint of Guinness with Angela Jones. Words became pictures. Pictures became characters. Characters became art. You are a truly gifted artist, my minds-eye with a paintbrush, and a long-standing family friend. Your passion for the story and the motley crew of dysfunctional characters blew me away, without knowing it, you convinced me to stay 'true' right up until the very end. There will always be a little piece of you within this book, Angela.

Beta Readers are an author's best friend. The most valued of folk who enjoy giving detailed feedback prior to publishing. I raise a glass of gratitude to: Julie Spillman (No17,) John Keating, Harry Wells, Rodney Burgess and Antonia Teixeira. Special thanks go to Colin Morgan at Coles Copying, who hand delivered my ever-changing manuscripts on his way home from work, time and time again. Top Man!

Finally, I'd like to thank Karen James for bestowing the two most precious commodities any human could ask for, Time and Patience. There is no end to love…

CPSIA information can be obtained
at www.ICGtesting.com
Printed in the USA
LVHW081322030519
616557LV00004B/291/P

9 781784 654740